LILAC DAYS

Lilac Days

The true story of the secret love affair that
altered the course of history

GAVAN NADEN
and
MAXINE RIDDINGTON

HarperCollins*Publishers*

HarperCollins*Entertainment*
An Imprint of HarperCollins*Publishers*
77–85 Fulham Palace Road,
Hammersmith, London W6 8JB

www.harpercollins.co.uk

Published by HarperCollins*Entertainment* 2005
1 3 5 7 9 8 6 4 2

A catalogue record for this book
is available from the British Library

ISBN 0007198639

Typeset in 11/14 Sabon by
Palimpsest Book Production Limited,
Polmont, Stirlingshire

Printed and bound in Great Britain by
Clays Ltd, St Ives plc

For Pam, whose colour will always burn bright.

ACKNOWLEDGEMENTS

Special thanks to: Edith, Art, Wayne, Hal and Gretchen Howitt for their rich memories and tremendous hospitality, and to the late Honourable Mrs Frances Shand Kydd, a dignified woman and unique free spirit.

Thanks to: Harvard University Press; Imperial War Museum; Spilsby Library; Horncastle Library; King's Lynn Civic Office; all the staff at King's Lynn Library; Jon Day at Beaulieu Library; The British Library; Brian Harris; Redwood Library in Newport; and those at www.heacham-on-line.co.uk

To our agent, the irrepressible Ali Gunn at Curtis Brown and her assistant, Stephanie.

Maggie Turnbull, our trusted friend who had the courage to read and criticise each draft, make invaluable suggestions and then feed us Sunday lunch (such light pastry!).

Gavan's thanks: To my wonderful children, Holly and Oscar. To Cary, in deepest France. To all my friends and family who have helped more than they will know during the writing of this book, especially Alf Fisher, Marcus Van Horn, Tom Ward, Ross Langford and Ronnie Bentley. And to my big sister Gayle, who has been the truest of friends. Thank you and I love you.

Maxine's thanks: To my boy, Tom, for being the best and for understanding his mad mum. Also to Kim, Val and Ridd for keeping the Gumley fires burning; Steve Adcock, my forever friend; Sue Lewis for the Heacham house and so much sistering; Mick and Sheila for making Mum happy. Mum – for teaching me what love really means. Dad – wish you were here.

And finally to Graeme Clark, too beautiful for this world. We will never forget you.

ONE

'Travelling Alone'

Two small boys thundered headlong down the narrow corridor bursting with passengers and luggage, their excited squeals echoing throughout the steam train. Even the slow monotonous pulse of the engine, and the piercing shriek of the whistle heightened the anticipation of what lay ahead. They were heading home. Home to the west coast of America. Home to sunshine and their grand-parents, Grossmutter and Grossvater.

Dressed in matching suits, Sunday best ties and new shoes that pinched, Jack and Ned skidded to a halt at the entrance to the first class carriage. Only the bark of a deep voice yelling, 'Boys!' stopped them in time. Jack surreptitiously elbowed his younger brother in the ribs and stood ramrod straight to attention, as the porter edged closer in his snowy white uniform. Ned crumpled to the floor howling, theatrically gripping his side.

Not far behind, exhausted from wrestling with a borrowed case and too little sleep, struggled Edith Travis. Losing her balance, she stumbled and strands of long dark hair broke free from the tight bun on top of her head, flicking at her face. She ignored the glare of the porter, but for effect said, 'What a carry-on! You are a naughty pair.' The tone of her voice told her sons she didn't mean a word of it.

The train pulled away from the platform under a steam-filled milky sky blurring the faces of those waving farewell. Edith at last loosened her grip on the case's rough leather handle and wiped the perspiration from her forehead. Once more she could hunt for her tickets.

The boys ran towards their mother and circled around her floor-length skirt, flicking and punching each other to the rhythm of the wheels against the rails.

They watched her searching for the tickets, fingers buried in deep pockets bulging with string and the pointless toys that all boys love. They giggled at how silly she looked, especially as they remembered seeing her handing over the tickets the moment they pushed through the barrier and entered the vast open space of the platform.

Jack was seven years old and knew the way to his mother's heart, having committed to memory the ticket collector's words, 'Carriage F, seats A, B and C – five carriages down.'

'It's here, Mommy,' he said, proudly pointing towards a long seat, barely wide enough for the three of them. Edith's legs momentarily buckled at the thought of resting. Now the meagre size of their living, eating and sleeping space overwhelmed her. For the next three days they would be squashed together like sardines in a tin. Consoling herself with the thought that they were at least not travelling coach class, with days and nights stuffed in an upright chair, she placed a napkin on her seat. Edith beckoned to her sons to drag their case the final few yards, half-heartedly attempting to push it forward with her foot until the boys grabbed the handle.

With Ned posted as look-out, in case the burly porter returned, Edith jumped on the seat and reached up to the ornate overhead luggage rack. But the case was so heavy that she was unable to hoist it above waist height. So when a gentleman deftly took the handle and handed it to the porter to put in the luggage carriage, it was a great relief.

Edith nodded thankyou and hoped he hadn't seen her climbing on good upholstery in her shoes. The gentleman smiled kindly and winked at the boys. She watched enviously as he walked past the large brass kerosene lamps that were already burning bright in the evening light, through the door to the sanctuary of the first-class Pullman car.

The 3,000 miles of track joining the east and west coasts of America had long been completed by men paid the princely sum of $1.25 a day. An old Illinois Central Railroad poster was pinned to the back wall of Edith's coach. She scanned the words and smiled knowingly. 'Wanted!' it read. 'Labourers. Men with families preferred.' She squinted to see the small print, which lured supposedly reliable individuals on the promise of 'regular work, good weather and affordable land'.

Ten years of marriage from the tender age of sixteen had taught Edith that some men's dependability evaporated when they took a wife. She absent-mindedly touched her ring finger and fiddled with the smooth gold band. Life would be so much simpler if only she could stop thinking about the boys' father.

The other travellers chattered nervously, at first in whispers and then a little louder, as the train picked up speed. A row in front, an elderly lady was knitting with garish green wool as though her life depended on it. Her shoulder was nudged by her husband's each time he flicked over a page of the novel he was reading, Ford Madox Ford's *The Good Soldier*. There was an unlit pipe held in his mouth. They remained silent except for the rhythmic clicking of needles and his incessant sucking noises.

The boys clambered over the back of the seat, as their mother stared through the window at New York's disappearing skyline. They soon discovered that with a nimble twist of the wrist the upper berths hidden in the walls folded flat into bunk beds. Ned could not resist wriggling inside, and the moment he was safely in position, Jack slammed the berth on his younger brother. Screams of terror could be heard throughout the carriage as sheets and blankets cascaded on to the floor. Edith closed her eyes to avoid the glares of the elderly couple, who had turned round disapprovingly. She prayed for this long journey soon to be over.

The carriage offered little in the way of privacy except for a single thin curtain around her bunk, which Edith would use to shield her modesty throughout the forthcoming night. Her mother, with her usual pragmatism, had counselled against such a long journey: 'It is no place for a woman, never mind one with children.' As usual, however, Edith had smiled knowingly and carried on doing exactly what she wanted.

Now she withdrew three apples from her Gladstone bag, one for each of them. She hoped that munching would keep Jack and Ned quiet for a while. She gazed at their innocent faces, knowing in her heart they were her good boys.

Reclining in a large gold brocade armchair in the first-class carriage, Maurice Roche sipped Earl Grey tea from a finely painted china cup and spread the *New York Times* out over his long legs. He leaned forward to pick at the neat flags of crust-less sandwiches, unable to conjure much hunger after a heavy lunch at the polo club.

Glancing down at the newspaper, he was appalled by the terrible headline, '*Lusitania* struck by a submarine: probably 1,000 dead.'

He knew the giant ship well, as his mother Fannie had sailed aboard her many times between New York and Liverpool. The liner was the pinnacle of luxury and capable of outrunning any other vessel. Maurice read how the voyage had ended in such tragedy, despite emergency measures being in force for some time. Yet, passengers had only recently been warned of the danger by the German Embassy in a newspaper advertisement which stated:

Travellers are reminded that a state of war exists between Germany and her allies and Great Britain and her allies; . . . in accordance with formal notice given by the Imperial German Government, vessels flying the flag of Great Britain, or any of her allies, are liable to destruction in those waters.

And now 123 Americans had been killed after the liner was fatally torpedoed by a German U-boat. Maurice wondered what the poor souls who had drowned had thought in those last minutes . . . The war in Europe seemed to be edging ever nearer, and he felt sick to the pit of his stomach at the thought of what lay ahead.

Among the dead was one of his old New York friends, the millionaire Vanderbilt. Maurice's shock made the news seem all the more unreal. The *New York Times* article said he had died a hero because, despite being unable to swim, he had placed his life belt around a woman's waist. His own death was assured. It was typical of the man to behave in such a heroic manner, thought Maurice.

Three years earlier, Vanderbilt had at the last minute been lucky enough to cancel a trip on the *Titanic*, and now this had happened. It made no sense at all.

'Such tragedy. The poor families,' he murmured.

He was glad to be alone at last, although the garishness of the first-class carriage did nothing for his already pensive mood. The past weeks had been a hectic round of socializing with pretty women and stupid men. He was bored by insipid conversation and borrowed views. Now aged thirty, he could not muster any enthusiasm for yet another party given for no particular reason. So when he was asked to travel to California on behalf of his alma mater, Harvard University, to report on the latest technological innovations, he felt he would be doing something useful. Over $50 million had been spent on the Panama–Pacific International Exposition – a world fair in San Francisco – to celebrate the opening of the Panama Canal. Publicity claimed that the bay was being illuminated by forty-eight massive searchlights out in the water, and the harbour looked as if it was lit by hundreds of fireworks.

The creator of this show, Walter d'Arcy Ryan, had ordered a train to pump out steam, so the lights would appear romantically hazy. This so-called 'steam scintillator' was something Maurice had to see.

Needing to stretch his legs, Maurice rose, nodded politely to the snoozing men with their sagging cigars and headed for the observation deck at the rear of the train.

Edith awoke with a jolt, realizing that her mouth was slightly open. She sat bolt upright and tried to recall any sounds she might have made, covering her embarrassment by coughing into her handkerchief.

Despite the carriage being full, she sensed she was alone. Certainly her boys were suspiciously quiet, and she cast an eye towards the stove where the blazing wood had turned to glowing embers and the heat was on the wane.

Edith looked around for Jack and Ned, but they were nowhere to be seen, even after she had checked down both ends of the corridor. Rubbing the sleep from her eyes, she became more concerned as she strode down the carriage, pushing aside any bags blocking her route. Although desperate to call out their names, she bit her tongue, not wanting to make a fuss.

Outside the gentlemen's saloon, she tapped quietly on the door until the porter emerged, half exposing a rotund, white-haired man reclining on a high-backed chair, his feet outstretched, one shoe polished to perfection and the other still awaiting a shine.

'Yes?' the porter said, surprised to see a woman in a place that was the preserve of men.

'I do apologize,' said Edith, noticing the smell of beeswax drifting from the room. 'I've lost my children – two boys, five and seven, dark hair, tall for their age.' She emphasized her words with a sideways slant of the head. 'Have they been down this way?'

The porter looked blankly at Edith while his customer, annoyed by the intrusion, was glaring irately. He shook his head and pointed towards the dining-car. 'I expect they have wandered off down one of them carriages, Miss.'

Edith stepped away as the elderly man lamented loudly, 'They'd better not be disturbing anyone again.'

At the back of the train, several passengers gathered on the small veranda of the observation deck. Some held their hand against their forehead to get a better view of the passing scrubland dotted over the claustrophobically high banks. Sandwiched in among the smartly tailored suits and women with binoculars sat her two boys, looking skywards. Edith opened her mouth to shout their names, but the whistle sounded and drowned out her words.

Above Jack and Ned, leaning against the rail, stood a tall handsome man with his hand held open. On his flat palm lay a small silver coin. He then closed his hand, held out two fists and motioned for her sons to pick one. After a brief discussion with his brother, Ned grinned and tentatively tapped the man's right hand. 'That one!' he yelled. Slowly the man opened his fist to reveal an empty palm. 'Ah,' he said. 'Good try.' The boys looked dejected. Then, reaching for Ned's ear, he pulled a shiny coin out from behind his lobe. 'Need to clean those tabs of yours a bit more often,' he smiled, flicking the dime in the air. Both boys shrieked and scrabbled to catch the whirling silver.

As the coin landed, Edith bent down to take Ned by the arm. 'Where have you been?' she said in an irritated tone. Both boys jumped to attention and stared sombrely at their shoes.

Maurice bowed his head. 'Charming young men you have, m'am,' he said, trying to distract Edith from her anger.

But Edith remained too cross to reply and merely raised her hand in acknowledgement.

'I hope your luggage is still in place,' he said. 'Good to see you're not standing on the train seat any more. That's a serious offence.' He laughed easily.

8

She looked more closely into his blue eyes.

'Oh, of course, that was you,' said Edith, blushing. 'I am sorry, it has been a very long day.'

'I should have realized you'd be worried,' he said. 'I've got a twin brother who always egged me on. We were constantly disappearing into cubby holes and playing silly pranks.' He tossed the coin in the air. 'I guess I'm still a kid at heart.'

She smiled and thought how natural he seemed.

'I'm an only child, so I never had that pleasure,' she said. 'But maybe I was lucky. You know what siblings are like – best friends one second and fiercest enemies the next. I can't understand it.'

'Perhaps I could explain over dinner tomorrow,' he said. Then, sensing he had been too forward, he added, 'If you and your husband would care to join me?'

'I'm travelling alone,' replied Edith.

'Well, perhaps you would consider the invitation anyway?' he said, catching the interest in her eye. 'Allow me to introduce myself. My name is Maurice Roche.' He offered his hand.

Edith, worried that her palm was damp, greeted him with her fingertips. His grip was very reassuring, as he took her small hand in his.

She asked him teasingly, 'And where on earth should we meet?'

Maurice grinned, 'How about the dining-car at eight o'clock?'

Edith thought how much nicer it was to dine in style with a good-looking man, than picnic with two small boys in a space the size of a cupboard. But she didn't want him to know that.

She released her grasp and firmly guided Jack and Ned

back in the direction of their carriage. From over her shoulder she said, 'Thank you, Mr Roche, I would be delighted. And I am Edith Travis.'

It had been a long time since she'd been alone with a man. After her disastrous marriage to Forrest, Edith had avoided the company of men. She could not quite forgive herself for being taken in by someone who proved to be little more than a *bon viveur*. She had sensed he was trouble but had agreed to be his wife when, at sixteen, she was barely more than a child.

She was a home-bird by nature and had never left her small town in California, whereas he had travelled, appeared worldly wise and had just turned twenty. Both her mother and father vehemently disapproved of the alliance but that only added to his appeal. She was certain their love was like no other and they would be together for ever. He promised to take care of her and said he hoped their babies would have her eyes. She knew then that she could not live without him.

When he proposed, nothing else mattered, not her mother's tears nor her father's silence. And as they eloped, her father, waiting by the gate, rushed up and gave Edith the money he had saved for her wedding day. He crushed her and whispered, 'I hope God will forgive you. Leave if you must, but remember, this will always be your home and I will always be your Papa.'

Before she was twenty-one, both her children had been born, close together and all consuming. Her relationship with her husband soon grew strained, and Forrest found it hard to compete for attention. Still a hot-blooded young man, he let his eye wander to other women; and he took little interest in his sons, preferring the company of the bottle and the betting track. Suddenly he started disap-

pearing for long stretches at a time, refusing to inform
Edith when, or even if, he would be back.

Edith's life as Forrest's wife was one of domestic chores,
child-minding and worry: a world away from what she
had imagined. Money was scarce, and good company
scarcer. She was lonely, and lost her spark, no longer
having the fight to believe in Forrest, or his dreams.

When he strayed what shocked her weren't the whispers in the store or the assumption that she would welcome
any man's attention, but rather the overwhelming desire
to be free of him. Side by side in bed at night, she no
longer craved Forrest's slowly beating heart. Nor did she
want to lay her head gently on his chest just to feel his
breathing any more. Instead, she prayed for him to quickly
fall asleep, her own heart pounding each time she felt his
outstretched hand or the weight of his body on hers. Like
a child afraid of the dark, she screwed her eyes tightly
shut and hoped it would soon be over. She grew to loathe
herself for such complicity in the lie that their marriage
had become.

But each day, as her love weakened, she needed to feel
wanted again. Embarrassed by having to ask her parents
for money, Edith could stand the uncertainty no longer.
So she made her husband his favourite soup one last time,
wrapped the boys up against the winter cold, and left.

Surprising even herself, she booked into a cheap guest-
house, consulted a lawyer and found the courage to
demand a formal separation. Only then could Edith
breathe again.

As the train rolled into Cleveland, Edith beckoned the
porter to retrieve her luggage so she could press her
favourite cream and purple cotton dress. With its pretty
bow and high collar that flattered her neck, she hoped

she would not look too shabby next to the other diners.

Strangely, she thought it lucky she had few clothes with her, as it made the decision about what to wear for Mr Roche so much easier.

Part of her wanted to impress, but there was part of her that was afraid of being hurt again, and that gave her strength. 'He will have to like me for who I am,' she told her boys, twirling in a dizzy circle in the newly ironed dress.

By next morning, as the train pulled into the bustling Chicago station to swap engines and crews, Edith sighed with relief. It had been a miserable, noisy night, and no one looked rested. The coal-fired stove, restocked with fuel, had burnt so fiercely that the heat had been unbearable. Only a faint draught from the ill-fitting arched window provided any respite, and Edith had moved closer to the gap and gasped in the cool air throughout the night.

Yet, with almost a thousand miles completed, a small murmur of contentment spread through the carriages. The next stop in Omaha would break the back of the journey. To celebrate, Edith took a bag of marbles from her bag and handed them to her boys, 'No more running off,' she ordered, watching as the two flicked the glass balls across the floor.

Feeling restless, she busied herself filing her nails and then retrieved her favourite hat pin from the back of the seat. The boys had been using it as a spear, and the hook had become embedded in the material. The old lady in front cast her knitting aside and, bored with her husband's lack of conversation, turned to Edith.

'My grandsons are the same age, I find a few sharp words keeps them in order,' she said curtly.

Edith smiled. 'Is it always this hard?' she asked.

'It never stops until the day they are gone, and then your house is silent for ever,' she replied, softening.

'That's something I won't like,' said Edith.

'None of us do, when we're only left with this,' she replied, looking conspiratorially towards her sleeping husband.

Edith laughed. Here was a woman after her own heart. The women chatted easily passing the time until Edith feared she must get ready. She looked at her watch and pointed with her finger to indicate how quickly the time had passed. 'I need someone to look after my boys tonight,' she said hopefully.

'Why's that?' inquired the lady.

Edith lowered her eyes. 'I have a dinner engagement.'

The old lady nodded. 'I see,' she said, glancing towards her husband who was now snoring loudly from behind his book which lay covering his face. 'Leave the boys with me, I could do with some company. You go and have a wonderful time.'

'Oh, I don't know . . .' Edith muttered.

'It seems a long time since either of us had some fun. Let me get mine by caring for little ones again. You go off and forget about them for a while.'

Edith trusted her lined face. 'You're very kind,' she said.

'And you're very pretty,' said the old lady, reaching into her knitting bag and producing a tiny pot of rouge. 'A man likes a flushed cheek, if you don't mind some advice,' she whispered, pressing the make-up into Edith's hand.

The first-class Pullman dining-car was the most sumptuous carriage on the train and Edith waited nervously at the entrance to be shown to Mr Roche's table. She felt as if

13

all eyes were upon her. Not because she was beautiful, but because she didn't belong.

The *maître d'* ran his finger down the guest list and looked back at her. Edith was sure he was about to say, 'I don't believe so', and felt she should apologize for wasting his time. Instead he said, 'Of course. Please follow me.' He guided her along the plush carpet and past tables with twinkling crystal glasses and silver cutlery laid out like jewels. Ornate velvet drapes were drawn tightly in front of the windows and Edith knew she was in a very exclusive cocoon.

Maurice was drumming his fingers on the white linen cloth when he saw Edith being ushered towards him. She looked more beautiful than he remembered. He adjusted his necktie and smoothed his hair a final time. With each of her steps, he felt his heart pound.

As she neared, he stood to welcome her.

'Mrs Travis, I'm so glad you came,' he said kissing her hand and then gesturing towards her seat.

'Thank you for inviting me,' she said shyly,

'I like your dress,' he said. 'Purple is my favourite colour.'

'And mine,' she smiled, seeing he was wearing nothing of that hue but grateful for his compliment. 'I hope I'm not too informal,' she said, admiring a woman at the next table in a glittering evening gown.

'You're not. You're perfect.'

She tried to concentrate on the menu but found herself continually glancing up at Mr Roche. His skin was lightly tanned and smooth, as if he took care of himself. She liked the way his eyes crinkled when he said her name. Most of all, she liked the way he was looking at her now.

'Would you like some champagne . . . Edith?' he said,

as if suddenly lost for words. Edith thought she saw him redden and wondered why he, of all people, should have any self-doubt.

'Please,' she said, remembering the last time she drank it, with Forrest at their wedding, and the way the bubbles made her nose tingle. The waiter bought a bottle of Krug and started to tear off the foil. Maurice held up his hand. 'Don't open it. Just leave it there,' he said, pointing to the table.

Edith wondered if she had made some terrible *faux pas*, but then he grabbed hold of the bottle and held it up to the light.

'Half the fun is in the pop!' he said.

He wrapped a cloth around the bottle's neck and, as if gently swaddling a baby, brought it to his side. As he stood to twist the cork, Edith noticed a fine golden watch hanging by a chain from his silken waistcoat. He was surely a man of considerable means.

'To trains,' he toasted as the champagne foamed into her glass.

'And the strangers you meet,' she said.

After dinner, when he suggested going to the observation deck, she felt light-headed enough to agree. 'Let's see if we can spot the lights of Cheyenne,' he said, offering his hand.

Walking towards the windy deck, Edith realized she had not brought a wrap and hesitated. Maurice urged her on, removing his coat and placing it around her narrow shoulders. Then he gently slipped his arm around her waist. As he pointed out the distant landmarks, she thought she felt his fingertips press lightly into her flesh. She took another sip of champagne, in case it wasn't true.

TWO

'The Silvery Moon'

Gazing at the hazy wall of heat shimmering around the Rocky Mountains, Maurice felt truly happy. From his large window seat he could see gnarled fir trees clinging to the side of the Never Summer Mountains and the rugged expanse of the new national park, opened despite opposition from early settlers. The determination to succeed shown by these proud men and women who had survived on the grit of self-belief and isolation brought to mind a story Maurice's father loved to tell.

In his adventurous bachelor days, Jim Burke Roche came to America to hunt wild grizzly bears in the two million acres of Wyoming's Yellowstone Park. He brought with him a party of similarly bullish English gentlemen, each keen to bag a bearskin for his country house. When they heard tales about how the park shook at night with spirits of the dead, they laughed them off as wild and superstitious nonsense.

Cavalierly setting off across the yellowing rocks and bubbling thermal lakes, they hoped to hone their hunting skills stalking bears, bison, moose, mountain lions and

16

perhaps, although no one dare admit it, American Indians.

Early on in the expedition, stoked by several drams of Irish whiskey, Jim decided to be the first to land a prize animal. He sneaked off from the rest of the party and, after two hours of fruitless hunting, set up camp alone. Bedding down for the night, oblivious to danger, he was convinced he would be rewarded at first light with a bearskin to surpass anything his companions could bag.

When the rest of the shooting party realized Jim had disappeared, they panicked and spent hours frantically searching in the outback for their esteemed host. As night fell, they huddled around the flickering light of the camp fire, increasingly paranoid and utterly convinced that Jim had met a grisly end. To the eerie sounds of coyotes howling through the night, their imagination ran riot.

'The dead spirits must have got him,' said one, 'and then tore him into tiny shreds.'

However, in the pitch darkness, they feared more for their own safety than that of their lost travelling companion. In the morning, not wanting to stay a moment longer than necessary, they headed back to civilization and informed the authorities of Jim's death. Reports circulated throughout New York, and then London, that the future Lord Fermoy had perished, and with him his family title.

Meanwhile, Jim, angry at being deserted but very much alive, limped back on a lame and slow horse in one piece, but without a bearskin. Once safe, and having eaten his first full meal in days, he relished the furore surrounding his mysterious disappearance. He dined out frequently in New York society on the strength of this brave adventure, always embellishing the tale of his intrepid lone survival with details of the many bears he slew, but had to leave behind.

'A lesser man would not have survived such hardship,' he told Jennie, Lady Randolph Churchill. 'Three full-size grizzly bears came at me as I slept, but I had fortune on my side and managed to kill each one with a shot between the eyes.'

Such stories intrigued one particularly beautiful American woman, called Fannie Work. A friend of Lady Churchill, she begged to be introduced to the fearless pioneer. Their meeting led to a passionate affair and, despite fierce opposition from both sets of parents, the couple were married within weeks. Fannie, headstrong and young, needed to prove she had made the right decision. She soon left America and set sail for Jim's family home in Ireland.

Maurice smiled at this vivid memory of his father's first encounter with his mother. Love comes from the most unlikely places, he thought.

For the past few years Maurice had avoided getting too involved with women. Having grown up with an identical twin brother, he preferred his own company much of the time. His good looks and wealth made it easy to attract the opposite sex, yet the women in his set often disappointed him. Their ambitions seemed limited to marrying well and being rewarded with diamonds. He wanted more than that in a wife.

He lay awake in his bunk considering the simple pleasure of last evening's dinner. There was nothing extraordinary about it, but that was what he liked, the honesty. There was no drama, yet it was exciting. Edith was funny. And so very real. Being with her was like a rush of fresh air.

Between Ogden and Salt Lake City he got out of bed, turned on the light and hastily scribbled a note. He pressed the bell hard to summon the porter.

'First thing in the morning, take this to Mrs Travis and

ask the lady for an immediate reply,' said Maurice to the weary porter. 'Tell her it is most urgent.'

Before the dappled sunlight drifted through the shutters, Edith was brushing her hair dry in the privacy of the ladies' saloon. She was tired but happy after another night of broken sleep and wondered how she could engineer another meeting with Mr Roche.

Suddenly, Jack bounded in.

'You have to come now!' he announced, pulling on her arm.

'What's happened?' she asked, afraid there had been an accident.

'He's sent a porter,' said Jack.

'Who?' asked Edith.

'That very rich man.'

'And you . . . you're not supposed to be in here,' she said sternly, a smile creeping around her mouth.

Edith ran back to her carriage wet-haired, her skirt hitched towards her knee, so that her stockings were clearly visible. The shocked porter averted his eyes and awkwardly handed her the folded note. She snatched at the ivory-coloured paper and, with a mumbled 'Thank you', turned away.

'Any reply, m'am?' the porter asked.

'Tell him . . . Let me think . . . I will have to see to the boys first . . . Lord, who will watch over them tonight? What will I wear?'

'Is that a yes, m'am?' asked the porter dryly.

'Yes!' she said. 'Most definitely a yes! But tell Mr Roche next time he must ask me in person.'

She stretched up on to tiptoe and threw her head back.

'Certainly, m'am,' he replied, suppressing a smirk as Edith pirouetted down the carriage.

As she spun, Edith slid her fingers around her wedding ring and tugged until the gold band came free. She placed it carefully inside her skirt pocket, hoping no one saw.

Back in the compartment, Jack jumped on to Ned's bunk and tried to shove dirty socks into his brother's ear. Then they both hid under the sheets, screaming and giggling until an unsuspecting porter came to fold the beds away.

'I'll come back later, when the young men aren't so busy,' he tutted.

Edith nodded sagely, and then, when he was gone, crumpled into a fit of giggles alongside the boys on the bunks, still clutching Maurice's letter in her hand.

'I'm hungry,' said Ned, holding the sheet to his chin.

'I'm double starving,' said Jack.

Edith hunted through her bag and found a couple of dried figs and a small pack of unshelled pistachios. Her supply of fruit and nuts had finally run out.

Counting the change in her purse and knowing she was going to eat well again that evening, Edith smiled. 'Come on, boys. Mommy is going to buy you a proper breakfast! Let's go to the restaurant.'

As the boys ate, Edith idly flicked through the pages of the *San Francisco Chronicle*. She needed to find a job, something to pay for their upkeep and occupy her mind. She could not rely on her parents' goodwill for long.

Neither of the boys was good at settling, and getting into a new school was going to be a trial. Jack was by nature a shy, hard-working boy, while his elder brother was more outgoing and a gifted musician. Ned's talents gained him instant admiration from adults but meant he suffered at the spiteful hands of jealous children. Starting over had made Edith panic at first, and she wasn't convinced going home was the right decision. But that was where they were headed. She'd had her fill of worry and for the moment saw no other option. She feared her father's morality and her mother's servility would eventually drive her away again, but for now they were all she, and the boys, had.

During mid-morning the train pulled into 'Junction City' at Ogden, Utah, just a few miles from where the Transcontinental Railway was finished. The old town had long since died away, but a few mills, iron works and breweries were still in business. It did not make for a pretty view, but the boys were happy and dodged in and out of the station columns and up and down the steps, their collars held high against the howling wind.

Edith listened as a porter described the best route to the emerald lake.

'It'll take you about half an hour, up that hill,' he said pointing into the distance.

'Then about the same back down. You'll have seen nothing like it. We'll be here a little while, so get going.'

Jack and Ned had run off down a side track, and Edith calculated that she had little chance of getting them to complete the hike in time. It looked at least four miles to the peak of the mountain. And the wind was blowing a gale. They would probably all get a chill.

Instead, she ventured into the general store, where a set of paints and inks caught her eye. They were positioned next to a picture postcard of the lake, poetically described on the back as 'A silver rim about the jewel, framed by stupendous mountains, dark at their base, and ending in flashing summits of snow.' It made her wish she had been more determined in her sightseeing.

As she placed the card back into the rack, she saw the unmistakable outline of Maurice Roche, wrapped in the coat he had draped around her only the night before.

In his day clothes he appeared more at ease, as if a weight had been taken from his shoulders. Suddenly aware that she was staring, Edith picked up a glass bottle of ink and pretended to study its contents, but as he turned to face her Edith became flustered. Trying to catch his attention by waving, she let the bottle of ink slip from her fingers and an ebony pool splattered over the hard stone floor.

'My dear Mrs Travis,' he said, stepping towards her.

'Mr Roche, I'm so sorry,' she replied, helplessly watching the black liquid flood over her fingers.

She bent down and started to pick up the broken glass, too embarrassed to talk, as the mess spread further.

'Don't move,' he said, 'you'll cut yourself,' and hurried to find help.

The storekeeper came running from the back room armed with a broom. 'Stop yer fiddling, woman. All breakages must be paid for.'

Maurice took a dollar bill from his pocket and placed it in the storekeeper's hand.

'Don't fuss, it's only coloured water,' he said.

'Your change, sir,' said the storekeeper, picking several silver coins from his pocket.

'One moment,' said Maurice. 'I'll take that set of paints and this postcard as well.'

'Very good,' said the storekeeper with a grin. 'And is there anything else the lady wants to break while you're here?'

'Please wrap them,' said Maurice, unable to suppress a smile.

Glancing at his watch, he walked over to Edith and said, 'I must send an urgent telegram before the train leaves.' He placed the gifts beside her. 'Please give these to the boys. And have this as a better memory of today.' He then left without a backward look.

She hated herself for being so clumsy and feared that her embarrassing charade would make him have second thoughts about this evening's dinner invitation. But as she gathered her belongings, she saw him hesitate outside a small flower shop across the street.

The boys were thrilled with the set of pastel paints, and behind their bunk a still wet picture of the Salt Lake was attached to the wall, copied from their mother's postcard.

As the children played, the old lady, intrigued by Edith's liaison, fastened a pin through Edith's hair. 'That one is a bit of an aristocrat, you know. And a bachelor,' she said.

'Which one?' Edith asked naively.

'Your date.'

'I am twenty-six years old. I do not date.'

'Suit yourself,' said the lady. 'Sure smells of dating to me.'

'Do you know Mr Roche?'

'Of course not,' said the lady. 'He'd never have time for the likes of me.'

'You seem to know a lot about him, though.'

'For goodness sake don't tell me you haven't seen him in the papers.'

'Why should I?' said Edith, starting to feel foolish.

'That fancy man of yours is Maurice Roche, heir to the Work family fortune. His mother was the belle of New York City.'

Edith shook her head in disbelief and adjusted her velvet

suit jacket, brushing her hand nervously down the sides of her hips to smooth the long line of her skirt.

'Order the best – he can afford it,' advised the lady.

Maurice had taken time over his appearance, washing, shaving and ordering a manicure. He selected a navy suit, cut from the best Italian cloth, and a white wing collar shirt so well starched that it almost sat at the table by itself. His cuffs peered out from beneath the sleeves of his jacket, exposing heavy gold cufflinks engraved with his initials. His shoes were so new that they squeaked as he walked. He hoped Edith would not think there was a mouse on board.

Feigning a casual stance, he leaned back into his chair, a glass of champagne fizzing on the table and his untouched cigar balanced on a jade ashtray. After only a few minutes her absence began to make him feel uncomfortable, and afraid she might have changed her mind. He idly picked up the coffee spoon and rubbed it between his thumb and forefinger.

Then he saw her silky auburn tresses falling around her face as she made her way to the table.

Maurice stood up from his seat and held out his hands.

'I might still be inky,' she teased.

He smiled, and took her hands without looking.

They linked arms, walking the short distance to their table as a piano player in a darkened corner struck the opening chords to 'By the Light of the Silvery Moon.' Maurice leaned over to pull out Edith's chair, and when she brushed past, she could smell fresh soap and sandalwood.

She stared at the extravagance of the expansive seven-course menu, which included Mountain Brook Trout and

Antelope Steak. What would Forrest think if he could see her now?

Maurice shifted uncomfortably in his chair and produced a small gold box tied with a satin ribbon.

'This is something for you,' he said.

Untying the ribbon, Edith gasped. 'They're so beautiful,' she said, looking at the delicate arrangement of small flowers.

'May I?' he asked, standing to pin the corsage on to her hair.

'Thank you so much,' she said, shivering at the touch of his hand.

'Have you been to the Waldorf Hotel?' she asked, reading the menu.

'Yes,' he said, 'many times.'

'Is it as good as the pudding?'

He paused. 'It's all a matter of taste, but I'd go for the pudding most times.'

'It says here it's rich and subtle and a little exotic.'

'Just so,' he said, 'but the hotel does have a wonderful restaurant called the Palm Room, full of famous faces.'

'Is that what you like about it?' she said.

'I'll take you there one day and you can find out for yourself.'

She put the menu down.

'You don't believe me, do you?' he said.

'It's not that I don't want to.'

'Edith, I will take you.' He held her hand. 'I promise.'

'I'm very complicated,' she said.

'Good,' he said. 'I'm not.'

'Oh, Mr Roche,' she mocked, 'how you disappoint me.'

They both laughed. Before long they were dancing.

In the early hours of the morning, the waiters wanted

to get to bed, but Edith and Maurice continued to dance between moves in a bad game of chess.

The library carriage had been deserted for some time, but they were in no rush to say goodnight. They joked that the strong coffee was keeping them awake, although they both knew it was a lie.

Maurice unbuttoned his jacket and laid it over the back of a leather chair. He rolled up his shirt sleeves to expose his strong tanned arms. Edith saw the light hairs on the back of his wrists, the freckles and curve of his forearm. As if he knew what she was thinking, Maurice sat down and stroked his hand across her cheek, tracing the outline of her lips with his thumb. She pressed his hand hard against her mouth, kissing the tips of each of his fingers. Neither said a thing.

It was the first time they had been silent.

THREE

'Nothing Surprises Me'

Edith's mother knew, after thirty years with one man, that to get what she wanted required cunning. Pouring the last of the schnapps into a tall glass, she began talking fondly of the old country.

'We had a good life,' she said.

'America has given us better opportunities,' said her husband. 'I love this land.'

'Yes, people in our very street have never learned to read and write,' said Frau Hund, refilling his glass.

'They are indeed to be pitied,' he said. 'They must learn to take the chances given to them.'

'You are right but imagine never knowing the pleasure of poetry, or escaping to another world when yours is bleak and unforgiving.'

Herr Hund nodded sagely.

'We relied on the library in New York when we first came,' she said.

'It was a godsend,' he said, wiping his moustache. 'The language was hard.'

'It would be wonderful to have such a place here in

Marin County.'

'Most certainly,' he said.

'Mein Mann, you are so wise.'

He kissed the top of her head. 'Play me one of your sweet tunes on the piano,' he said, unaware of what he was agreeing to as the haze of sleep overcame him.

Within a week, Frau Hund had started a small library, using a stall in the centre of the town. It was stocked with two dozen books, which she loaned out for a cent each. If a cent was beyond the customer's reach, she would readily lend her much-loved copies in exchange for an hour's work in her vegetable plot, or a few eggs. Then, when she had collected enough money, she would buy, swap or borrow newer books to add to her collection.

News spread quickly and her stall became a meeting point, its popularity earning her a small income. Frau Hund's passion and enthusiasm were infectious, and the stall soon outgrew itself. She searched the county for better premises, until she had found a tiny store with good light, proper shelves and a desk.

Each morning for a week she laid Herr Hund's breakfast out then set off to clean, dust and hand-paint the library inside and out, to make the room ready for her treasured collection of books and magazines. She bought two old desks and four chairs, and above the door she nailed a wooden plaque with her name written across it. When she pushed back the shutters and opened for business, it was one of the proudest days of her life.

Herr Hund could never get to grips with his wife working and still regarded the library as a hobby. 'It's just pin money,' he said, 'nothing of significance.'

Of greater concern to him was the onset of a dark, brooding tension across the country. Suddenly, it seemed as if the war in Europe was spreading to their side of the ocean, reaching the orange groves and neat picket fences of Marin County. There was an enemy to hate and it came from his homeland. It was the Hun.

The Germans were pressing hard to forge an alliance in America's own backyard with its neighbour, Mexico. Ordinary Americans, scared of invasion, were taking matters into their own hands. German language courses were banned and children sang 'We're going to take the Germ out of Germany' as they played in the street.

At a time when many Americans flexed their burgeoning muscle, Herr Hund felt powerless and emasculated. He was too old to fight and an alien in the country he called home. But the nation was turning against his family. The escalating anti-German feeling thrived on fear, and many believed there were enemy infiltrators in every walk of life.

Herr Hund was very struck by the case of a Marin County man, Johannes Koolbergen, who testified before the federal grand jury that Germans were trying to blow up the American railway system. In a sworn affidavit, Koolbergen claimed that the German consul in San Francisco, Franz Bopp, was masterminding attempts to destroy American tunnels, munition buildings and ships.

Koolbergen testified that Bopp offered him a considerable amount of money to blow up the railroads. However, the Marin County man alerted the authorities, and, turning double agent, started collecting evidence against Bopp.

Although terrified, Koolbergen met Franz Bopp and accepted two hundred dollars as a down payment for his services. Then in an elaborate twist, Koolbergen went to Canada and, with the assistance of the authorities, pretended to blow up a railway tunnel.

Government agents arranged for a bogus report to appear in the newspapers, falsely claiming that the tunnels in the Selkirks mountain range had caved in.

Bopp was completely hoodwinked. Believing that everything was going to plan, he wrote a coded telegram to Koolbergen: 'Would like to send some flowers to your wife, but do not know her address.' He wanted to congratulate his new recruit and arrange to pay him a further one thousand dollars. A few days later, Bopp was arrested and indicted for violating US neutrality.

Following this sting, Marin County was placed on alert. People tiptoed about their business, believing they could be attacked at any moment. Neighbours no longer trusted one another, especially the Germanic- sounding Hunds, and suspicion supplanted friendship almost overnight.

Although the plot had been foiled, Herr Hund felt tarred with the same brush, and believed the same prying eyes were watching him as the evil Bopp. His innocent activities provoked such unnecessary interest that he lay in bed at night waiting for a knock on the door that might incarcerate him.

Frau Hund, once proud to live in America, was made to feel a sense of shame because of her birthplace. She watched people walk past the library averting their eyes from her sign when previously they would have come in. Her adopted homeland was growing sick from hatred of its own.

This was not the time to be separated from family, and Edith's homecoming gave the Hunds something to look forward to. With their girl back, said Frau Hund to reassure her husband, they would be all right. A few days before Edith's return, Frau Hund made a detour on her way to the library, stopping off at the local drugstore where she was a regular customer. She intended to buy some sheet music for her husband who had always loved Beethoven's peaceful 'Moonlight Sonata'.

The store seemed no different from any other day, with its rainbow wall of assorted apothecary jars, sweet-smelling biscuits and tempting ices. But Frau Hund felt uncomfortable walking past the townswomen huddled together in a corner who looked away as she smiled. The usual gossip and cheery greetings were replaced by an awkward silence and, when her back was turned, she felt a hiss of distaste. Undeterred, Frau Hund bought some flour and salt and tried to attract the attention of the shop-keeper busy writing on his blackboard. He was crossing out 'Sauerkraut' and, in big bold letters, replacing it with 'Liberty Sausage'.

Frau Hund ignored his silly censorship and politely requested the sheet music. Without looking at her, the shopkeeper said, 'We won't be selling German goods here.'

'I beg your pardon?'

'Don't you understand English? I said we won't be having any of that kraut crap in this here store.'

'Is that so?' said Frau Hund, carefully putting down her basket of groceries, the eyes from all corners of the store burning into her back. 'Then you won't be wanting my German money either,' she said. Bidding everyone 'Guten Tag', she walked out.

Before he put his key in the lock, Herr Hund heard his favourite sound in the world – his wife playing the piano.

Then the music mysteriously stopped. He walked round to the side of the house and tapped on the glass to encourage her, expecting to see her laughing face. Instead she was slumped over the piano keys, her head bowed and shoulders heavy from silent sobs.

He ran inside and called, 'What has happened, Liebling?' But she could not look at him.

When her tears had dried, Frau Hund put on her coat and shoes and, without a word, took her husband's hand and they headed into the darkness.

He was there first. Red paint had been splashed across the library's front door, which swung drunkenly off its hinges. It had been kicked in. As he walked up the steps, glass crunched underfoot. The windows were all smashed. Inside, piles of books had been ripped from the shelves, set alight and now lay in a pitiful smouldering pile.

Herr Hund shook his head, unable to utter any words of comfort for his wife who crouched down low to rescue the door plaque, which had been wrenched from its fixings. The 'D' of their surname had been crossed out, so that it now read 'Frau Hun'. She sat on the steps, staring into the night, clutching the plaque to her breast.

Herr Hund began brushing away the burning ashes and scooped up as much of the glass as he could, ignoring the pain of cuts from stray shards. He tried his best to re-hang the door and then jammed it shut in frustration, slipping the key into his pocket. Frau Hund put her arm through his and they walked home through the streets, conversing quietly together in their native German tongue, knowing anonymous ears were straining to listen.

Edith had been up late on the last day of her journey and hadn't yet gathered together her belongings. There was an excited cackle in the aisle from Jack and Ned and the slapping of goodbye handshakes. As the porter passed through the carriages shouting, 'Ten minutes to Oakland,' she started to worry.

The Sacramento wheat fields had long gone and been replaced by the magnificence of San Francisco Bay. Yet Maurice had still not come to say farewell. She did not want to appear presumptuous, and just hoped they would bump into each other on the platform.

She pinned Maurice's corsage to the lapel of her coat and marched the boys to the washroom. As the train pulled into the station, she slipped a wet comb through their hair.

'You must look nice for your Grosseltern,' she told them.

At the far end of the platform she spotted her parents. Herr Hund looked much older since last winter, and her mother's hair was now silvery grey. The boys released themselves from her grip and ran headlong into their Grossmutter's skirt, while their Grossvater leaned down to tickle them both.

'It's good to have you home,' he said.

'My, how our boys have grown!' her mother said, ruffling their damp hair.

As Edith's father lifted Ned high into the air she caught a brief glimpse of Maurice in the crowd, talking animatedly to a black porter. But her view was obscured as Jack held his arms out to be spun like his brother.

As Herr Hund struggled with the young boys, Edith hovered close by, fearing her son might be dropped.

'Careful now, he's quite a weight,' she told her father.

'Nonsense, child,' he scolded, grunting as he threw Jack into the air.

When out of breath, Herr Hund stopped playing and kissed Edith self-consciously on the forehead. 'Good to see you too,' he said.

Edith hugged him, straining to look over his shoulder to see what had happened to Maurice. But then her mother grabbed her by the arm.

'These big boys are bound to be hungry. Let's get them something to eat before we do another thing.'

'Really, Mama, it's fine,' protested Edith.

'What about you, darling? How are you? Do you need something? We have plenty.'

'No, I am fine as well. Please, Mama, just for a moment. I just need to say goodbye to a friend. Can you give me two minutes?'

As she turned to search for Maurice, her father's voice boomed, 'Hurry up, Edith, we'll miss the omnibus.'

Suddenly she remembered what it was like to be home.

'Please, Papa, just a minute.'

'We have had a long journey and your Mama is tired. We must go. Now!'

Edith ignored her father and took her children, one in each hand, and marched across the concourse towards the exit, but Maurice was nowhere to be seen. The boys pulled on her arms, desperate to get back to their indulgent grandparents. They were just in time.

Herr Hund was already signalling to a passing omnibus and they had to run to catch it. The driver held his hand up to prevent an old negress getting on and waved Edith and her family through. Only when they were seated was the elderly lady summoned on board.

The lady started shuffling along the aisle, heading for where several other negroes sat on broken seats at the back. Edith stood up and asked if she would like to sit down. But the lady shook her head and kept moving on down to the rear of the bus.

'What are you doing?' hissed her father.

'What is right,' she replied.

'Not here,' he said.

Despite the now empty seat, Edith remained standing,

stubbornly refusing to give way as the bus swayed along the bumpy road back to Golden Gate Avenue and the house where she was born.

A juddering hit the Hund house like a hammer slamming into stone. The bed shook, the floors danced and from downstairs the sounds of smashing crockery echoed along the corridor. Edith awoke, eyes staring, heart pounding.

'Quick! Quick!' yelled her father from another room. 'It's another quake.'

Falling to the floor, she scrambled on her hands and knees into the hallway, hearing distant screams from the street. She reached for the door as the glass in the window cracked and then shattered.

Ned's plaintive face peered round a door. 'What's happening, Mommy?' he asked.

'Get Jack,' she ordered.

'Can't!' he said. 'He's sleeping.'

Edith took his hand and pushed hard with her foot at the base of the bedroom door. Jack was lying terrified in his bed, a pillow over his head.

'Come on,' she said. 'You can't stay there.'

'Don't want to,' cried Jack.

The walls juddered in and out like drum skins and a large slab of plaster fell from the ceiling on to the foot of the bed. It was enough to strike fear into the young boy's heart, and he sprang into the safety of his mother's arms.

Ten minutes later, the shocks had subsided and the family were sitting around the kitchen table brewing strong coffee and wrapping the children in blankets to stop them trembling.

'Haven't we suffered enough?' asked his wife, stroking the boys' hair.

'This is nothing,' said Herr Hund, repeating one of his favourite stories. 'Nine years ago, before you boys were born, we had a shake so big it shook your boots from your feet. The whole of San Francisco was split in two. Thousands died in blazing fires and flattened buildings. It was like an almighty gunpowder explosion had hit the city. There was a dust cloud so big it took weeks to settle.'

'That's what I call a real earthquake,' said Ned.

'Over ten thousand refugees came to Marin County, and most never left,' said Herr Hund. 'Except one.' He motioned towards his daughter.

Patting Edith's knee, Frau Hund shot a disapproving look at her husband, indicating that it was time for him to stop talking. There was no point pretending that they hadn't expected circumstances to turn out differently for Edith, but rubbing their poor child's nose in her mistakes was not allowed.

'Our girl is back, that's what matters,' said Frau Hund.

Edith trod gingerly around the house, praying for the floor not to give way. Satisfied that the danger had passed, she pushed each piece of furniture back into its rightful place and washed and cleaned until she had polished the quake away.

For weeks afterwards, Edith noticed that her father was quieter than usual. He sat alone, even at mealtimes, his eyes reddened, taking little interest in life. She assumed that the quake had awakened painful memories. At night he would meticulously check all the doors and windows, often sleeping in a chair by the fireside rather than retiring to bed. His brown eyes had dark circles underneath and the laughter had left his face. Not even Jack and Ned could make him smile.

Whenever she left the house, his voice rang out, 'And

where are you going alone? It's no place to go wandering about.'

One night, after her father refused to eat with them, she saw him scraping his meal into the chickens' scraps. Edith knew she must try to get her proud father to talk.

When Jack and Ned were finally asleep in their shared bed, and the house was quiet, Edith wandered through into the kitchen to make hot cinnamon milk and her favourite apple cookies. She enjoyed this peaceful time of day and lingered, slowly weighing the flour, adding the ingredients one by one and greasing the tins. As she sat down in front of the log fire waiting for the biscuits to cook, Edith saw her mother holding a copy of *Jane Eyre* to her breast and periodically pretending to read.

'They're asking when the library will be open,' Edith said, raising the steaming milk to her lips.

Her father looked out of the window. 'The library is finished,' he said, with no emotion. 'I am not having your mother persecuted. We came to this country to be free, to escape such horror.'

Her mother placed her book face down and moved wearily over to her husband's side. They sat together, each wiping away the other's falling tears. Then, reaching for one another, they held on tight. Edith took the cloth from the stove and bent down to remove the baking tray from the hot oven, as the smell of burning apple filled the kitchen.

With her back to them Edith whispered, 'It's not ruined.'

She placed the hot cookies on the table and eased them out of the tin on to a wire cooling rack.

'I will run the library,' she said, wiping her fingers down the sides of her apron. 'I was born here, let's see people deal with that.' She pushed the baking tray into the deep sink, the sound of sizzling metal almost drowning out her father's angry voice.

'I cannot allow it,' he said. 'It is not safe for a woman.'

Edith scoured the tray back and forth, vigorously removing every trace of grease. After drying her hands, she arranged the cookies in a circular pattern on a clean plate and slowly replenished the mugs with milk from the jug, taking her time to grate fresh nutmeg over the top.

'I have lived long enough to know what people are capable of. Nothing surprises me any more,' she said softly.

She held the plate towards her parents and nodded her head in reassurance. Her mother unwound herself from her husband's arms and embraced her daughter. Then mother and child sat together on the bench and nibbled the apple cookies in silence.

Herr Hund watched for a long time. Then he walked across the kitchen and opened the dresser drawer. Reaching inside, he removed a large iron key. 'I will not fight with you as well,' he said, handing Edith the library key.

The next day, Edith prised open the newly fitted lock and stepped inside her mother's Aladdin's cave. Sitting cross-legged on the floor with a fine paintbrush in her hand, she practised drawing words across the canvas to ensure they would fit. When her mind was clear, she took from a bag her sons' precious paints. The material absorbed the first brush stroke and she slowly added to it, building up the letters until they boldly stood out. Finally satisfied, she hung the sign up? to dry and surveyed her handiwork.

'Travis Library. Open.'

A fat ginger tom cat lay basking across the library steps in the sun. When Edith tried to shoo it away it refused to move.

By teatime Edith had rescued enough books to fill the front shelves. Exhausted, she slumped into sleep on the floor. She awoke with a start to discover the cat rubbing its slinky body against her arm. Edith relented, feeding it cake crumbs mixed with a splash of milk. The sound of people passing by made her wonder if she had been naive in believing she could alter anything with a pot of paint and change of name.

As evening's shadows fell, the screech of a bicycle braking on the dusty path brought Edith to the front door. Although the door was open, the lady cyclist knocked. Older and much taller than Edith, she carried a large wicker basket under her long arms.

'I teach school,' she announced, a trace of an Irish accent lining her voice.

She extended her hand and Edith warmly shook it. 'Edith Travis,' she said. 'I'm the new owner.'

'Pleased to meet you,' said the teacher. 'I was ashamed to live in this town when I saw what they had done.'

'Never let injustice win,' said Edith, paint spots spattered over her weary face. The teacher smiled and said, 'My children will be delighted you're back in business.' Edith, clasping her hands, said, 'why don't you bring your class and they can choose some books for free?'

'That's very generous,' she replied.

'I don't know how I've survived without this place.'

'Me neither,' said Edith.

Edith wanted to make the library her own and added quickly to her Mama's extensive collection. From across the states she bought newspapers and society magazines published in response to America's insatiable appetite for information. Recognizing people's natural desire to escape from war, she stocked lavish society magazines with the latest fashions, beauty tips and travel pieces. Such journals proved to be hugely popular and she soon built up the library's custom once again.

Early one morning, ahead of the day's bustle, Edith was reading the *Washington Post* when she noticed a report in the society pages. A shudder rushed down her backbone as she glanced at the headline: 'Mr Maurice Roche from Elm Court gives dinner to 100 at Newport.' She abandoned her cataloguing and sat down to read the full story. It said that Maurice had entertained the likes of the Vanderbilts and the Russian sculptor Prince Paul Troubetskoy at the Hill Top Inn in Newport, Rhode Island. 'There was an evening of animation when myriads of blue and red electric bulbs in the foliage illuminated the grounds and tables on the lawn. The event was a large dinner followed by dancing and supper.' Checking to see that no one was looking, and ashamed of the act she was about to commit, she tore the page from the newspaper, folded it in quarters and tucked it inside the garter of her stocking.

Back home, Edith feigned a headache and on her mother's instruction went to bed early with a remedy of pressed garlic and ginger. 'Swallow this down with salt on your tongue,' ordered Frau Hund. Edith downed the tart mixture, closing her eyes, but all she could see was Maurice dancing with beautiful girls on a lawn.

Unable to sleep, she took the newspaper clipping and carefully unfolded the curled edges of the large page. Sitting on the bed, she pulled open the drawer of her side table, took out her pad and paper, and started to write a letter. She did wonder whether she was doing the right thing, but she could not stop herself.

Dear Mr Roche,
Please forgive this intrusion, I read of your exploits in the newspaper and it provided me with your address. I am intending to come to New York on business alone and wondered if you might care to meet? I am sure my journey east won't be as exciting as the last time. But if you spare the time, none of that will matter.
Kindest thoughts, Edith Travis.

FOUR

'Give Me the Chance'

With no thought for privacy, Maurice had stopped on the sidewalk and ordered the porter to unlock each of his cases. Shirts, shoes, brochures, even underwear came tumbling out, everything except the errant slip of paper.

He had already searched frantically through his pockets and emptied every one. But the piece of paper with her address had somehow gone. Where the hell was it?

What a fool he was for not finding Edith, what an absolute fool! He had scanned the crowds hoping to see her face. But she was gone.

Maurice spent the next two weeks in a haze, wandering around the San Francisco exhibition with a complete lack of purpose. At every corner he expected to see Edith smiling back at him, saying it had been a joke and she knew where he'd be, but with each passing day his efforts at self-delusion became less convincing. Missing the chance to meet Edith was bad enough; to do so by losing her address made him feel stupid and angry.

When Maurice finally had to return to Newport, it was with a heavy heart. He longed so much to see her again that he found it impossible to settle back into normal life; he was always daydreaming of what might have been. Eventually, using his connections with the Vanderbilts, he took a job as a lowly clerk in Hoboken, New Jersey. Just being near the railways reminded him of meeting Edith on the train and gave him comfort.

Maurice tried to explain this unusual career move to his perplexed twin brother Frank by claiming, 'Loafing is all right for a while. But a man needs to do something worthwhile.'

'And this has nothing to do with that girl you met on the train, I suppose?' said Frank, raising an eyebrow.

'Don't be ridiculous,' said Maurice.

'You're just a typical love-sick Roche. Let's hope you don't get yourself into a mess, like mother,' Frank replied.

Fannie Burke Roche's love life had never run smoothly. As a wild, rich and beautiful woman, her infatuation with Jim was never going to last long. When the money ran out, partly owing to Jim's extravagance, she soon tired of Ireland and in 1891 fled with the twin boys and their elder sister back to America.

Her wealthy father agreed he would help but only on condition she divorce Jim. With the lure of her father's millions as bait, Fannie found a judge in Ohio, Delaware, who was happy to sign the paperwork. She was a free woman again.

Or so she thought.

After their separation, Jim did not see Fannie for over a year and he had no idea that his marriage had been annulled. It was only on flicking through a copy of the society handbook, *Debrett's Peerage*, that he discovered what Fannie had done. Jim's pride was wounded, he hated the idea that his former wife could use the American courts to divorce him without his knowledge. Incensed, he fought back and sued Debrett for libel, claiming that Fannie was subject to British law and that the American court ruling was invalid. In his eyes she was still his wife. Debrett conceded and reinstated Fannie in their next edition.

'It's up to us to re-establish the family name,' said Maurice.

'So says the man who inherits a fortune, but works on the railways. Honestly, Maurice, you take this duty thing a bit too far. Stop worrying and get on with life.'

Maurice knew that his brother was right. He had taken the job on the railroad in the hope of seeing Edith. It was ludicrous, but all other efforts to trace her had failed.

The circular indentation on Edith's finger had been softening and fading since that night on the train when she took off her wedding ring. Now nobody would know she had ever been married. Yet when her divorce papers came through, Edith was shocked by the sombre finality of it all. After ten years with Forrest it was hard to believe there was another way to live. She read the decree that formally ended her marriage, then hid it underneath the mattress of her cast-iron bed. A chapter in her life was over, and yet she was back where it all started, with her parents.

She handed her father a mug of black coffee while he sat quietly in the corner of the library, his hands resting solemnly on the table. Herr Hund had started coming there to protect Edith and found that, despite himself, he enjoyed the cultured atmosphere. He liked the well-thumbed books and took to scrutinizing the newspapers in the hope that by Christmas there would be good news from Europe. He scoured the war reports in the forlorn hope there would be an end to hostilities. Instead he read of thousands of casualties who had been suffocated by deadly chlorine gas. There was no end in sight to the barbarity.

Each day his presence made Edith more restless. She looked forward to going home and sitting on the front porch with her boys at her feet. One night, after gathering the keys, she motioned for Herr Hund to put down his paper, but instead of turning out the light, he was drawn to another article. She jangled the keys in the hope that he would fold away the newspaper. When he still didn't move she tried to provoke him. 'It makes no sense to me why people fight,' she said, poking the article with her finger.

'It is because they disagree,' he said. 'Look at you and Forrest.'

Provoked, she shouted, 'Will you never stop blaming me? I will not be the last woman on earth to fall in love with the wrong man. Would you rather I stayed with a drunkard than try to make a better life on my own?'

'You made a promise,' he said calmly.

'So did Forrest,' she said.

'You would not listen, I tried to warn you . . .'

'Papa, I was sixteen years old. Yes, I was wrong, but do not punish me for the rest of my life.' Her anger turned to exasperation. 'I need to do this my way. Do not hate me for trying.'

'I could never hate you.'

'Respect me then.'

'That is something which is earned,' he said, closing the newspaper and switching off the desk light.

From the way Edith had been watching the mail

deliveries, Frau Hund had convinced herself that the most marvellous news was imminent. So when a letter from New York arrived she put it on the kitchen table and kept a watchful eye. She couldn't help fingering the seal and she had to sew her most complicated cross stitch to stop herself from prying.

Edith came home first, followed by Herr Hund. As they walked in, it was as if the air had been sucked out of the room. Sensing the discord, Frau Hund tucked the letter inside the piano lid.

'You have a surprise,' she said, when her husband had gone to feed the chickens.

'Do I?' asked Edith, not in any mood for her mother's silly games.

'It came this morning,' Frau Hund said, opening the piano lid.

'Not more music. Mama I do not have time to learn any more tunes.'

'It is a note,' her mother said. 'From New York City.'

Edith was so startled that she grabbed at the envelope. Then, unable to wait, and turning her back on her mother, she read,

Elm Court,
Bellevue Avenue,
Newport R.I.

My Dear Mrs Travis,
Many thanks for your letter and I am delighted to hear that you are now on your way east, and that very soon I shall have the pleasure of seeing you. Unfortunately I have had to give up all idea of going to Chicago at present. I should like to have

found at least ten days and that is impossible.

I shall, however, be on hand to give you a welcome upon your arrival here in New York. I *promise* that. I have a motor and in your spare time can show you about. Of course, I know you will be very busy when you first get here, but I might be able to amuse you in some way. I hope you will give me the chance. Do send me a line to the above address and tell me just what train you are coming on. I want to be on hand to greet you.

Yours ever,

Maurice Roche.

At church on Sunday, Edith stood beside her father in his favourite pew as the organist played 'Rock of Ages'. This was when Herr Hund was most at ease. The other members of the congregation knew he was a righteous man, and didn't care about his origins. They welcomed him in as a good, God-fearing citizen.

Afterwards, as they wandered home through the cemetery, the mossy undergrowth gave Edith an unlikely spring in her step. Feeling brave, she turned to her father

'Papa, I have to go to New York soon,' she said.

His whole body stiffened. 'Out of the question,' he said.

Edith tugged on his sleeve, urging him to carry on walking, as if somehow it would set his spirit free.

'I need more periodicals for the library – you know how people love them,' she said, unable to look at him.

Herr Hund jammed his foot between the rungs of the gate. 'Is gossip and tittle-tattle worth more than your life? The trains are being targeted by bombers. It is not worth the risk.' His jaw locked tight and the muscle on the side of his head pulsed.

'I am not afraid,' Edith said warily, for out of the corner of her eye she could see her mother approaching with Jack and Ned.

'You never are,' he said. 'That is the problem.'

Herr Hund pulled the gate hard and marched ahead, whistling for the boys to follow him home down the narrow lane. But even they struggled to keep up with the speed of their Grossvater's gait.

Edith moaned to her mother, 'It is the same as ever. I am still the child. Why will he never let me go?

'Wait until your boys are men,' her mother replied. 'Then tell me that.'

'It's because I'm a woman,' said Edith.

'No, my dear, it's because you are his child.'

Edith rubbed her hands together in exasperation. 'He needs to remember what it is like to be young.'

Her mother appeared wistful for a moment and then said, 'That was a long time ago. I loved New York City. It was where my life began with your father. You must promise you will go dancing for me.'

Back home the boys were in playful mood, and time spent in their company had softened Herr Hund. Over lunch, Edith poured him a large shot of schnapps, and afterwards she refilled his glass and sat down by his side.

'Papa, tell me about the first time you saw America and how worried you were for us all.'

'I wasn't worried, my daughter,' Herr Hund said, 'I was excited. When we sailed into Ellis Island and I saw the Statue of Liberty, I thought I was looking at an angel. But then my dream soured as we waited on the barge for two days with no food or water. When we were finally cleared by the doctor I carried all our bags, holding the health certificate between my teeth.'

'But it was worth it, Papa,' said Edith.

His eyes burned bright. 'Of course. I thought I was coming to paradise. But just like the Garden of Eden, some places change.'

'Nothing stays the same, Papa. You gave me a different future as I must do for my boys,' she said.

'Maybe,' he said. 'But the war makes me think we have learned nothing.'

'The war will not last for ever,' she said.

Frau Hund sat down at the piano and began playing a German lullaby, as Edith kneeled at her father's knee and tenderly sang,

> Lullabye, lullabye my lovely one,
> Close your eyes and sweetly dream,
> Lullabye, lullabye my lovely one,
> Schlaf in schwarz-gearbeitetem silbrigem Strom.

He smiled and stroked her head, deep in his own thoughts; neither of them wanted the melody to end.

'If you must travel to New York, then go,' he said, dozily, with a wave of the hand.

Her mother gently replaced the piano lid and winked.

A telegram arrived for Edith the following day but preferring to read it away from prying eyes, she kept it hidden at the bottom of her bag. All the way to the library it was as if the telegram was burning a hole through the material and her hands shook as she tore at the paper.

Dear Mrs Travis, Many thanks for your letter. Will not be able to reach New York before Wednesday. Much love Maurice.

Telling her first customer that she would be back in a few minutes, she pedalled ferociously to the bank, withdrew her savings and ran to the railway ticket office just as it was opening. She knew she had to do it then, or she might lose her nerve.

'A return to New York please.'

'You off again, Miss Travis?' asked the ticket seller, recognizing her from the library.

'Yes, thank you, to see a friend.'

'It's a long way. Must be a good one.'

'I hope so.'

Maurice had risen early, long before the manservant came to open the drapes and place fresh coffee beside his four-poster bed. It had been a difficult night. Although usually a good sleeper, he could not stop his mind from racing long enough to drift off properly, and just before dawn broke, he turned his light back on and read.

The days before the rendezvous with Edith were passing depressingly slowly. Her chatty, unassuming notes were the highlight of his day. What had he thought about before he met the irrepressible Mrs Travis?

Her recent letter lay open upon the oak bureau, both sides of the wafer-thin paper covered with news. She wrote easily and with passion, sometimes every day. The more he read, the more Maurice liked her.

Flames from the marble fireplace created an eerie flickering across the ceiling, and the insistent tick from the pendulum clock on the mantelpiece urged him to waste no more time. He chose a leaf of cream notepaper embossed with his Newport address and, picking up his fountain pen, began:

My dearest Edith,

I was *so* glad to hear from you this morning and also that you have been passing your time in a profitable way. I am leaving here tomorrow and will take the night train Tuesday to New York, getting there Wednesday morning. I awoke to find the rain falling and went to church. I played some tennis today and have been with my mother. I am looking forward so very much to seeing you.

He had never been a good letter-writer, but hoped she would not mind. He re-read the lines for inspiration before adding, 'I think of you all the time – my best love. I will write again.' Despite the heavy rain, Maurice walked to the post office to mail the letter himself rather than trust his manservant.

Maurice arrived bleary-eyed at a snowy Grand Central Station. During the morning he had changed his shirt and tie twice and his shoes once. Now his expensive French cologne was causing the other travellers to glance at him with suspicion, and he was no longer sure the extra dab had been a good idea.

Catching sight of his reflection in Bloomingdale's window, he saw a man in a thick cashmere overcoat looking somewhat stockier than he cared for. But the temperature was below freezing and he realized he would have to forgo sartorial elegance for the sake of good health.

As he walked into the station's south entrance he checked the time on the elaborate Tiffany clock, surrounded by the Greek statues of Hercules, Minerva and Mercury. I hope the gods are smiling on me today, he thought.

His fingers were frozen from gripping a single scarlet carnation, and his stomach rumbled thanks to a loss of appetite that had been with him for several days. Quite unable to stand still, Maurice paced the entire length of the concourse, not once looking up at the gilded stars and constellations on the ceiling.

He heard the announcement that the Twentieth Century Limited train had pulled in. This was Edith Travis's train and Maurice felt the anticipation of being with her once again. As the throng of passengers filed by, Maurice scanned their faces, waiting for that exquisite moment of recognition.

But Edith failed to appear.

Not used to being kept waiting, he pushed his hands into his pockets and the carnation's stem twisted awkwardly. She must be delayed, he thought, straining to hear the loudspeaker. Perhaps one of the boys has been taken ill. Or Edith has had some kind of accident.

He retraced his steps to the clock, checking the time. As he watched the minutes tick slowly past, he heard a breathless voice from behind.

'Mr Roche. It is you?'

He glanced around and there was Edith. She had been running. Her shawl was falling over her shoulders and the feather in her hat had come adrift.

'Mrs Travis!' he said, laughing with joy.

He kissed her flushed cheek and took her suitcase. It hardly weighed a thing.

'I couldn't find my luggage or a porter,' she said.

He shook his head dismissively. 'You're here now, that's all that matters.' Remembering the carnation in his pocket, he pressed the wilting flower into her hand. 'So sorry,' he said. 'It's not what I intended.'

'That's much more than I am used to,' she said.

He offered his arm and they walked from the station to Maurice's car.

Inside the plush interior, Edith detached the flower's head and fixed it to the lapel of her coat, the smell of leather and polish mingling with the carnation's delicate perfume.

Maurice placed a heavy woollen rug over her legs and fired up the engine. Handling the car with ease, he smoothly shifted through the gears and manoeuvred away from the station.

'Have you ever skated?' he asked, hiding the fact he was a former ice skating champion.

'There isn't much snow in Marin County!'

'That's certainly not a problem today,' he said, over the noise of swishing windscreen wipers.

Twenty minutes later, Central Park stretched in front of them, a piece of English countryside inside the middle of Manhattan. Switching off the engine, Maurice moved swiftly around the front of the car to help Edith. The ground was slippery from the snow and they walked gingerly towards the Bow Bridge.

'They used to rig a ball up to the top of a pole to let you know the ice was safe,' said Maurice.

'What happens now?' asked Edith.

'It's all a matter of trust,' he smiled.

She gripped his arm tightly, and he reassuringly patted the back of her hand. They peered through the falling snow and followed the tracks of courting couples, entwined against the biting cold.

On the frozen ice a carousel of faces came in and out of focus as people snaked around.

'Want to give it a go?' said Maurice, sizing up a pair of skates.

'I guess so,' she said, still unsure.

'I won't let you go,' he said. 'Promise.'

On the bench, he gently held her leg and pulled the boots' leather laces tight to protect her ankles.

'How's that feel?'

'The left one's a little loose,' she lied, as he touched her again.

When Edith tried to stand up, her legs wobbled like a new-born foal's and she instinctively grabbed Maurice for support.

'Take it slow,' he said. 'Feel the ice.'

'I must look silly,' she said, stumbling.

'No you don't,' he said.

Edith's confidence came gradually. Her muscles relaxed and she pushed against the blades and began to look around the lake, rather than stare at her boots.

'I think you're ready to go solo,' he said.

'You do?' she giggled, startled but excited.

He released her hand. 'It's just like riding a bicycle. Keep going and don't look back!'

She took a deep breath and drove off hard. For a few seconds she thought she was flying. And then came the bumpy landing.

He stood over her with a flustered look on his face.

'Are you all right, darling?'

'You called me darling,' she said, blinking.

'I did,' he said, helping her up. 'It's terribly bad manners.' He smiled. 'Are you hurt?'

'Really, I'm fine,' she said, brushing off the flakes of frost.

'Come on then!' he yelled. 'Race you round once more!'

After an hour, the cold and ice had gone right through to Edith's bones. Shivering, she untied her boots and walked with Maurice carefully back along the pathway.

She had rented a small room in a downtown boarding-house at a dollar a night. It had one bathroom, shared with six others. As they drove away from the park, Edith decided she would ask Maurice to drop her off some distance away, so that neither of them would be embarrassed.

'Where are you staying?' he asked.

'With relatives,' she lied.

'I'll come and pick you up.'

'No, no . . . I can get a ride. Where are we meeting?'

'The Waldorf, of course,' he laughed.

Two blocks from the boarding-house, Maurice pulled over and watched as Edith stood in a doorway waving him goodbye.

'See you this evening,' he yelled.

'I'll be there,' she mouthed back.

Maurice headed straight for the elegant splendour of the Waldorf Astoria Hotel on Fifth Avenue. Its extreme comfort made it a particular favourite of New York's elite, the self-styled top 'Four Hundred'. Although Maurice was one, he thought them snobbish and faintly ridiculous but he played along.

The doorman opened his car door and a valet stepped forward to park the snow-covered vehicle. Maurice's luggage was hauled from the trunk and carried to his usual suite on the seventeenth floor. Walking through the hotel, Maurice stopped at the café to sit in the rosewood drinking bar. He wanted to soak up its gentlemanly atmosphere and give himself some Dutch courage. Leaning on the brass rail, he downed a large whisky and summoned the concierge.

'Can you reserve the best table in the restaurant for eight o'clock please.'

Maurice ordered another large whisky as he flicked through the pages of *The American*. He started reading an article, but it immediately bored him. He had been apart from her for less than half an hour but could still feel the way Edith had leaned into him around the frozen lake, the lightness of her frame, the slenderness of her wrist. He was a man obsessed.

Edith took the wrong bus and jumped off quickly when she saw the Waldorf disappearing into the distance. Unable to find transport back, she walked along the icy sidewalk, slipping whenever she tried to run. She knew she would be late.

Arriving at last, she wanted to warm herself, so she turned away from the check-in girl near the entrance and refused to hand over her coat.

'No, I'm fine,' she said, walking into the Palm Room, where she had to pinch herself.

The famous restaurant had, half hidden behind a trellis of vines, a delicate leaded glass ceiling the like of which she had never seen before. She stared at the tables of chattering diners awash with gold and diamonds that glinted in the candlelight.

'Hello again,' Maurice said, standing to greet her. 'I hope your car was warm, it's freezing out.'

She smiled. 'The car was very snug, I almost didn't want to get out.' Thinking that might sound rude, she added, 'I mean, I wanted to see you, of course.'

Maurice tried to put Edith at ease by talking lightheartedly about his turbulent family history; how, since the death of his domineering grandfather, the father of Fannie, their private lives had provided much gossip for the society pages. Perhaps it was the way she listened so attentively, or the effect of the whiskies, but Maurice soon found himself revealing much more than he intended.

'My rather flamboyant mother has divorced again,' he said. 'I think she is keen for people to know.'

Edith smiled. 'Does she have no shame?'

'Certainly she has no desire to be left penniless.'

'Never rely upon a man for money,' she said.

'In my circles, we men tend to feel a little hounded!'

She raised an eyebrow. 'Why's that?'

'Obsession with money,' he replied. 'My wealthy grandfather insisted my mother leave both her husbands, or forfeit the family fortune.'

'That's a rather unusual request.'

'Yes, but we are an unusual family,' Maurice shrugged. 'My mother would never do as expected. She'd attack anyone who threatened her position in the Four Hundred.'

'Could they really hurt her?' Edith asked.

'They could make life uncomfortable in her set. But she would never allow it to go much further. By sheer force of will she would win through.' He leaned across the table and in a mock whisper said, 'Edith, my dear, one so-called friend said my mother never refused a social engagement whether her husband was invited or not. She lives for parties.'

'Maybe your mother and stepfather didn't care to be alike. Love can take many different forms.'

He sipped his wine and smiled. 'My grandfather hated both her husbands. He even tried to pay the last one off, a Hungarian horseman called Batonyi.'

'Was he successful?' she asked.

'Not exactly. Batonyi was so angry at being bribed that he went for the jugular. It got very personal and he turned on my mother for not standing by him. He swore in court that she had an illegitimate child by a Wall Street magnate, then wanted a million dollars to withdraw the allegations.'

As Maurice talked of these vast sums of money, Edith began to appreciate the true extent of his wealth. She thought of her own meagre circumstances, which seemed so paltry and ordinary.

'Money can twist minds,' she said. 'Surely it is better to live a simple life than be consumed by greed.'

Maurice nodded. 'Batonyi certainly got too big for his boots. He thought he was invincible and decided to represent himself. A fatal mistake. Under cross-examination he crumbled, but by then my mother would have nothing more to do with him.'

Maurice stretched back in the chair and drained his glass of wine, covering over the top when a hovering waiter tried to refill it.

Both of them looked down at their hors-d'oeuvres, which lay untouched, and even though Maurice had stopped talking, there was no awkwardness between them. The dining-room suddenly seemed a very public place.

'Edith,' he began. 'Please don't be shocked, but I'm not hungry and you don't appear to be either.'

'I feel dreadful because it's all so wonderful but I can't eat a thing,' she agreed.

He took a chance.

'Would you like to leave?'

Edith pushed back her chair and stood up from the table. Assuming that his clumsy invitation had caused great offence and that the evening was over, he began a fumbling apology.

Instead, her hand was reaching out towards him.

In his penthouse, she stared out at the New York panorama, while he poured gin and tonic.

'I love the city,' she said.

He did not respond but stared back at her.

'Is there something wrong?' she said.

'I'm just looking at you,' he said, moving closer.

She held his gaze.

Maurice pulled her towards him. His arms held her close and he lightly touched her neck with his lips. His breath made the hairs on her skin flicker.

She pushed gently against his chest.

'I can't,' she said.

Maurice stepped back.

'I mean . . . I am scared,' she said, turning round and holding her hand out to his.

'Of what?' he said.

'Your knowing me,' she stuttered.

He cupped her head gently in his hands and he felt the cold of her cheeks.

'I already do,' he said, looking into her eyes and lightly brushing her lips. He led her with such tenderness, that her fear faded away.

As they lay together there was no sound, only touch. Their first time revealed a need that startled them both.

FIVE

'The Lewis Gun'

Maurice did not want Edith to leave New York. The desire to be together gripped him so tightly that he never wanted to let go. Existing for snatched days and nights was not how either of them wanted to live.

'I don't care, Maurice. I just want to be near you,' she said. 'Being thousands of miles apart just doesn't feel right.'

'I know,' he said. 'It's a huge change, but come to New York. It's a city you'll learn to love, and the boys will too.'

Maurice was desperate for Edith not to weaken once she was back in Marin County. But he knew she was a proud woman and found it hard to accept his offers of financial assistance. Writing from the Knickerbocker Club in New York, and taking great care not to offend her, he urged her:

My dear Edith. Do keep up your courage and things will come out all right. Let me know when I can be of some help. You must be very glad to have your boys with you. I trust you are all well. Much love. Maurice.

Edith's impetuosity drove her on, and she was determined to do this on her own. She loved everything about Maurice, but was resolved never to be beholden to him. On returning to her parents' house she knew the time had come to be brave.

It would be hard telling them, as they had done so much, but she needed independence. Once her mind was made up, she went about it in as gentle a way as possible saying she loved them both. 'I have to know I can cope on my own,' she said to her weeping mother. Finally, with her bags packed and in the hall, and the boys running round the rooms, she pulled her father to one side and thanked him for his generosity.

Herr Hund shrugged. He knew that no matter what was said, his daughter's mind was set.

'My girl, some things in life are hard to understand,' he said, shaking his head. 'And you are one of them.'

'Papa, I am my father's daughter,' she said, hugging him hard.

'I will miss you, Liebling,' he said rubbing her back. 'Do not be a stranger.'

'I love you, Papa,' she said. 'But let Mama keep the library, she needs to know you love her.'

'I will go there and think of you,' he promised.

Edith found a small apartment in Lakewood, south of New York. It was simply furnished but clean, comfortable and discreet enough for Maurice not to worry about being spotted. The rent was cheap, and she could afford the down payment with income she had made from the library. She didn't care what job she found as long as the boys were happy and their stomachs full.

Within a week, Edith was selling ice cream from a stall next to Lake Carasaljo's wooden kissing bridge. Oh, how her sons loved her! The joy they felt being handed over-filled cones and then sitting peacefully watching the still waters. Edith was happy. Being in the fresh air and seeing the excited children had a calming influence on her changing life. Her Italian immigrant boss was quick to grasp that her pretty face was good for business; but what he liked even more, being an astute businessman, was her optimism and hard work. He was so taken with her that he insisted she come and wait at the tables in his Italian café during the low season.

Mindful that the gossip columns were keeping a careful eye on Maurice, Edith told no one about their relationship. As a divorcee with two young children, she could embarrass him. It all had to be handled with care. Protecting her children was also important. She found a friendly school and smiled at the other mothers. They liked this stranger with her curled-back hair and natural manner. One friendly mother, Mrs Bankin offered to look after the boys if Edith was working late, which was a handy excuse for seeing Maurice. Edith at last began to feel she had her own identity.

Meanwhile Frank wondered why his brother's city trips were becoming so frequent. He knew Maurice had quit the job on the railway, but he seemed more withdrawn and secretive of late.

'I thought we could play tennis this weekend, invite a few people over – it's a while since we were on the courts,' Frank said.

'You'll have to count me out,' said Maurice. 'I'm in New York.'

'My doubles partner goes AWOL again,' said Frank, clearly annoyed. Disappointment encouraged his directness. 'What takes you there this time?'

'Boring business,' said Maurice, casually.

'You seem to be doing a lot of that lately. What's the big deal?' Frank watched his brother's face for a flicker of discomfort.

Maurice shook his head. 'Nothing dramatic, I'm afraid. Dull stocks and shares, that's about as exciting as it gets.' In order to cover for his lie, he stood up and ushered Frank into the pool room.

'Fancy a game?' he said, with false enthusiasm.

Frank was not convinced.

The more Maurice saw of Edith, the more he admired her new-found independence and the way she rose to each challenge without fuss. It was a lesson his wealthy society friends could do with learning. No matter how much money and good fortune came their way, many of his set moaned and complained about how difficult life was.

Watching Edith carve a life for herself, eking out her meagre earnings and shrieking with delight when she could at last afford a new rag rug, was a humbling experience for him.

When they could not be together, he wrote short loving notes of encouragement and support. She pinned them to her kitchen cupboard and each morning they would make her smile.

Edith adored these billets doux and wanted Maurice to include small details of his day, so she could feel even closer to him. He was not used to writing in any great detail, but tried to satisfy Edith's curiosity. 'My mother was glad to have me back and I am cooling off here since my return. I had an excellent swim in the ocean, the water was just right. Do take good care of yourself and don't worry about things. Much love.'

Their time together was spent simply, as Edith felt no need for fancy restaurants or Broadway shows. Instead they wandered around museums and art galleries and took the ferry to Manhattan. One weekend she wouldn't tell him where they were going, but insisted they left his car behind in Lakewood and headed for the kissing bridge. It was an afternoon where nothing happened, except being together.

Edith did not get an invitation to meet his family or see the estate on Rhode Island. But none of that mattered. They were happy with each other, and she thought that one day it would happen.

While they were apart, Maurice felt emotions he never knew existed. He needed to express his love whenever they parted. One night, upset at having to return to Elm Court after a romantic dinner at the Plaza Hotel he wrote to Edith,

> I hated to leave you in New York. I have thought a
> good deal of our two days together. I miss you very
> much and I hope you are happy my best love.
> I cannot say when I will get back to New York this
> minute, but I will know tomorrow. I hope it will
> be Monday morning. Let me know if there is
> anything I can do for you. God bless you.

However, Maurice had one secret which he felt unable to share. He wanted to keep things perfect between them, and knew that Edith would struggle to understand this deep desire. At first he coped with not telling her, but as the weeks went on he began to feel increasingly guilty.

Edith sensed his growing reticence and feared he was

perhaps feeling trapped by their relationship or, worse still, doubting her. For a long while she kept quiet, hoping he would relax enough to say whatever was on his mind.

Over a romantic dinner at the Claremont Inn restaurant, it all spilled out. She had decided that not knowing what was causing him such grief was far worse than whatever she was about to uncover.

'Maurice,' she began, 'is there something wrong?'

He was taken aback by her question and knew the time had come, but he did not know where to begin.

'Edith, I care for you so much,' he said.

She felt sick. This was it. She lowered her eyes.

'It's not you,' he said. 'It's me.'

'Oh, Maurice, spare me the kind farewells. Just tell me where I went wrong. I need to know.'

'What are you thinking?' he asked, ashen faced. He came and sat by her side. 'It isn't us, you fool.' He kissed her hand.

'It's not?' she said, laughing through the fear. 'Then what on earth is it?' she frowned.

He stuttered as he spoke. 'I am going to enlist,' he declared flatly.

The room went quiet for what seemed an eternity.

She spoke first. 'I have moved across a continent to be with you, yet now you expect me to cheer you off on a troop train, not knowing if you will return.'

'I would not feel a man if I did not fight,' he replied. 'A man must feel useful. I told you that when we first met, and it's even more relevant now.'

'But what use are you dead?' Edith asked, her voice raised enough for other diners to hear.

'Better death than a pointless life,' he said, standing to leave.

Edith stared at the floor, unable to think of a single word to say.

That night, Maurice lay awake, wishing he could make her understand that serving was not just an obligation. To him it was a matter of personal honour. Whatever he said seemed to make no difference; Edith always had the same response.

The following day, Maurice contacted the US army, but when he produced his papers they turned him away. Having an Irish father meant that he was ineligible to join the American services. Petty bureaucratic rules, however, would not deter him.

'I have to fight somehow,' he told Frank.

'This may be a long shot,' Frank suggested, 'but we could try to enter via Harvard.'

Maurice scoffed. 'What has Harvard got to do with the war?'

'They have a voluntary officer training corps with links to the main services. Get through basic instruction and you're in.'

A few weeks later, Frank was wearing the uniform of the naval reserve and Maurice that of the ROTC, the Reserve Officer Training Corps. Harvard was only too pleased to have them.

On 2 April 1917, the American Senate and the House declared war on Germany. President Woodrow Wilson stood on his podium and said, 'America is privileged to spend her blood and her might for the principles that gave her birth and happiness and the peace which she has treasured. God helping her, she can do no other.'

It had begun.

And Maurice, unlike Edith, was ready.

* * *

Maurice was thrown against the side of the truck as it hurtled along the dirt track of his new cantonment at Wrightstown, New Jersey. The other soldiers laughed, bouncing off their seats and hitting the floor, while he gripped on to the metal frame to keep his dignity intact.

Maurice, now thirty-two years old, worried about keeping up with the intensive physical training. Although fit and agile, he was up against much younger men, keen to prove themselves in combat. He knew he would have to rely on his knowledge of fluent French to give him a head start. Six commanding officers from the French army had been specially drafted for their expertise in trench warfare and to oversee training at the barracks.

Camp Dix was situated in woodland, sixty-five miles south of New York, in terrain chosen for its resemblance to the fields of northern France. Maurice thought the rows of tents made it look more like an Indian reservation in the movies than a theatre of war.

The camp was now accommodating 60,000 soldiers, far in excess of its intended capacity. Men were dismayed at the poor living conditions and at having to sleep in shifts to get a bed. Huts were thrown together in less than ten hours to relieve the overcrowding temporarily, but the haste in which they had been nailed up was evident. There was one small stove and a solitary dim bulb for every 250 men.

These claustrophobic conditions did not make for good morale. The night of 4 October 1917 ended with Maurice questioning the true nature of man's inhumanity to man. Soldiers from the 15th New York Coloured Infantry and the 26th U.S. Engineers almost engaged in a pitched battle. The engineers were men from the deep south who refused to accept black men in their army, so they pinned a sign in the lavatories: 'Nigger soldiers not allowed.'

The black men complained to senior officers, who had it removed. However, it was immediately replaced by a 'White soldiers only' sign. The black men tore it down and burned it in the yard, and then the tension erupted. Blacks and whites squared up to each other armed with clubs and stones, and only the intervention of a group of officers prevented a riot.

These were men fighting for the same cause. Yet they were unable to see beyond the colour of their skin. Maurice lay in his bunk knowing this was not why he had joined the army.

At half past five, he struggled from under the rough woollen blankets into the freezing washroom to shower in icy water. He ran the cut-throat razor up and down the leather strop until the blade sparkled. Lathering up as best he could, he pulled his skin tight and stroked the blade across his blue cheeks.

Fifteen minutes later roll call was followed by breakfast mess, a mixture of overcooked eggs and chewy cornflakes which had to be eaten hastily by six sharp, in time for the first class of the day.

Maurice was learning how to use a bayonet. He was ordered to aim for the enemy's neck. If the blade was thrust into the chest it could stick in bone and be impossible to withdraw. And a blow to the groin, while excruciatingly painful, rarely resulted in death, leaving the enemy able to fight back. 'The throat!' was the cry he heard each time he charged.

By midday, Maurice was sitting on a hard wooden bench eating a stew called by a different name but with the same taste as the day before. The milk pudding which followed was thick enough to hold a spoon upright. If an army marches on its stomach, he wondered how well they would fare.

His soft society hands soon became covered with calluses from hacking into unforgiving mud with heavy picks and shovels during the dreaded afternoon of trench digging.

'Come on,' said the soldier next to him. 'Get a rhythm going and it's much easier.'

'I don't know what I hate more, the pain of digging or having to read the endless manuals,' said Maurice, not moving.

The soldier smiled. 'Give me hard work rather than brain work any day. But it would help if we could hold a damn rifle, rather than just read about it.'

Maurice snorted and, raising the pick over his shoulder, struck the ground hard. He had promised to fight for his country, and whatever else, he would fulfil his part of the bargain.

He collapsed into the mess tent for dinner, every muscle aching. He brewed and drank two cups of strong coffee to sustain himself for the hours of French teaching that lay ahead.

At the end of each demanding day, Maurice retired to his narrow bunk exhausted, checked his gun belt and polished his hobnail boots, then clambered under the itchy covers and stretched widthways to prevent cramp. It was the only time in his life that he cursed his height. Before lights out at 9.45, he re-read Edith's letters to keep his spirits up. Using his suitcase as a desktop and forcing his eyes to stay open, he wrote back:

I was distressed to receive your letter addressed from the hospital – I sincerely hope that your operation was a success from every point of view. I cannot imagine how you came to get that inflamed gland. I wish I had time to write sooner, but if you know anything about the hours here we have very little time to ourselves. I have been taking this work very seriously. I often think of you and those happy times we had together and I am looking forward to the time when we shall meet again.

The mail was handed out each morning and Maurice looked forward to the treats Edith smuggled through to him. Despite candy being banned, she hid small packets of biscuits or wrapped a slice of Italian panettone from the café inside the parcel.

'Send it to your soldier,' her boss insisted, pushing towards her the largest piece he could find. She never failed to include something with her daily cheerful note. It was her way of showing her love and loyalty.

Although Edith winced at the word 'soldier', detesting the idea of Maurice fighting, she knew his honourable nature left him no option. To keep him, she would have to share his sense of duty. One thing was clear: she loved Maurice far too much to leave him. And so she sent him cake.

Discipline was maintained by strict rules, including restrictions on visits from sweethearts. As the training intensified, these were allocated rarely and only with special permission. Maurice knew that the more proficient he became at his army life, the closer he was to setting sail for Europe. Only being able to see Edith occasionally was making him miserable. Then lying on his bunk trying to remember the feel of her hair and the light in her eyes, he heard a mêlée in the corner of the tent. Men were gathering together in excited groups, slapping each other on the back.

'What's going on?' he asked the soldier next to him.

'We're on high alert,' came the reply.

'Is it an exercise?' Maurice asked.

'No. The real McCoy. Better pack your bag. We'll be going any day now.'

Maurice knew he had to see Edith one last time before leaving for France. It was unbearable to think they might never meet again. If he was caught, however, he could lose his rank of captain, something he had worked hard to achieve. Despite grave reservations, Maurice was prepared to risk all. It could be his last regret if he did not try.

The train station at Camp Dix was too risky for a rendezvous. Soldiers had been posted to watch the incoming trains and keep security tight. He decided to sneak Edith into a nearby station where there was less of a military presence. He scribbled a hasty note:

We are prohibited from going to New York unless on urgent business. Tell me what are your plans? I am pleased to hear that the boys are well and you have received your legal separation. Will you find out if there is a train service from Lakewood to Pemberton? I say that because the place is only five miles from here. Do find out about it – I am so anxious to see you. Just find out some town that lies between here and Lakewood on the main line. Let me know your finances. Much love Maurice.

Edith got everything in place and was waiting for the word when their plan was thwarted. Hundreds of men at

Camp Dix fell ill during a measles epidemic and needed round-the-clock care. Then Edith's sons contracted terrible fevers. Maurice was crushed with disappointment. He wrote to her trying hard to cover his true feelings: 'I was so sorry to get your letter this evening telling me of your boys' illness. We have been quarantined for measles.'

Maurice tried to persuade her to come anyway. 'It does not apply to officers – only the enlisted men. I am very well and have had a particularly interesting week with the Lewis gun.' It took a further week until her children were on the mend. Then she caught the first available train.

Edith was so excited waiting for Maurice behind Pemberton station that she hardly thought about being discovered. She had made a special effort to look pretty and wound red ribbon through her hair.

Taking a small mirror from her bag, she smoothed petroleum jelly along her lashes. She waited for the first glint of his buttons in the moonlight and the sound of his familiar stride, then saw the shape of his body silhouetted against the platform wall. He broke into a broad smile and ran the last few yards, arms outstretched.

'I have only a few minutes,' he said.

Kissing his fingers, she felt their new roughness against her face.

'Whatever happens, I will never leave you,' he said.

'You know I love you,' she said, her voice faltering. 'Write to me always.'

The distant voice of his accomplice yelled, 'Captain Roche!'

They held on for as long as they dared. He stroked her soft face and she buried her head in his neck. She felt the touch of his fingers over her hair, and he carefully untied her bow to let her curls fall down around her shoulders.

He lifted her face, kissed her lips and then turned away.

She watched until nothing moved and all she could see were dark stationary shadows. Reaching up to re-tie her hair, she found that the ribbon had disappeared.

Standing alone, Edith suddenly felt very frightened.

SIX

'I Cannot Understand'

The relief at being under way showed in Maurice's face. The stomach-churning fear that he had felt standing on the docks with the rest of the expedition force, left him as soon as he boarded SS *Olympic*. The waiting had been terrible, and as he marched on deck, he crossed himself and prayed all the men would be coming home.

Ominously, the *Olympic* was the sister ship of the ill-fated *Titanic*, and although she had made many successful transatlantic crossings, the wartime journeys were proving treacherous. The threat of enemy gun-fire remained ever present. Only a few months before she had been attacked in the English Channel by a German U-boat firing a torpedo at her bows. The *Olympic* turned and rammed the enemy hard. Maurice was reassured by the vessel's supremacy in the waters and hoped it would last.

He threw his kitbag on to his hammock next to the bulkhead and found a space alongside three other officers, already squeezed into the same small cabin. Maurice introduced himself and quietly settled down with a page of White Star Line paper embossed with 'On board S.S.

Olympic'. The first time he wrote to Edith he had only seconds. 'It was wonderful seeing you. Bless you. My love.' He took her hair ribbon from his top pocket, kissed it and tied it around the end of his hammock.

Time was short, and the men busied themselves practising drills, to ensure that they would always be ready for the enemy. Otherwise, thankfully, the journey was uneventful. Maurice wrote, as he was about to disembark:

I can't thank you enough for giving me the opportunity of seeing you again and you looked as beautiful as ever. It was kind of you to send me the wireless of good wishes. I hated leaving just as you arrived. We had a perfect crossing, practically no storms. I miss you very much. Bless you, much love.

A week later, Maurice was cleaning his Springfield rifle to the chilling hum of battle in a muddy field in France. He was with the 78th regiment in charge of the supply train, stationed outside a small town to the south of Calais. The troops, known as the Lightning Division because of the white flash emblazoned across their crimson insignia, had commandeered hay barns, lofts, attics and the YMCA. Comfort enough for any man at war, thought Maurice.

The ringing of bells, children selling figs and oranges and the occasional clip clop of donkey carts gave a deceptive air of normality.

Occasionally, the more sedate officers would even arrange an expedition to collect butterflies and wild flowers. Yet, in the distance, the continuous sound of blasting guns was a constant reminder of the reason they were there.

Maurice wiped away the blob of grease from his rifle and checked along the sights. He had to be as meticulous as possible, for his life now depended on it. A small fleck of dirt could clog up his rifle's mechanism and jam the trigger. He obsessively oiled and polished the metal, going over and over the drill to be followed in the event of attack. He did it until his head hurt and his fingers found the parts without looking. If he was to face death, he did not want to think in those few seconds. He wanted to be certain his actions were automatic. And if the time came to die, he prayed to God his last thoughts would be of Edith. As if to reassure himself, he pulled on the trigger and his rifle gave an encouraging click.

His unit advanced slowly towards the front, to relieve the British around St Mihiel. It was hoped the half a million Americans fresh from training would attack and demoralize the enemy, before a huge offensive in the Meuse–Argonne region. To control the Strasbourg to Lille railway, gunners launched wave after wave of attacks and achieved a small advance for the first time in many years. Thousands of German soldiers were taken prisoner. Maurice, as the supply commander, worked tirelessly to ensure the troops had what they needed at the front, but it was fraught with danger.

Contact with the outside world was erratic. It was an insular, bloody time, with soldiers so fatigued that they slept where they stood. With each onslaught the ground shook and the fields and sky merged into a mass of white explosions. At night the flashes of gunfire lit up the scattered twisted corpses of men who had walked through no man's land to their death.

Plans to use the railways were stalled while the Allies regrouped and devised new strategies of attack. Maurice was making continual trips to the front, supervising men and maintaining supplies. But advancing through the torrential rain and torn-up roads was almost impossible, and the infantry got bogged down in rivers of mud. Over the following weeks, the American assault ground to a standstill.

During breaks in gunfire, Maurice wrote to Edith.

Your letters have only just reached me. We have
had some hard work at times and I have also seen
the horrors of this war more than once. I often
think of all you did for me. So far the men in my
company have fared very well and have had no
casualties. Will you ever forget the day you came
to Camp Dix? I can picture you so far from the
struggle. Do take care of your boys. It is your
job.

Maurice kept sane by thinking of Edith. Amid the chaos and the terror her smiling face made him feel there was a purpose to his sacrifice. It was to keep her and her boys safe, and during the fiercest of the fighting she became his reason for being. Yet he feared he was becoming hardened and callous from the appalling sights he had witnessed, so he made light of the fighting.

I wonder when this terrific war will ever end.
I think it will come this fall; others state it will last
two years. I love getting letters, so do write often.
You will be pleased to hear I am so well and lucky
every time I go to the front. Much love and God
bless you. Maurice.

The morale and sheer number of American troops had done much to revitalize the fighting spirit of the Allies, and with exhausted Germans demoralized and suffering heavy casualties, hope lay on the horizon. When the war commander General Pershing ordered American and British forces to take the Argonne, the result looked like a foregone conclusion. Victory would be imminent.

It was a bloody scene. In appalling conditions thousands of Americans were killed in a series of bitterly fought exchanges. Maurice was one of the lucky ones. Many of his fellow officers fell this time, including several classmates from Harvard. Although victory looked within their grasp, he began to wonder if he really would see Edith again.

Edith did her bit for the war effort by following the lead of America's head of food, Herbert Hoover. He urged people to eat frugally so the boys on the front could be well fed. To avoid rationing, he demanded Americans go without wheat on Mondays and Wednesdays, and pork on Thursday and Saturdays. Edith considered this good sense and drew up a weekly food rota, seeing it as nothing more than an inconvenience, given what Maurice was going through.

Ned and Jack planted a victory garden and kept it well watered to ensure the vegetables grew. Much to her amusement they had taken to chanting 'Yeah, we're Hooverizing' at every mealtime.

Like many sweethearts and wives, Edith wanted to express the pride she felt in her man's bravery. Yet, unlike the other women, she had to keep her relationship with Maurice a secret. She could tell no one. So, rather than openly display a special war flag in her garden, as others did, she draped it discreetly from the mirror of her dressing table. Pinned across the stars she attached a small cloth on which she had embroidered: 'Captain Maurice Roche, 78th Division'. Each night in bed, with his framed picture on the side table, she watched the flag flickering gently in the breeze, and all the time it moved she knew he was with her.

When the Armistice came on 11 November 1918, Edith ran out into the street and found the boys marching up and down with sticks slung over their shoulders like rifles. She screamed, 'Peace, we have peace!' until tears ran down her face. They danced back inside and crammed their mouths with food until they could hardly breathe. The whoops and hollers of victory echoed around the neighbourhood as people partied throughout the night in celebration. Days later, Edith, Jack and Ned joined thousands in a victory parade to mark Germany's downfall. She now felt immense pride that Maurice had played a part in America's victory and hoped the days would be few until they could be together.

But there was to be no quick homecoming for the troops. The sheer might of the Americans had succeeded in overwhelming the German forces, but to get the millions of men home would be painfully slow and take longer than most of them had spent fighting. As for Maurice and his men, they had been told they must stay as a peacekeeping force. However, there seemed to be little for them to do.

Sitting quietly on the outskirts of Sedan, the sounds of gunfire now thankfully quelled, Maurice felt a long way from home. He wrote to Edith:

We are presently awaiting the time to go. Ever since the Armistice our division has been in the rest area

practically doing nothing. The next time you see me
I shall be dressed in civilian clothes with bow ties.

The war had changed the soldiers and the protracted
peace made it hard to believe anyone still knew they were
there. Maurice wrote to Edith on Christmas Day:

I am thinking of you today. You are at the other end
of the world. But I pray that you and the boys are
having a Happy Xmas together. It has been a nice
day here and we have had a good lunch and spent
the day sitting around. I hope this finds you well
and also the boys. I received your Christmas card.
Thank you for your kindness in remembering me.
Much Love, Maurice

He wanted to go back home, but not to the life he had
known before. He suspected that the frivolous existence
he had led at Newport, Rhode Island would have no
meaning for him now.

I am sending you a photo that was taken by a
Frenchman the other day. It isn't too bad. You will
see I have survived the war. I certainly have given
up all idea of living that useless New York life.
I am looking forward to seeing you after this
shameful war is brought to a close. You have been
wonderful in every way.

Although an uneasy peace had been restored and he had
survived the horrors, Maurice carried a huge burden. He
reproached himself for not fighting with the British army
from the onset of war. He had felt demeaned watching his

fellow men die, unable to stop the catastrophe. But the greatest blame lay in his own survival. He hated himself for having failed to do his duty properly while others made the ultimate sacrifice. He wrote:

> I shall never forgive myself for not having gone to war before I did, with the English. I may go out to New Zealand. I will let you know when we definitely sail. As yet we have no date; not having even made arrangements to pack. With much love.

Such revelations dismayed Edith, who wrote to assure Maurice that his efforts were valiant and heroic. But it made no difference, and she feared he might never get used to life back in New York.

He was not thinking straight. She had heard stories of men who returned from war as strangers to their wives, shadows of their former selves. The trauma of what they had witnessed altered their minds for ever. Was this happening to Maurice, she wondered? She wrote pleading with him not to make any rash decisions. 'Just come home and get used to normal life again,' she urged. 'Let me take care of you.'

Weeks turned to months and as he waited to be demobilized, Maurice thought deeply about what she had said. He knew she was, in her way, suggesting a life together.

Edith had never pressed him to become man and wife, and they had never talked about it, yet he felt there was an expectation that he would propose upon his return from war. From his family, there had always been immense pressure on him to 'do the right thing' and marry well, rather than selfishly follow his heart.

And no matter how hard he tried, marrying a divorced woman with children would not sit easily with his

81

conscience. Someone of his position needed a wife with an unblemished past. His family's reputation had suffered too many times in the wake of scandal.

Marriage to Edith would mean ridicule. He loved her, but doubted his own strength to cope with such public condemnation. The last thing he wanted was for his private life to be splashed across the papers.

'What shall I do?' he asked his brother when they met on leave in France.

'Find another girl,' said Frank phlegmatically.

'I don't want anyone else,' Maurice said.

'But you know she will never be accepted as one of us. They will make both your lives miserable,' Frank replied. 'When father dies you will be Lord Fermoy, and the aristocracy are more unforgiving than the Four Hundred.'

'I need her, Frank.'

'I can see that,' he said.

'What can I do?' Maurice asked.

Frank sipped cognac, and watching old men playing boules in the distance, gave his twin the most practical advice he could. 'You're a rich man. Offer her something – a life she could never expect without you.'

'What do you mean?' Maurice brooded.

'Don't marry her, but make her your de facto wife, Maurice. Mrs Roche in everything but name,' explained Frank, hardly believing what he was saying.

Maurice nodded in agreement. 'I could see a lawyer, get it put in writing, so that Edith feels secure.'

'She seems very independent,' warned Frank. 'Tread carefully. Talk to her.'

'I've wasted enough time, Frank I need to act. I want to be with the woman I love,' he said.

It was a normal busy evening in the Italian café. Edith could hear the phone ringing but decided to ignore it, not wanting to interrupt the complicated order she was yelling through to the kitchen. The phone kept going, and she walked wearily over to lift the receiver. Despite the crackly line, she immediately recognized her mother's voice.

'Mama, what is it?' she asked, dreading the reply.

'Your father is very ill. I think you should come home,' she said.

After the briefest of conversations Edith replaced the receiver and ran.

Marin County, she had heard, was in the grip of a virulent flu epidemic. Herr Hund had caught a simple chill but rapidly declined and one day, after working in the library, he collapsed on the way home. Now he lay grey and unmoving in his bed, a damp cloth pressed across his burning forehead. His breathing was shallow and he moaned out loud. He was one of the first victims.

The deserted streets of Marin County looked like a war zone. As Edith and the boys crossed the county line, officials demanded to see their certificates of good health to ensure they were not infected.

The authorities, terrified of the epidemic, had taken over large hotels and turned them into makeshift isolation units to house the vast numbers of sick and dying. Emergency laws were introduced, and those spotted not covering their face were thrown into a holding area. Even church services were abandoned, so that people did not gather together and increase the risk of contamination. And there were no cars anywhere. People were told to walk in the fresh air. Most obeyed, too afraid to resist the escalating level of government control.

Edith saw Dr Howitt before she went in to her father.

'He hasn't long left,' he said softly. 'I'm very sorry. He is a fine man.' The touch of his hand on her arm was comforting.

'Thank you,' she said, feeling helpless. 'He always trusted you.'

'I've known this family for a very long time. I remember your delivery. I've never seen a more proud father,' he said.

Edith could not speak.

'Now,' he said, seeing she was getting upset. 'Keep the boys away and always wear your mask. Influenza is highly contagious and very dangerous.'

'He loves them so much,' she said suddenly, remembering how her father took her and the boys in when she most needed help.

'Call me any time,' Dr Howitt said, snapping his bag shut. 'My practice is still right around the corner.'

Edith went back upstairs to where Frau Hund sat rubbing honey on her husband's parched lips and tried to persuade her to take a break. But her mother would not leave. Neither woman spoke much, Edith occasionally going downstairs to check on her sons and escape the cloud of decay lying heavy within her father's room. Ned awoke to sing a new rhyme he had learned:

> 'I had a little bird,
> Its name was Enza.
> I opened the window,
> And in-flu-enza.'

In the early hours of the morning, as dark turned to dawn, Herr Hund squeezed his wife's hand and died.

* * *

Edith could not return to live in New York. Her mother was refusing to eat or sleep, and just sat in Herr Hund's favourite fireside chair as if frozen with shock.

'She is grieving,' said Dr Howitt, kindly. 'A life shared cannot be quickly undone.'

'I can't leave her,' said Edith. 'We're all she has.'

He nodded, 'You are a good daughter. But remember you too have suffered a loss.'

'I'm fine,' she lied.

'Come and see me anyway,' he smiled, getting into his car. 'It's good to get away from the house for a while.'

Edith kept the tears at bay until the doctor had gone, and then broke down. She longed to see Herr Hund standing tall by the back door, calling her name and smelling of tobacco. But instead there was a never-ending silence. Each night she went to bed exhausted and awoke to feel the same weariness. Dark circles ringed her eyes and she became snappish with the children.

Edith gave up the Lakewood apartment where she had been so happy and wrote a letter resigning from the café. Her mind was under siege and she thought she would never find peace again. She felt nothing but utter desolation. Struggling for direction, she walked to the library each day for the sake of something to do.

Pulling herself out of bed one morning and finding nothing in the larder, Edith went to the corner store and bumped into Dr Howitt. He smelled of oil of cloves.

'Hello,' he said brightly. 'How are you?' He doffed his hat and she noticed his salt and pepper temples.

'Coping well,' she replied, though her face told another story.

'I've spent the morning removing decayed teeth,' he said. 'I don't know who hates it more, me or the patients.'

'I think I can guess,' she said, the smile on her lips feeling unfamiliar after all this time.

'I've been keeping an eye out for you,' he said.

She looked away.

'You have a lot to deal with,' he said, idly checking through a barrel of oranges. 'When was the last time you went out?'

'New York,' she said.

'Bad for your health,' he said. 'Staying in . . . not New York.'

She smiled for a second time.

'Much better,' he said.

'I have to get along,' she said. 'I can't leave mother for long.'

'Of course,' he said, disappointed. 'Give her my regards.'

When Edith arrived back home there was a box of fresh oranges on the doorstep with a hand-written note: 'Keep your strength up. Doctor's orders.' He must have dropped it off on the way to the surgery. She carried it inside, wondering when she might thank him.

Dr Henry Howitt, thirty years older than Edith, was born in Guelph, Ontario, after his family emigrated from Derbyshire, England. Henry came to California hoping to make his fortune picking grapes. Working hard, he bought and sold small plots of land and with the profits dedicated himself to his first love – the study of medicine. For a while it seemed that luck was always on his side.

But tragedy struck when he was out boating with his girlfriend, Rhoda Perkins. Their canoe suddenly capsized, she went under, and Henry dived through the pitch blackness to reach her. But each time he did so she struggled, and her body became too heavy for him to move. After ten minutes Henry was exhausted and near to drowning himself. Only the quick thinking and prompt action of a gallant passer-by saved him. Rhoda's body was recovered later, and Henry never forgave himself for being unable to rescue her.

From that day on the promised he would do all he could for the helpless. So, with the money he made, he graduated from Stanford University and then went on to finish his studies in Germany. It was a shared affinity with the old country which first drew the Hunds and Howitts together.

When she arrived at the surgery Dr Howitt was filing a large pile of medical records, his table littered with notes. He looked up, pleased to see her. 'As you can tell I am without a receptionist,' he began, awkwardly moving files to clear a space on his desk.

'It is a little chaotic,' Edith said, amused by his embarrassment. 'What happened to the last lady?'

'She couldn't stand my orderliness,' he joked.

'Oh, how unkind,' she replied. 'Did she find it complicated?'

'Not really. I threw the files on the desk in a heap and she sorted them out.'

Edith laughed.

'She got a little tired of me,' he confessed. 'And now look. I'm in a mess.'

'You certainly are.' She skimmed her hand over the top of the papers. 'You could do with a little assistance,' she said.

He stood still and looked straight into her eyes. 'So could you.'

She swallowed hard. 'I know,' she whispered relieved to be free of the pretence, if only for a moment.

'Perhaps I can help,' he said, benignly. 'Would you consider working here a couple of days a week and we could talk about your troubles?'

'My father was right about you,' she said.

Edith started working during the mornings and found that many of the patients were men who had returned home disabled from the war. She was humbled by their bravery and lack of self-pity as they struggled inside and waited patiently to see the doctor.

One man, Edmund Frome, would scream at night, thrashing his arms in terror at an invisible foe. During the days he would hide in doorways and peer along the street until it was safe to go. If he heard a tyre burst or a door slam, his face would twitch and he would dive for cover. Mr Frome had been labelled a shirker because he had crumbled in the face of battle.

After clinic, Dr Howitt stayed to explain what soldiers like Frome had been through.

'They're suffering from battle shock,' he said. 'Night after night they saw their friends shot in front of them. Some were buried alive, and almost suffocated. It's hardly surprising their minds gave out. And for that they are reviled.'

'I heard men were shot for cowardice,' she said.

'And many committed suicide. What a tragedy.'

The tortured state of these soldiers' minds made Edith fret about Maurice and what he had seen in France. His recent letters made her think something might be wrong between them.

She wondered if he resented her leaving New York, for he had not commented on her taking a job with Dr Howitt. One letter dated two months before had only just arrived after being forwarded to California. It seemed oddly distant, and Maurice was again prevaricating over what to do.

Maurice was struggling to make sense of the conflict. The terrifying days of combat and the screams of dying comrades had been replaced by a long wait where nothing ever happened. He was still in France, surrounded by the same people, yet they no longer had the terrorizing call to the front. He found it impossible to understand how such extremes could exist so closely together.

He felt useless. And the longer he stayed, the more Maurice was drawn to the battlefields. He would stare at the open ground once filled with death, trying to make sense of what had taken place. But he found none. To return to America and his life of luxury after the crudeness of war would be a betrayal of what he had seen and done. To desert fallen colleagues who could never go home was too much to bear.

On May 7th we leave for the embarkation area en route home. I probably should be more pleased than I am to be returning but I have gotten used to the life over here, the peaceful days and I am glad to be living the sort of life which is most satisfactory. Besides going home means making a new start and as I am always undecided about things I cannot tell what fate has for me. I wish you would send your next letter to 23rd st 53rd st – a sort of 'welcome home' letter. I expect to take the summer off anyway.

Edith wrote back and explained why she had left Lakewood at such short notice. She hoped he would understand, but it was hard to judge how much he would take in and what he really thought. He seemed to be cutting himself off, and it worried Edith.

On Sundays she tended her father's grave, where she watered the plants and tidied the grass. It was a good place to think before returning to the demands of two hungry boys and an uncommunicative mother. One Sunday morning, a flustered Edith was working in the kitchen, the heat from the pans fuelling her simmering temper. While peeling potatoes, she spotted Jack and Ned taking turns to shoot arrows at the mail box.

'Get on with your chores, you two,' she yelled, not caring who heard. 'There'll be no dinner until they're done.'

Jack got down on one knee like the Agincourt archers he had seen in his grandfather's encyclopaedia. Carefully closing one eye and lining up the target with the tip of his arrow, he released the string, and watched it arc into the air. It gave a satisfying thud as it whooshed through the mail box's opening.

'Jack Travis!' his mother screamed.

He opened the box so as not to damage the arrow and pushed his hand deep inside. Alongside the tip of the smooth willow, he felt the familiar shape of a letter. He knew then that redemption was within his grasp. Running back to the kitchen, the letter held high above his head, he shouted, 'Mom, there's a letter from Mr Roche.'

Edith dropped the potato knife and, wiping her hands down her apron, prised the letter from his fist. 'Jack,' she said, 'you're supposed to check the mail, not kill it. Did you forget yesterday?'

'I guess,' he said, adding quickly, 'but now you have a Sunday treat.'

'Go away, you cheeky thing, and lay the table for dinner – be good and thorough.'

Herr Otto (*top left*) and Frau Helen Hund (*top right*) arrived in New York in 1893 from Bremen, Germany in search of a new life. They moved across the country to California and started a private library service. Both were heartbroken as they watched their only child Edith (*bottom left, central figure*) elope to New York with her sweetheart at the age of sixteen, but they were there to pick up the pieces when her marriage failed and Edith returned home with her two sons, Jack and Ned (*bottom right*).

Edith and her sons travelled from
New York to California aboard
the transcontinental train, where
they encountered the Irish-
American millionaire and
socialite Maurice Roche. He was
drawn to the young boys' sense
of fun, which reminded him
of his own childhood, and he
was attracted to the beautiful,
plain-speaking Edith. It was the
beginning of a passionate and
consuming relationship.

Overwhelmed by a sense of duty, Maurice left to fight in the First World War, leaving Edith (*top right*) bereft and still a single woman. She found comfort and respectability in marriage to the honourable but reserved Dr Henry Howitt (*bottom left*), but missed the excitement and passion of her affair with Captain Roche (*top left*).

Maurice left America for England to inherit the title of Lord Fermoy and entered the glittering world of English high society. He became a Member of Parliament and Mayor of King's Lynn *(top)*, near the King's residence of Sandringham, unaware that Edith had given birth to a baby girl in California, nicknamed Lambie *(left and below)*. It was unclear if Maurice had fathered the child.

Edith's husband, Dr Howitt, had a placid nature. He loved his work as a doctor and enjoyed being a family man (*top left*). Edith, although still struck by wanderlust (*top right*), became increasingly over-protective of her young daughter, dressing her up in dainty clothes (*bottom right and left*) and refusing to let her play outside alone.

Maurice's exploits featured regularly in New York gossip columns and prompted salacious headlines.

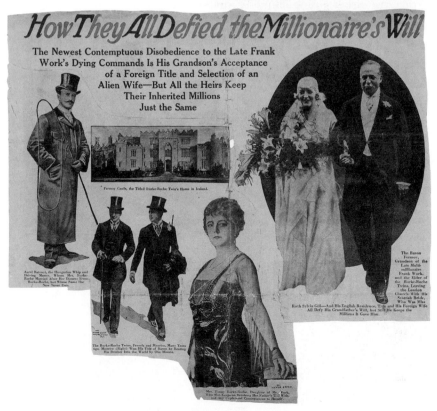

How They All Defied the Millionaire's Will

The Newest Contemptuous Disobedience to the Late Frank Work's Dying Commands Is His Grandson's Acceptance of a Foreign Title and Selection of an Alien Wife—But All the Heirs Keep Their Inherited Millions Just the Same

Fermoy Castle, the Titled Burke-Roche Twin's Home in Ireland.

Aurel Batonyi, the Hungarian Whip and Driving Master, Whom Mrs. Burke-Roche Married After Her Divorce From Burke-Roche, lost Whose Name She Never Uses.

The Baron Fermoy, Grandson of the Late Multimillionaire Frank Work, and the Elder of the Burke-Roche Twins, Leaving the London Church With His Scottish Bride, Who Was Miss Ruth Sylvia Gill—And His English Residence, Title and His Foreign Wife All Defy His Grandfather's Will, but Still He Keeps the Millions It Gave Him.

The Burke-Roche Twins, Francis and Maurice, Many Years Ago, Maurice (Right) Won His Title of Baron by Beating His Brother Into the World by One Minute.

Mrs. Fanny Burke-Roche, Daughter of Mr. Work, Who Also Rejoices Breaking Her Father's Will With and Any Unpleasant Consequences to Herself.

Maurice's desperate search for a wife was resolved when he asked the talented young Scottish pianist, Ruth Gill (*left and middle*), to marry him. He could now continue the Fermoy line. At forty-six he was twice her age, but she gladly gave up her burgeoning musical career in order to better herself. Ruth's physical resemblance to Edith as a young woman was unmistakable.

CARTE POSTALE

Here we are taking the cure. I hope that you have had a pleasant summer in Cal. We leave here next week on our way to Scotland. Do write me and tell me what you are doing and if you are going to the Olympic games; they ought to be interesting.

Have no news, am hard at work losing weight.

With love,

414. - VICHY
Un coin du Nouveau Parc (Jardin Anglais)

Mrs Howitt

311 Lincoln Avenue,

San Rafael,

U.S.A.   California.

Postcard sent to Edith by Maurice whilst on holiday with Ruth.

Maurice was instructed by his wife that their child had to be born in Scotland. In accordance with her wishes, he took Ruth back to her parental home, where she gave birth to a daughter, Mary Cynthia (*top*). He continued to write discreetly to Edith. On his birthday, during his holiday with Ruth in France, he sent a postcard with a small poem enclosed (*bottom right*) to reassure her that she was always in his thoughts.

CARTE POSTALE

Correspondance   Adresse

August 2.

Dear Edith.
Here I am listening
to the music at Deauville.
Wish you were here too.
Hope you are all well. Love, MR.

Sun rises 5.11.   Sun sets 8.43

MAY
1936

15

FRIDAY

'Twas the first day that the
   midges bit ;
But though they bit me, I
   was glad of it :
Of the dust in my face, too,
   I was glad.
Spring could do nothing to
   make me sad. *E. Thomas.*

She sat on the wall by the chicken coop and looked at Maurice's familiar handwriting on the large blue envelope. Putting the letter to her lips, she kissed where he had written her name. Opening along the lines of the fold, she took out the few sheets of delicate paper.

The thought of him being on American soil was tantalizing, and she shivered with anticipation.

Yet it was not what she expected. She read the address and saw it was sent from Newport, Rhode Island. Maurice was home! How strange that he had not sent a telegram or tried to telephone. He wrote:

> Although we had a long journey over we got here
> safely. Camp Dix has changed so much – the place
> looks so worn out and so untidy! You wouldn't
> know it at all. Perhaps I am queer. People weren't
> very nice to me abroad, they hardly ever sent me a
> line, perhaps I haven't made good friends. My
> brother is expected back this week and I am
> waiting to see him. I have no interest in Newport,
> that life is finished for me. It is ridiculous to be
> dancing one's life away at my age. I am trying to
> get a job at Harvard University this winter, perhaps
> I may get it. I came up to New York for the day.
> I took a friend to the Plaza. It all brought back so
> many memories of our meals there together. Will
> you ever forget it. With much love and a good hug,
> yours ever.

Contained within the brooding letter was a separate document, folded and pushed to the base of the envelope. Unravelling the paper, she saw Maurice's signature and one other illegible name, with a space indicating where she should add her own. There was a legal looking stamp by the side of the names, and at the bottom, pinned with a small silver stud, was a cheque for $1,000, made out to her. She turned the document over to try to make sense of it all.

As she read each line, her disbelief turned to alarm. Maurice had instructed lawyers to communicate with her. The document was a contract. An agreement to bind her to Maurice, to be sealed with money. There was no mention of love or happiness, or what she might want, just a large sum.

I am nothing more than a business transaction to him, she thought. Provoked into a blind rage, she tore the cheque from the contract and threw it to the floor, pressing her heel hard into the paper.

The sizzle of boiling water spilling on to the cooking range and urgent shouts from her mother brought her running back inside. As she looked around at her family, Edith felt that Maurice's crude suggestion had insulted not only herself, but everything she believed in. He had struck a blow at the heart of who she was. Her soul was not for sale, and she would forgive no one who thought such a thing. She took the pan off the heat and bent down to open the iron door of the range. The heat from the coals hit her full in the face and she drew back, prodding the glowing pieces with the poker to make them red hot. Taking Maurice's letter and the contract she threw them in, and watched as the edges of the paper first curled brown and then caught alight, with green and blue flames dancing along his handwriting, eating up his signature until there was nothing left but ashes.

She had no appetite for lunch, and as the faint summer sunshine flickered through the windows, her anger turned to sadness, Edith sat at her father's desk and penned a letter. 'Dear Maurice, After all this time and that is how you see me. As if money could impress me or make me want you more. I have always loved the man you are, not your wealth or your position. I think it best if we never see each other again.' She signed it 'Mrs Travis' and enclosed the cheque.

Maurice had spent months dreaming of sleeping in his old four-poster bed, of stretching out and feeling the clean cotton sheets against his skin, the soft down of the pillows and the firmly sprung mattress. Now when he sank into his bed, he lay awake most of the night.

The Army was proving hard to leave behind.

He rose at first light and paced around the grounds of the estate until the household showed signs of life. He wanted solitude, and try as he might to muster enthusiasm, social invitations filled him with dread. Quiet suppers alone in his room or the company of a good book appealed far more. Deadened inside and angry when approached, Maurice tried to suppress his feelings. He did not want to reveal this side of himself, especially to Edith, for he thought it ugly and weak.

He feared she would see this as part of his aristocratic nature. He adored Edith's natural exuberance and spirit, yet sometimes felt unnerved by her forthrightness and impetuosity. His proposal to her was to be an expression of love and a way for them to be together as a couple. He had racked his brain over how to do the right thing in an impossible situation, and wanted so much to please her. By legally formalizing the arrangement he hoped Edith would believe he was committed to her.

He had done no such thing. As he read her curt farewell,

his hands shook and his head span. Her anger sprang from every word. This was not how he had expected the contract to be received. Now lost, he wanted to explain, tell her it was all a mistake, let her know she had got things wrong. Finding it hard to get his breath he sat by an open window. He tried to call Frank, but there was no reply. He felt utterly alone, and this time did not welcome it.

In the days that followed he stayed in the house, writing letter after letter to Edith, desperate for a reply. At first he tried to skirt round the problem, hoping her temper would cool once she understood what he meant.

I do hope you will find it possible to come east this
fall. I cannot understand why you wish to say
farewell to me and want me to think differently of
you. I always thought of you as being a fine, strong
woman and you always show great control. Why
do you write as you do? I am returning the cheque
to you. I don't want you to think of it ever again.
I wish you were here this afternoon. It is raining
hard and I have nothing to do. With much love.

Yet as time went on and still no reply came, he realized she was not for turning. He begged her to understand, trying to rekindle their love by confronting the problem head on. He wrote:

I am so very sorry to hear you have something on
your mind and things have not been as you hoped.
I am anxious to hear what are your real troubles.
I think I know. I might be able to advise you in
some way. I hope you will give me the chance.

The timing could not have been worse, for Maurice was now drawn into protracted family matters. His uncle, Edward Fitz Edmund Burke, the second Baron Fermoy, was dying, and as he had no male heirs, the title would pass to Maurice's elderly father. That would leave Maurice as direct heir to the Barony.

Since Maurice's parents' divorce, his uncle had never liked Fannie, seeing her as a posturing American in search of a grand title and position. Edward Fitz never forgave her and reacted by stripping the Fermoy homes of all their assets. He shipped valuable oil paintings, mezzotints, antiques and precious fittings over to London to be auctioned off. He wanted nothing of value to be left, making his inheritance worthless to Fannie and her descendants.

Maurice, weary of the endless recriminations, hoped they could all pull together. Amid the outrage and animosity, if his family was to retain a semblance of respectability, they must learn discretion.

He only wanted to protect Edith from the worst of his warring family, and to give them both a chance of a normal life. He had tried to have it all, and failed in spectacular fashion. Now, his mis-guided but well-intentioned action would for ever haunt him. He was ready to inherit the title, but it was a hollow victory without Edith by his side.

In the surgery, Edith worked obsessively in order to forget Maurice. Dr Howitt became the focus of her day's activity. Every time her mind wandered to Maurice or his damned cheque, she busied herself filing, rearranging notes or completing the kind of menial tasks that had always bored her before.

'What else can I do?' she asked.

'Would you like to assist with my next patient?' Dr Howitt replied. 'If you're not too squeamish.'

'I won't know until I try,' she said nervously.

'I like your spirit,' he said, finding her an apron.

It did not take long for Dr Howitt to wonder how he had managed without Edith Travis.

One Friday afternoon after another stream of patients had been dispatched, there was a lull and Edith began sterilizing a batch of instruments. Dr Howitt wandered in, his brow beaded with sweat. 'Try putting back a dislocated shoulder on one of those cattle farmers . . . it's not easy!' he exclaimed.

As Edith poured the boiling water into a tank, a giant of a man walked out of the surgery, his arm in a sling. 'Thanks, Doc,' he called. 'I'll be sure to send around the best steak.'

'No wrestling those beasts for a while,' Dr Howitt shouted after him.

Edith laughed, grabbing the tongs and arranging the cleaned instruments on a steel tray, ready for use.

Dr Howitt turned and said, 'It's good to see you laugh.'

Taken aback by his having noticed, she lowered her head, pretending she had not heard.

'I hope you regard me as a friend,' he said, holding out his hands to take the instrument tray.

'You're very kind, Dr Howitt,' she said, walking back to stand behind a nearby trolley.

'Please, call me Henry,' he said, rolling down his shirt sleeves in the same way her father used to do, meticulously unfolding each layer until the cuffs came together.

'There's a new comedy playing at the theatre on Saturday evening,' he continued, in a matter-of-fact tone. 'I always feel awkward going alone.'

Henry Howitt's wife, Alice, had died ten years earlier while still a young woman and he had spent much of the time since grieving for her. He had always dismissed the advice from concerned friends that it was time to move on.

Edith looked into his expectant face. He had been so good to her over the past few months. Leaning against the drug cupboard, his white coat unbuttoned and tie slightly astray, he had the air of a genial uncle.

'I'd love to come, thank you,' she said.

Edith knew he was a different kind of man from Maurice and she was still smarting from the way Maurice had so badly misjudged her. How could he possibly think she would settle for the life of a kept woman? She had waited for nearly a year, praying he would come home from a war she never wished him to fight. But instead of enfolding her in his loving arms he sent her a contract. A deal. A pay-off.

It was time to show him who she really was.

The auditorium was full as Dr Howitt took Edith's arm and escorted her in. He had bought seats on the front row of the stalls, and she could feel the staring eyes widen at the doctor and his receptionist out together.

As they sat side by side, one of the surgery's regular patients engaged Dr Howitt's attention and began regaling him with a jumble of symptoms and ailments so preposterous that she was clearly lucky to be alive. Just as the curtain rose, the doctor politely but firmly suggested, 'Come and see me first thing on Monday and we'll sort it out.'

Edith giggled into his ear, 'You're a saint.'

'Hardly,' he coughed, grateful the lights were low enough to hide his reddening face.

As the play progressed she stole sidelong glances at Dr Howitt and studied his angular features and the way he sat so relaxed in his seat, as if he was without worry. For those few hours in that small theatre, Dr Howitt's sanguine manner made Edith forget.

Afterwards, he walked her slowly home, past the library and the churchyard where her father and his wife lay buried.

'I've had a really nice time,' he said, holding open the gate. She sensed an unaccustomed nervousness.

'Please, there will be coffee brewing and it's early yet,' Edith said. 'Mother will be so glad to see you.' She leaned on the gate and it creaked as always.

He closed it and followed her inside. 'I could fix that for you,' he said.

They were married four weeks later in a simple ceremony, with Jack and Ned as page-boys. Her mother wept, this time tears of joy. 'He is a wonderful man,' she said. 'Papa can at last rest in peace, knowing you have found true happiness.'

Edith hugged her tight and trusted she was right.

More than anything else, after her divorce, Edith wanted security. And with Henry that was exactly what she had found. Now she had an interesting job, a lovely home and a steady man. She and the boys were safe.

SEVEN

'New York Is Awfully Cold'

The second Baron, Lord Fermoy died aged seventy on 1 September 1920, at Dongelly in Wales. He had no male heir, and so the mantle passed to Maurice's father, James Boothby Burke Roche.

Maurice had rarely associated with his eccentric Irish uncle who lived most of his life in the golden valley of Rockbarton, Bruff, south of Limerick. And now he knew all illusions of a peaceful life would quickly ebb away when he eventually became Lord Fermoy. The title, with all its grandeur, heritage and responsibility, meant an end to his freedom.

The hereditary Fermoy title was first bestowed by Queen Victoria in 1856 for lifelong political service. Edmund Burke Roche – a relative of the philosopher, Edmund Burke – was personally honoured as a much respected Member of Parliament for County Cork and, later, Marylebone. He had married Elizabeth Caroline Boothby, and their crest showed a winged sea eagle atop a collared lion with a greyhound bearing the family motto, 'My God is my Rock.'

Maurice had always enjoyed certainty and the looming title would allow him to be part of an ancient unchanging tradition. But it would also bring accountability on a scale he had never before encountered. As heir to the title he now had more than the weight of the Roche reputation pressing down upon his shoulders: he had to set the standard for future generations of the Fermoy barony. History would view his successes and failures and his life would be scrutinized. It made him want Edith's unquestioning love more than ever.

Maurice had spent hours in France dreaming. He loved Europe, longed to travel and even live abroad. He always imagined Edith by his side promenading down Parisian boulevards, stopping for good expresso and brioche in sunny street cafés. Yet he had come back to a world without her. She continued to ignore his letters and Maurice didn't know what more he could do.

Looking in the mirror, he noticed flecks of silver sprinkled throughout his hair. Owing to his war experience the face staring back at him was that of a considerably older man. In a renewed attempt to impress Edith, he instructed top New York photographers, the Pach Brothers, to take a series of portraits. They were known for their work with Hollywood stars, and Maurice trusted them to make him look like a younger man again. He came to their studio dressed in his favourite suit and, after light make-up was applied to his skin, there was not a blemish to be seen.

Maurice hoped that when Edith got the photograph she would see that he had not changed. Playing down the effort he had gone to, Maurice wrote, 'I shall send you a picture of myself. Perhaps it isn't quite as good as you liked, but it is better than nothing. When you get this please let me know if this is the correct address, for I feel it isn't sufficient. Do let me hear soon.'

Every morning he flicked through his letters in the hope that one would be postmarked Marin County, but it never was. She steadfastly refused to answer. It seemed there was nothing he could do. He wrote again, this time more insistently: 'I hope that you got the photo I sent to you – it was the last I could find. How I wish I was out there with you. New York is awfully cold – ten degrees above zero. Do let me know how you are. I long to see you again.'

When the days turned into weeks, Maurice's patience evaporated.

'I'm going to California to see her,' he told his brother in Newport.

'It will make no difference,' Frank said. He had grown weary of Maurice's dramas and Mrs Travis's intransigence. 'She's made up her mind. To be honest it could be a blessing,' he said, wanting to change the subject.

'First I'm shackled by the wretched money, and now it's the barony,' Maurice fumed.

'You are lucky to be next in line for the title,' said Frank. 'All that privilege and status. It may be an accident of birth, but you should consider yourself honoured.'

'Said by a man with no accountability,' snapped Maurice.

Maurice paced around the richly decorated room, wanting to smash the glass lamps and overturn the antique armoire. Frank moved out of his way. There was no point in confronting his brother in this mood.

Maurice stared at Frank and saw a perfect reflection of himself. After all these years, they were still identical. There, he suddenly realized, looking him directly in the face, was the answer to his dilemma.

'We are the same,' he stated. 'No one can tell us apart.'

Frank raised an eyebrow. 'Yes. What are you thinking?'

'Listen, Frank, if Edith and I went to live in Paris, nobody would be any wiser.'

'And where does that leave me?' asked Frank, fearing that Maurice was more out of control than he had imagined.

'You could take my place, become Lord Fermoy and inherit everything,' said Maurice. 'You'd be happy, you always wanted to be the eldest.'

'You're mad,' said Frank. 'This is the brandy talking.'

'Nobody would know – people get us mixed up all the time.'

'My God, you're serious!' he said. 'For Christ's sake, Maurice, it's not that simple,' said Frank, standing shoulder to shoulder beside his elder brother. Identical on the outside, he knew they were very different inside. But he did not recognize this part of Maurice, a man possessed by what he was being denied; a lost creature, driven to the point of renouncing his birthright and beliefs.

'Maurice, you need to get hold of yourself,' said Frank, gripping on to his arm. 'If you don't marry well, that could be the end of the title. Money is fine, but you cannot buy position.'

'Grandfather understood that everyone has a price,' he said, grabbing Frank's wrist. You're no different. Name it, dammit!'

Frank tore himself free and shook his head in disgust. 'Go to her then. I don't know who you are any more.'

Maurice stormed out of the house and fled to Atlantic Beach. He threw himself beneath the waves, fighting against the shock of the cold and swam through the deep water. A buttery moon guided his path and he breathed heavily in the still, clammy air. For a second, with the world encompassing him, he realized how small he really was. Soon, the icy water forced him to seek the shore and he surfaced at the ocean's edge.

As his eyes adjusted to the dark, Maurice crouched down on the sand and sifted through a pile of pebbles. Tossing them from one hand to the other, until he had one smooth stone which felt right to his touch, he drew back his right arm and threw the stone hard towards the foaming waves, as he and Frank had often done as boys. It skimmed the surface bouncing once, twice and then a third time before sinking silently to the bottom.

His mind was made up.

Maurice asked his driver to stop a little way down the street, so he could walk the rest of the way. He wanted to see Edith's neighbourhood in all its fullness. He took his time, sauntering slowly, listening to the comforting sound of the wind and feeling the heat of the sun burning his brow. Abandoning all good manners, he peered into each porch and open doorway. An old man stooped low to feed a tired dog chicken livers, while next door a woman sewed stockings. Across the street, a gaunt young man with a soldier's crew cut played 'Danny Boy' soulfully on his harmonica to soothe a crying baby. They all cautiously eyed the fine gentleman in his fancy suit and shiny shoes heading towards the Hund House. But no one said hello.

Maurice walked on slowly, then crossed the street to stare for a while. A white thigh-high picket fence bordered Edith's house, and a thin pathway led to a mustard-coloured door. The garden, dominated by a large mulberry tree, was dotted with a patchwork of flowering shrubs. But before he could summon the courage to cross over, a lilting woman's voice drifted from an open window. She was reading from a children's story book. Maurice smiled to himself as she stopped speaking. He heard a loud sigh and then two boys darted out through the gate into the street.

Since he had last seen them, Jack's limbs had lengthened into a youth's and Ned's stride had become decidedly gangly. Maurice realized how long it had been since he held Edith in his arms.

'Hello, young men!' he said, as they ambled up the road. 'Is your mother at home?'

Jack turned and shook his head, not recognizing Maurice.

'But I heard someone in the house,' he said quizzically.

'That's our grandmother,' explained Jack, who was aware that he had seen this man somewhere before, but unable to place him.

Hearing a stranger's voice, Frau Hund craned her head round the doorway and saw the imposing figure standing by her gate. She tapped her foot on the step to attract his attention.

Maurice walked eagerly up the path. 'Forgive me for intruding,' he said, tipping his hat. 'I am a friend of your daughter's, from New York.'

Frau Hund, suspicious since her husband died, stepped back to the safety of her doorway to regard the city man. He wore an ostentatious gold signet ring on his little finger, and his expensive attire and rounded vowels made her unusually nervous.

'It's a pleasure to meet you, Frau Hund,' said Maurice, extending his hand.

She brushed down her gingham pinafore and straightened her hair. When they shook hands he looked her straight in the eye, hoping to make her feel special. She knew then exactly who he was.

'You're a long way from home, Mr Roche,' she said. 'Would you like some iced tea?'

Maurice smiled when she said his name and nodded gratefully, as the fine Marin County dust was making the back of his throat feel dry.

They sat like trial lawyers on opposite sides of the kitchen table, sipping tea in monotonous unison.

'We just lost touch after Lakewood and I happened to be in the neighbourhood,' he said awkwardly.

'What a coincidence,' said Frau Hund wryly.

'I hoped you would help me,' he said. 'I must return shortly.'

'You have the face of a sad man,' she said. 'My daughter has mentioned your name. May I tell her why you are here?'

Maurice decided he was getting nowhere.

'I would be most grateful if you would tell me where I could find her,' he said.

'It sounds urgent for someone who just happens to be in the area,' she said.

Maurice drained his cup and stood to go. Frau Hund went to the front door and yelled for her grandsons.

'Take this man to Dr Howitt's surgery,' she ordered the boys.

'Is she not well?' Maurice asked.

Jack giggled. 'Come with me,' he said, pulling Maurice by the sleeve.

'No, me!' shouted Ned.

'Some things never change. Stop arguing, boys!' said Frau Hund. 'Good day Mr Roche, I hope you find what you are looking for.'

Frau Hund saw Maurice place a hand on the back of each of her grandson's heads and she opened the door for him to leave. 'Edith will tell you what you need to know.'

Jack pestered Maurice all the way.

'Are you the man from New York?'

'Yes,' replied Maurice.

'Where have you been?'

'I've been away fighting in the war,' said Maurice.

'So what's it like to shoot a man dead?' asked Jack, holding his fingers in the shape of a pistol.

'Worse than anything you can ever imagine,' he said.

As they approached the Cottage Hospital, Maurice took two dimes from his pocket and handed one to each of them.

'Bye, boys,' he waved.

The waiting room was crowded with people talking in hushed whispers. All the seats were taken, and a family of four leaned against the back wall. An elderly couple held hands and stared blankly at the floor, while a young man grimaced and rubbed his leg.

Edith was at the front desk. A heavily pregnant woman with two unruly toddlers at her heels stood before her. Edith knew the woman as the unfortunate wife of an unfaithful labourer who had given her syphilis. The shame heaped upon this poor woman had already driven her to a number of charlatans who failed to cure her. She was now being treated by the doctor with painful arsenic injections. It was not surprising that the woman, stroking her swollen belly, seemed oblivious to her children's cries. Edith knew that were it not for Henry, the woman could be paralysed, blinded and even go insane. And she was only one of many such women Henry was treating for this silent plague.

Each time Edith spoke to the lady, both children squealed and pulled on her skirt to be held. The woman's face remained impassive, her eyes cold with rejection, and she roughly lifted one child and rocked him on her hips. Edith cooed at the other baby.

A bell rang. Edith checked her list and said quietly, 'It's your turn to see the doctor.' The woman struggled through to Henry's consulting room, children in tow.

Edith tried not to think about her, but it was hard not to feel upset on seeing such pain and suffering. Then, out of the corner of her eye she glimpsed a stranger staring at her. He stood watching her every move, as if he too benefited from her kindness.

She took a closer look and, as her eyes focused, a shock jolted through her body and her mouth fell dry. Edith gripped on to the desk to steady herself because a few feet away, as glorious as the last time she had laid eyes on him, was her very own Maurice Roche.

Knowing she had only a few minutes before her husband rang for his next patient, she left her desk and walked to Maurice. Heart thudding and hands sweating, she was unable to speak.

'Hello, my love,' he said, a smile breaking across his tanned face.

She felt her eyes fill.

'You wouldn't answer my letters,' he said.

Inquisitive heads turned to see the doctor's young wife and the attractive outlander who had been dawdling in the corner, engaged in dialogue. Conscious of their eyes, she found the strength to say, 'Please, let's talk outside.' She guided him out on to the hospital's porch. 'It's easier here.'

Standing awkwardly on the top step, he looked earnest.

'I have something to tell you.'

Edith dug her hands deep inside her apron pockets to stop herself from touching him.

'I never meant to hurt you, I was clumsy,' he said, ignoring the stares through the screen door. 'I am so very sorry.'

Even though he had rehearsed many times, the words came out in a rush, 'I have been talking to my brother and I know it sounds preposterous but we're going to swap lives.'

Edith looked bemused as he carried on. 'We can have the life we always dreamed of. We can live in Paris and send the boys to the best schools. Edith, we need to be together. I have lived too long and seen too much without you.'

Reaching into his pocket, Maurice produced a small velvet box, his hands shaking as he opened it. Inside was a crushed red ribbon.

'Since we last met I have treasured this, and promised myself one day I'd bring it back to you.' He suddenly looked very sombre and stepped in close. 'Edith Travis, will you do me the honour of being my wife?'

Tears came to her eyes.

He leaned forward to embrace her, but instead of the warmth of her lips, all he could feel was her pushing hard against his chest.

'Edith Howitt,' she sobbed. 'I am Mrs Edith Howitt.'

There and then his world exploded. More than it had ever done on the battlefields of France.

EIGHT

'A Bit of Heaven'

'My dear Edith.

I am writing to wish you all the luck possible and every happiness. I shall often think of our first meeting on the train and the other happy times in New York. I do hope that if you and Dr Howitt ever come to New York you will let me know and I may have the pleasure of meeting him. Well, Edith, I can't believe that you are married. I know that you have a fine husband and that he will make you very happy – now that your future is assured I want to wish you very good luck. Do take good care of those two fine boys of yours and give them the very best education you can. Send them to college if possible for it is worth it every time. I wish you could drop me a line from time to time, for I shall always be pleased to hear from you and how everything is going. Well, goodbye Edith – please remember me kindly. Hope this finds you all in the best of health and enjoying the beautiful country of California.'

Maurice and Frank had come sailing to escape. But it was impending death, not life, that had drawn them to the ocean. Their father was gravely ill. The Fermoy title was for the taking, and Maurice had only to decide in which direction to go. But following Edith's rejection, he found it hard to know what he wanted. Even simple decisions required a huge effort. He hoped that out on the waves, where the cobalt sea meets the never-ending sky, might be just the place to inspire his destiny.

They dropped anchor to fish off the stern and lunched on the crab and lobster they caught. Several bottles of bootleg beer stood empty, bought from a smuggler's ship anchored safely outside the three-mile limit patrolled by federal agents. The illicitness of the alcohol seemed to have added to its potency, for both brothers felt woozy. The sway of the water and the heat of the sun soon loosened Maurice's tongue.

'I still can't believe she could do that to me,' he said.

'It was a cruel way to find out,' Frank said.

'She must hate me,' Maurice said.

'I doubt that,' said Frank. 'It took courage to see her.' He patted his brother's knee. 'Try to summon some of that now.'

Maurice gritted his teeth and shook his head. 'I am so weary with it all.'

Frank smiled. 'You need time and a good night's sleep. I heard you pacing again last night.'

'Sometimes it all seems too much . . . and now father is ill.'

'You have fought worse times.'

'But now I just want peace,' said Maurice.

Frank put his arm around his brother. 'You should get below for a while, you're burning up.'

110

He guided him towards the cabin and Maurice collapsed on to the bunk, falling into a dreamless sleep.

Some time later, he was awoken by the shock of his head cracking against the side of the cabin. The roar of water and wind tossed the boat like a toy in the ocean.

Frank was shouting, 'Get the main sail down!'

Maurice struggled to keep his balance, holding on to the side of the bunk. Blood trickled down his cheek and he wiped it away, triggering a wave of sickness. Water flooded down the steps, filling the tiny cabin as he scaled the slippery ladder two rungs at a time, wondering what dangers he would find when he got up top.

Barely able to distinguish between boat and ocean, Maurice crouched down on all fours and crawled across the deck. His eyes adjusted to the murky light as sections of rigging and rope came into focus. He could just make out his brother fighting with the jib. It flapped uncontrollably like a fierce mythical creature intent on fleeing his grasp, but Frank would not surrender.

A rush of sea water slapped Maurice hard across the head, stinging his eyes and sending his stomach somersaulting. The boat lurched and he heard Frank's panicked scream above the thunder, 'I can't release the sail.'

Maurice hollered back, waving at his brother to hang on, as he dragged himself to the helm.

Inching his way to the bridge, he grabbed the wheel. It lurched drunkenly one way and then the other, cracking against his fingers as he struggled to take a grip. A huge wave smashed into the starboard side, tossing both men across the deck.

Instead of air, Maurice was sucking in water. Amid his spluttering, an agonizing pain flashed through his ankle as it bashed on to a brass block. The throbbing from his leg filled his body as a wall of waves thundered against the side of the boat. He just wanted it over. At that moment he did not care whether he lived or died. Slowly, as his mind went blank, the fear left him and he lost consciousness.

The next clear sound was Frank yelling, 'Come on, Maurice, we can do this! About! Now! Tack!'

Frank had released himself from the mast and was manfully working the ropes. As he strained to get the boat under control, Maurice realized the ocean's swell was subsiding. Dragging himself to the side of the boat, he leaned precariously over to counteract the boat's listing. The gusting wind rippled against his body and they once again took control of the mainsail.

They were going to make it, and Maurice, seeing the thumbs-up sign from his brother, was surprised at how glad he felt.

Their father died at his home at 5 Artillery Mansions, Westminster of a heart attack brought on by a virulent attack of flu. It was a sorry way to go after all his years of adventuring. His long wait for succession had been followed by one of the shortest peerages in living memory, at a mere sixty days.

Maurice felt he had to tell Edith. Not out of any hope of rekindling their love, but because she had a right to know and for the support she had shown. He had a new future ahead, and he wanted her to see he had made the right choice. It was a simple note that bore no malice. He thought it would show that he held no grudge and hoped in some small way she would be proud of him. Visiting Marin County had given Maurice a perspective he never expected. Seeing Edith's home town, how she lived and worked, meant he could always picture her.

My father died recently so I have come into the peerage of Ireland and I am now Lord Fermoy. Why have you never given me a line as to what you are doing, or how you have been? I hope things have gone well for you and your boys are turning out to be fine citizens. Wishing you the happiest of times. With love.

As a peer of the realm Maurice prepared himself for the journey to England, where he would claim his title. But as he packed his cases, his lawyers alerted him to the fact that things might not be that simple. His grandfather, Frank Work, had stipulated in his will that Maurice and Frank must always live in America and marry American girls. If the twins wanted his millions, they had to earn them – his way.

As a dirt poor boy from Delaware, Ohio, Frank Work had fought hard for his money. He was a tenacious child who at the age of ten, after an unfair whopping from his school teacher, climbed onto his horse and rode out of town. He had in his pocket a single gold coin and proclaimed he would become one of the wealthiest men in New York City. And he wasn't wrong. He worked his way up in a gas-fitting store until he owned the company. Then he invested in stocks and shares, becoming an advisor to the millionaire, Vanderbilt. When he died in 1911 he had an estate worth $13 million. But the older he got, the more he enjoyed making life difficult for his family. He wanted his daughters and grandchildren to share some of his earlier struggle.

Maurice picked up the telephone and dialled his lawyers, determined to sort out the mess.

'Yes, yes, I understand,' he said, 'but none of my grandfather's heirs, especially my sister, Cynthia, who stands to benefit from his entire fortune, has any opposition to our claim.'

'Your grandfather's will has many unusual clauses. It could be tricky for you,' said the lawyer.

Maurice leaned forward in his seat. 'The terms of his edict are outdated and illegal. That's what I intend to prove in court. Good afternoon, sir,' he said, replacing the receiver firmly on the hook.

Maurice thought it would be hard to enforce the punitive measures of the will, especially as he was already receiving a subsistence income of $250,000 a year from the estate.

But there was a further $3 million each at stake.

The two brothers discussed their chances of overturning the will during lunch.

'I can't see we have anything to lose,' said Frank.

'Sanguine as ever,' smiled Maurice.

'Look, the old man was never going to go without a fight. He loved America and wants us to do the same.'

Maurice nodded. 'We both fought in the war, what more could he ask?'

Frank fiddled with his fork. 'Mother will have a field day if we win. You know how she and grandfather fought.'

'Which shows how pointless it all is. We must always be friends, Frank. You're really all I have.'

'Twins, Maurice,' he said. 'However you torment me, I will always come back for more.'

They set about untangling the old man's intricate demands. By the time Frank Work had died at the age of ninety-three, he had added fourteen complicated codicils. He had been particularly vile towards his daughter, Fannie, banning her from having anything to do with James Burke Roche, or her second husband Aurel Batonyi. She could never leave America, or exhibit horses, and in return she was to receive $80,000 'pin money' every year.

Fannie characteristically did the exact opposite of her father's wishes, and after he died she moved to Paris, where she stayed in the best hotels and resorts, spending money like water.

When the Fermoy title passed to Maurice, she proudly announced, 'I am Lady Fermoy, for ever.' The title she had so long coveted was handed to her without a murmur, as the third baron had gone to his grave insisting their divorce was not legal in Ireland. Technically she was still Mrs James Boothby Burke Roche and entitled to all the privileges of that position, including immunity from the law. Feeling almost invincible, Fannie flitted around the French capital enjoying the fashion houses, cognac and a very good life.

Frank also had an affinity with France and wished to accept a position with the Guaranty Trust Company in Paris. It was therefore vital for the will to be overturned.

'It's ludicrous we can't visit our own mother abroad or live and work where we please. What did we fight for, if we don't have freedom?' said Maurice in the reception of Nolans New York lawyers.

'Lord Fermoy and Mr Roche?' announced one of the partners, a besuited man wearing pince nez. They both stood to shake his hand.

'Here goes,' whispered Frank boyishly.

It was a risk, they were told, but nobody so far seemed prepared to contest the claim, and their elder sister

Cynthia, having declared her allegiance to America, had signed a waiver permitting her brothers to travel abroad.

Sitting in the lobby of the Waldorf Astoria, Frank moaned, 'Prohibition! We can't even have a drink to celebrate.' They ordered Turkish coffee and piled in the sugar.

'To Grandfather Work,' proposed Maurice, the thick dark sweet liquid burning his lips. 'May his stubborn spirit live in both of us.'

Edith was pleased that Maurice had the decency to let her know about his title. She also felt rather honoured.

She placed the letter with his others, and pushed them to the back of the drawer of the writing desk Henry had given her as a wedding gift. Turning around, she blushed to see him standing behind her chair and slid the key under a blotter.

'I need to talk with you,' he said.

'I was just writing the grocery list,' she lied.

He kissed her cheek. 'Always organized.'

She rose and began sorting through the boys' school bags.

'I have been thinking about your mother,' he said. 'The house is much too big for her. It won't be long before we have a child of our own and she could be such a help here.'

He reached towards Edith, but she pretended not to notice and carried on emptying stones and bits of twigs from the satchels on to the desk.

'You are still young,' he said, reassuringly. 'These things take time, that's all. Try not to worry.'

'It may not be my fault,' she bristled.

'It is neither of us, darling. It will happen. Trust me.' He brushed her hand with his. 'I have to go. I'll probably be late.'

116

He did not kiss her goodbye. 'Think about what I said. It would be company for you when I'm on call.' The click of the door signalled he was gone.

There was not much time for conversation in the Howitt household. Henry enjoyed planning his cases during the early morning stillness. He would grab a quick bite to eat and flick through the medical journals, before heading out in his black Chevvy automobile to make house calls. He rarely came home before dusk, often later if there was a birth or death. And during the evenings, having eaten his supper, he would sink into his favourite chair and gradually fall asleep. Edith would watch tenderly the rise and fall of his chest and the way his nostrils flared as he slept. He did not snore, but made gentle sounds with his lips as he breathed in and out of his open mouth.

As the house sank into silence, she stared at their wedding picture on the wall. Henry was sixty and she was thirty; they could have been father and daughter. He was looking at her, she had her arm through his. The boys stood to attention in front, and Frau Hund, always afraid of the camera, had on her stern face. Blinded by the flash, they had all collapsed into a heap when it was over. Edith and the boys giggled and held their stomachs, whilst Henry quickly got up and cajoled, 'Come on now, enough of this silliness.'

As Dr Howitt's wife, Edith had taken on certain responsibilities. Not just at the surgery, but in the community. She had to learn the art of conversation when it neither interested nor appealed. She would be inundated at fêtes and fairs with a stream of ailments and old wives' tales. She must answer the telephone politely at all hours of the day and night, however cranky she was feeling. Most of all, she had to know the whereabouts of her husband and the precise moment he would arrive at any given emergency. Despite having never taken the Hippocratic oath or aspired to a political life, she was entrusted with the role of the ultimate confidante, keeper of secrets and negotiator. And finally, when out with Henry, she had to be invisible.

For all his compassion, Edith sometimes felt Henry carried his dedication a little far. Especially lately, with the new Prohibition law.

Stopping people drinking alcohol was supposed to be the answer to society's ills. Without drink there would be less crime and corruption, fewer social problems and ill health. People would have more money in their pockets, not just from spending less on beer and spirits, but because of the drop in numbers imprisoned at the taxpayers' expense.

Edith watched stony-faced as the Sons of Temperance marched through Marin County warning of the dangers of drinking, and their preachers sang and quoted from the bible while cursing the evil alcohol.

Travelling preacher Dr Carolyn Geisel cried, 'Oh, my America, will you listen to us, the motherhood of the land? Will you continue to take our boys from our arms, grind them through your saloons into the penitentiary, and from the penitentiary into hell? Something must be done to save our boys from utter destruction.'

Edith did not believe that a few drinks at the dinner table or in the company of friends would lead to any such thing.

As with all doctors, Henry had his part to play enforcing the strict prohibition laws. However, he could legally write up to a hundred prescriptions for alcohol every ninety days, strictly for medicinal purposes. The number of patients who suddenly felt they could benefit from whiskey and wine to soothe their ailments doubled overnight. The hospital waiting room soon became more popular than the saloons.

'The queue is right around the street again, Henry,' said Edith dryly.

'I feel as if I am running a speakeasy, not a surgery,' he moaned.

Unlocking the door, she saw an expectant sea of faces. 'It's a bad law, you can't blame people for trying to flout it,' Edith said, annoyed at Henry's self-righteousness.

He gathered up his notes. 'I did not become a doctor to dose people with whiskey.'

'But telling them how to lead their lives is acceptable?' she said crossly.

'I will not be branded a criminal,' he said. 'Send the first patient in, please.'

Then, when she was almost out of earshot, he added, 'I don't know why you like to drink, it's hardly lady-like.'

She said nothing, closed the door and called out the first patient's name. Fuming behind her receptionist's desk, Edith slid out her notepad and wrote, 'Dear Maurice, Perhaps we could meet?'

Henry took his pipe from his mouth and put it by the front door step then wandered over to the middle of the garden to play baseball with the boys. Jack swung his bat wildly around his head and taunted his brother, claiming that he could hit a home run without even trying. Ned refused to rise to the bait and glared back before winding up his arm.

With Henry so distracted, Edith thought it a good time to broach the subject she had been putting off for quite a while. Looking up from where she was tending the vegetable patch, she began lightly, 'Dearest, it's been so long since I saw my friends in Lakewood and they have started nagging me to visit.'

Henry seemed not to hear as he stood waving his arms in an effort to keep the boys apart. 'Ned, come on now. Be a sportsman,' he said.

To stay calm, Edith counted silently in her head and tried to sound measured. 'I can't ignore them for ever. But it's a long way and you're so busy . . .'

Henry pointed at Jack and yelled, 'Hey, look at Babe Ruth over here!'

'Mother could help with the boys and around the house,' she said, undaunted, as Jack squared up to Henry for another strike. 'And I hope you don't mind, but I've already asked Miss O'Farrell to cover.'

The mention of the surgery guaranteed Henry would at last stop to listen, and he looked perturbed at the idea of his junior nurse stepping into Edith's shoes. He tossed the ball between his hands.

'So you have to be kind to her,' Edith chided. 'You know she's a little in love with you.'

Henry winked and threw a gentle pitch towards Jack, which he batted straight into Ned's open glove.

Edith clapped enthusiastically and let out a loud sigh, 'Darling, I must let them know. It's rude to keep people waiting,' she said from over her shoulder.

Henry turned towards her. 'Of course. You deserve a break from us men.' He ruffled Ned's hair. 'When are you leaving?'

'Next week, if I may.'

'Come back, won't you?' he said, half-jokingly.

* * *

120

Maurice was only weeks away from leaving America and, delighted by Edith's note, decided it could do no harm to meet her before he sailed for England.

In truth, he had thought of little else.

He stood dressed in a new sealskin coat and Oxford dress shoes, holding tickets for a new motion picture, *The Sheikh*, starring Rudolph Valentino. The film was scandalizing New York with the story of a young woman kidnapped and seduced by a desert sheikh. In a twist Maurice found amusing, the sheikh turns out to be an English nobleman.

Edith had mentioned the time it took for good movies to reach the Marin County picture house, and he wanted it to be a surprise.

For old times' sake, they arranged to meet in the foyer of the Plaza Hotel. This time Edith was not late, but she did look very different. Her hair was cut into a bob and sleekly framed her face. She wore natural-coloured stockings and low pumps that flattered her legs. She looked tanned and youthful.

Smiling, he kissed her on both cheeks and immediately remembered the softness of her skin.

'Oh I almost forgot!' he said, presenting her with a box of French chocolates.

'My favourites,' she laughed. 'You are thoughtful, thank you,' and she kissed him again.

She thought it would feel awkward between them, but it felt as if they had never been apart.

'You are as beautiful as ever,' he ventured.

She blushed. 'It is wonderful to see you.' Neither could stop smiling.

'Shall we have tea?' he suggested.

'I much prefer to walk,' she replied. 'If you don't mind?

I've never stepped out with a real baron before. Should I curtsy?'

'Always,' he teased. The ice was broken.

They wandered to Central Park, walking so close they were almost touching.

'Come with me,' he insisted, leading her towards the horsedrawn carriage rides by the west entrance. Edith stroked a jet black mare's mane.

'Horses sense much about a person,' he said, watching the beast nuzzle Edith's pocket.

'I haven't got anything, girl,' she said, 'unless you like chocolate!'

'Not a good idea,' Maurice frowned.

'They must be very different from your polo ponies,' she said as the horse shook its head, rattling its well-worn livery. She had come to regret never seeing Maurice's home, and always being on the outside of his life.

'And much less highly strung, I assure you,' he said, gesturing towards the carriage. 'Shall we?'

She clapped her hands with glee. 'I have always wanted to do this,' she said.

'I was just in time then,' he laughed.

The driver held out his hand to help Edith up into the buggy, but the steps were slippery and she lost her footing, falling into Maurice's arms.

'Good job your husband was there to save you,' said the driver.

Huddled together under the domed hood of the carriage, Maurice wrapped a rug around their knees. As the wheels bumped over the path, they brushed together. He noticed Edith's legs were shaking.

'Drive on,' instructed Maurice, slipping the driver a dollar bill.

'There's no skating on the lake,' she said.

'Weren't we freezing that day!' he said.

'I've never skated since,' she said. 'Lost my nerve, I suppose.'

The cherry trees looked candyfloss pink and when they were at the fountain, the driver pulled on a rein to turn the carriage and shouted, 'Come on, my girl.' The carriage swayed and Edith braced herself against Maurice's side. Their eyes flicked towards each other as they edged apart and smiled.

'I have missed you,' he said, unable to look at her.

'Maurice . . .'

'When I saw you today, I knew how much.'

She reached over, not intending to touch him, but he leaned forward and grabbed her hand.

'We both made mistakes,' he said. 'But we are here now and that is what's important.'

Unthinking, he kissed her cheek and felt the smallest shrug of her shoulders.

'But I want so much for you to forgive me.'

'I do,' she said. 'I couldn't do it any other way.'

Then he kissed her and she did not pull away.

He gave the driver a full day's wages to keep on going. Rudolph Valentino would have to wait.

Leaving America was always meant to be a huge adventure for Maurice. He never dreamed he would feel so melancholy. But standing on the deck of the the *Mauritania*, as scores of people on New York's Chelsea Docks waved hats, newspapers and scarves, he could think of only one person.

The bitter-sweet days he spent with Edith were all that filled his mind. As they lay hidden away in his suite, he shunned sleep, unable to accept that each day they woke brought them closer to the day they would part. He longed to spend every last moment looking at her. Time to trace the line of her nose, or listen as she read Emily Dickenson to him, trying not to cry. Time. The thing they could never have.

He had begged her to come with him. Leave Howitt, send for the boys and her mother when they reached England.

'You know how much I want to, but you know I can't,' she said. And for that he loved her all the more.

The ship's four huge funnels roared as the liner glided into the Atlantic Ocean, bound for Southampton, England.

A popular song played round and round his head. 'The kind of light that brings love. The love that brings real harmony. I sigh, I cry, it's just a bit of heaven. When my baby smiles at me.'

NINE

'The English Are a Cold Race'

In his 200-dollar first-class cabin Maurice thought how unfortunate it was that his first duty upon setting foot on English soil was to attend the wedding of his cousin George. The thought of a romantic union made him feel quite jealous. But his relatives were more than happy to welcome the fourth Lord Fermoy into their inner circle.

He had hoped to attend the service alone, but his mother would have none of it and arranged invitations for Frank and herself. Fannie could not resist the opportunity to gloat about her title to those Irish relatives who had spurned her for abandoning her former husband. The two sides of the family had not been together since Maurice and Frank were children. It was set for a hostile reunion.

In the magnificence of St George's church in Hanover Square, as the sun streamed through the Flemish stained glass, Maurice watched the bride, Aletta Venter, walk serenely down the aisle. He then chivalrously distracted her nervous fiancé with a good luck tap on the shoulder. Captain George Burke Roche stared straight ahead, grateful for the vote of confidence. When his bride reached him, his gaze shifted, as if hypnotized by the shimmering Russian pearls of her head-dress.

'So what brings you here?' asked Countess Hochberg snootily, during the lavish wedding breakfast at nearby Brown's Hotel.

'I am going to follow my family calling and stand for Parliament,' Maurice announced.

'How quaint,' she said, sipping champagne and feigning interest until she moved seamlessly on to Viscount Goschen.

A quirk of the Irish peerage had allowed both his father and grandfather to contest a seat in the House of Commons, and Maurice had been handed the same privilege.

'They're all very smooth,' whispered Frank. 'We've got our work cut out to infiltrate the English.'

'So far, they're only too keen to tell me how they won the war,' chuckled Maurice.

With their mother busily matchmaking – apparently trying to pair either of her sons with the elder daughter of a major-general – Maurice moved aside to hide behind a flower arrangement. The string quartet began playing, and when he saw her signal for both brothers to walk towards her, he caught Frank's eye. Fannie was not here for social chit-chat and needed close chaperoning. The brothers held out their arms for the first dance and she was soon whisked away to the safety of the open floor.

Shortly after the newly-weds left for their honeymoon, Maurice decided to stretch his legs. He slipped away unnoticed into the balmy evening light and wandered through St James's Park, where the great weeping willows cast ghostly shadows on the grass. He paused at the wooden bridge by Bird Keeper's cottage, looking to his right and the stark façade of Buckingham Palace. The flag was lowered: the King was not at home. Lighting a cigarette, he watched the ember glow in the twilight as the sound of Big Ben's tolling marked the hour.

Maurice undid his silk tie and stuffed it inside his waistcoat pocket. Enjoying the freedom, he strode through the exit and found himself on Westminster Bridge, next to the Houses of Parliament.

Here at last was his mission: to serve the British people and be at the very heart of government. But as an Irish American only a few weeks in England, Maurice knew he had his work cut out to show he meant business. There was little trust of the Irish right now, following their recent demands for independence.

On the way home, Edith felt queasy after collecting the week's supplies. The winding roads did not help, nor the heat of the day. Since returning from New York, her mind had wandered and her body felt different.

As her stomach lurched she felt a crushing tiredness and knew only too well what was the cause. It was possible to forget the tell-tale symptoms of this malady, but the moment they returned, they were unmistakable. She had, after all, been pregnant twice before – but never with the doubt that now raged through her mind.

She was carrying an innocent child, and if the father was Henry there was nothing to fear. She would go into labour, he would deliver their baby, and they would be happy.

But what if the child belonged to Maurice? He was a lord who needed an heir, not a bastard. His distinctive face and beautiful huge blue eyes, all those things she loved about Maurice, now threatened to expose her betrayal. She shivered with terror. What lay ahead was a brutal choice.

To do the unthinkable would leave her damned. She would have to travel out of state, find an understanding doctor, and risk her own life to end her child's.

And what if she was wrong?

Tormented by the deceit, the more attentive Henry became, the more she hated herself. Whenever he worked late, Edith would unlock the bureau and re-read Maurice's letters.

She would hold them carefully, so that when her tears fell they would not trickle on to the paper and smudge his writing. She cried because she loved him . . . because it was impossible . . . and now she wept because she might be carrying his child. Undressing for bed, she turned sideways and stared into the mirror, looking for the tell-tale swelling of her belly.

To comfort herself, she wrote and told Maurice of her birthday celebrations. It had been a tedious occasion of idle chit-chat with stuffy neighbours, but she made it sound fun, with games and dancing. Yet she would have sacrificed it all to have him there.

Edith had grown to love his conviction and desire to do what was right. She knew that while these things drew her towards him, they also kept them apart. She conceded that his greatest power was his determination. 'You are so brave taking on the English in their backyard. I know you will succeed in whatever you want to do.'

His response had been typically generous.

It was a great pleasure to get your letter this
morning with the blue ribbon from your party.

Edith it is nice of you to say all those nice things. I've certainly tried to 'make good'. It has never been easy to do all those things oneself without any person to help.

I am looking forward to our next meeting. Little did I think that I wasn't going to see you again after I said 'good-bye.' I only wish that you had come back one week earlier when I was in New York. We ought to have an everlasting friendship and even though we are both getting grey haired there are plenty of years to come. Bless you, much love and a big kiss.

Hearing Henry's car, she slipped under the covers and reached for her unread book. She felt sick wondering how and when to tell him, knowing that before much longer he would guess. As he quietly climbed the stairs so as not to disturb anyone, she made up her mind it was to be tonight.

'I thought you'd be asleep hours ago,' he said, kissing her forehead. He still had his stethoscope around his neck. 'Did Ned keep you up with his nightmares again?'

'No, I just wanted to see you, that's all,' she said. Her hands were icy cold and she pushed them beneath the blankets.

'Mr Grogan insisted on showing me his new artificial leg or I'd have been home sooner,' he laughed, slipping off his shirt. Edith saw his familiar stocky frame reflected in the mirror, and felt her palms go clammy.

'There's something I have to ask you.'

He sat upright. 'Of course I'll try and get tickets for the travelling opera, I've just been a little busy today.'

'No,' she said, 'it's something else.'

'It always is!' he exclaimed.

She forced herself to look him straight in the eye.

'I've been feeling a little under the weather lately,' she began.

'Really,' he said, studying her face for clues.

'Yes, I feel sick, I can't face food, the smell of my favourite perfume now turns my stomach . . .'

Perched on the end of the bed, he drew down her bottom eyelid. 'You are very pale,' he said. 'Any other symptoms?'

'I feel so tired all the time.'

'Edith are you trying to tell me something?' he said, expressionless.

She patted the top of his hand and nodded.

He held his arms out towards her and shouted, 'We're having a baby! Is it true?'

'Yes,' she said.

'Do you want a boy or a girl?' he asked, wiping the tears on his arm as he hugged her.

'I don't mind,' she said, 'I just want you to be happy.'

'Edith. Darling,' he said. 'You have made me the happiest man alive. Thank you, my love, thank you.'

'Why can't we have a party?' said the boys, wide-eyed and hopeful. 'It's not every day we get to have a baby.'

Edith looked at Henry, 'I don't see why not. But let's have a day out first.'

Frau Hund made rye and pumpernickel sandwiches with chicken and home-made pickle, pressing them into fancy star shapes with a metal cutter. Then she snipped the stem from a home-grown lettuce and left its head to stand in cold water while she rubbed raw onion around the inside of a bowl, chopping in several red tomatoes already ripened on the windowsill.

Impressed by her mother's expertise, Edith refused to give in to the nausea she felt after peeling six boiled eggs and scooping out their middles. She mashed the yoke with melted butter, salt and freshly milled pepper, before refilling three of the eggs and fixing the halves back together with toothpicks. The remaining eggs were stuffed with green and black olives and individually wrapped in wax paper. And just in case the boys got extra hungry, she packed several thinly rolled molasses cookies.

Henry's car was crammed full as they drove to the river. It was a hot day, and Edith fanned her brow with a large straw hat decorated with pale blue ribbons. She liked to think that when she wore it tilted to one side it gave her an air of mystery. Still pale from morning sickness and the smell of hard-boiled eggs, she breathed slowly.

Near Mount Tamalpais, twenty minutes' drive from the surgery, stood a giant oak tree. Henry took Edith there in the weeks before they married. It had a gnarled and solid appearance and thrived among the mass of Redwood trees. They found that by climbing into its branches they could see the Farallon Islands twenty-five miles out to sea, the Marin County hills, San Francisco Bay, and sometimes even the snowy peaks of the Sierra Nevada. Henry liked to sit underneath it and close his eyes as if asleep. He called it 'our peace'.

After they had parked the car, Edith made for the tree, lowering herself lethargically on to the rug beneath its familiar shade. Grateful to be out of the sun, she sipped on a drink of over-sweetened lemon juice, her mother's remedy for 'settling the baby'. Henry placed the hamper by her feet and said, 'You'll feel better out of the heat.' He then went back to the car and returned with two small fishing rods.

Using a little bread and ham for bait, he set the boys up by the banks of the river, patiently threading the hooks and showing them how to cast the line into the middle of the waters.

'Du bist gut?' asked Frau Hund, worried by her daughter's sombre mood.

Edith nodded, fearful that the blankness of her eyes might betray her dark thoughts. 'It's the baby blues – you know – it will pass,' she replied.

They were interrupted by Ned yelling from the river bank, 'Can we eat these fish?'

'Sshh!' said Jack. 'You'll scare them off.'

Ned waved his arms and mouthed, 'Can we, Mommy?'

'If they're big enough,' Edith mouthed back, holding her hands twelve inches apart.

She lay back, her head resting on the cushion her mother had bought to keep her comfortable, while peering through the leaves of the tree to the mountains of clouds beyond. Her eyes grew heavy in the dappled light, and Frau Hund's call to eat barely registered, until Ned shook her hard.

'Eat, Mommy,' he said passing her the eggs.

Edith waved his hand away and pointed at the water's edge. Jack's rod was twitching on its rest and she squealed, 'Jack, you've got a bite!'

Jack dropped his sandwich, saying, 'Sorry, Mommy, gotta go,' and raced off. Jumping to his brother's assistance, Ned yelled, 'It's a darn whale!'

Henry wiped away a mouthful of crab meat salad and shouted, 'Lean back, boy, and reel it in dead slow.'

Ned was now holding on to his brother's waist, screaming, 'It's gonna eat us! I tell you it's a monster!'

Henry raised himself slowly and walked to the hollering

boys. He could see the snout of a huge trout poking from the water. Ten minutes later, they all ran back to the tree proudly carrying the wriggling fish.

'Make a fire, boys,' suggested Henry, as he deftly gutted and boned the fish. Jack and Ned dashed off to forage for sticks and tinder.

Henry sharpened two large sticks and speared the fish along its gut. It was not long before they were holding the trout just above the glowing logs and watching the shiny silver skin turning earth brown.

As for Edith, she shook as the smell of ripe flesh filled the air. She leaned back against the tree's knotted bark and closed her eyes, feeling Henry's cool hand stroking her brow. 'She's exhausted, poor lamb. She'll have to give up work sooner than she thinks,' he said.

Edith pretended to be asleep, imagining and wishing she was somewhere else.

After a casual meeting with fellow peer Lord Rothermere, the chance to stand as a Member of Parliament came rather sooner than Maurice expected. The two men agreed on many political principles and Maurice, intrigued by Rothermere's Anti Waste League, offered to campaign on his behalf.

Disillusioned with rampant post-war spending and high taxes, the party was made up of die-hard peers and MPs known for their anti-communist stance and fierce opposition to the coalition government. Maurice admired their fearless and determination to change the face of British politics.

Maurice's conviction and drive convinced Rothermere that this new Irish American peer was worth more than just a backroom position. He therefore asked Maurice to consider standing for Parliament at the forthcoming Westminster Abbey by-election.

Maurice's charm meant that men and women warmed to him and his early speeches had a naturalness few could resist. However, the journey was not all smooth. Maurice's rise provoked jealousy, and he was seen by some as an interloper, a rich quasi-aristocrat trying to muscle in. Disagreements between the British and Irish made Maurice a pawn in the Anglo-Irish tension, and he was used as an example by those keen to downgrade Irish peerages. The gossip-mongers claimed that Maurice had no intention of going anywhere near Ireland.

'He's only been here five minutes and thinks he knows the British people. New money may well talk in America, but breeding counts here,' they whispered. 'He doesn't even sound British.'

In the face of such indignation, Maurice acted with dignity and diplomacy, deciding to bide his time. He withdrew from the election race, informing the newspapers, 'As I only arrived from America two months ago it would be bordering on presumption to accept a nomination for any constituency at the present time.'

He would have to win people's confidence another way.

Privately he was seething at how he'd been treated. He was working hard and fast to ingratiate himself with the higher echelons of London society, but a few jealous voices were halting his chance of selection.

Considering whether he had made the right decision to cross the Atlantic, he wrote to Edith wondering why he was being subjected to such vitriol:

It is never easy to do things oneself without any person to help. The English are a cold race – and

there isn't much heart here for strangers. My
brother is soon off to Egypt. I've been. It's up the
Nile. He will have a wonderful time. Bless you and
much love and a good kiss.

It had been a hectic few months, and after the ups and
downs of politics he tired of London's pace. He missed
the outdoor life, clean air and green fields to hike in. Most
of all, he missed the ocean.

Over a lavish lunch in esteemed company at Claridges,
one of his favourite hotels in the heart of London's
Mayfair, he lamented to the Duke of Connaught about
his lack of a country retreat.

'In New York I could always drive to Newport and get
away,' he said. 'Here I am in the capital from one week
to the next and I need a change of scene.'

The Duke knew what he meant. Since his wife Louise
died four years ago he had divided his time between
Clarence House and his Bagshot home, where he indulged
his love of horticulture.

'Have you ever shot grouse?' the Duke said.

'Never,' answered Maurice. It had been a while since
he had hunted, and the prospect of shooting on wide open
land was very appealing.

'Scotland is magnificent,' said a compatriot, 'I'm afraid
we can't shoot pigeons anymore, but the grouse are plen-
tiful on the estate. Come up for the Highland Games.'

'It's most generous of you,' said Maurice, surprised by
this kindness from such a recent acquaintance.

'And I'll invite some nice young ladies to keep you
company.'

'It's been quite a while since I danced. I may have two
left feet, but I'll be delighted,' he laughed.

Maurice was not the only rich bachelor whose love life was the subject of speculation that lunchtime. 'Bertie should be back before long,' said the new acquaintance.

'I heard Prince Albert had surgery for an ulcer,' ventured Maurice.

'Lady Elizabeth Bowes-Lyon is giving him a hard time. Twice he has asked for her hand in marriage and both times she's refused,' his companion revealed.

Maurice knew a little of the younger prince's health problems, but was interested to learn of his recent romantic troubles.

'I understand her eye is fixed on the elder brother, David . . .'

'The heir to the throne?' said Maurice.

'The gossip says Elizabeth will not accept Bertie's hand in marriage until she is assured David is no longer a potential beau.'

'It's hard to wait for someone to make up their mind,' agreed Maurice. 'May the best man win,' he said, raising his glass.

Maurice boarded the overnight sleeper for the 400-mile journey from London to Inverness in Scotland. He was due at a 'Saturday to Monday' houseparty and then intended to do some shooting. When he had received his invitation he laughed at the snobbish British aristocracy's pompous desire to show they had no need of work by extending the weekend for a day. A driver was waiting to collect him, and they drove sedately along deserted roads, all the way flanked by purple heather, until they were deep into the highlands.

Maurice was hardly indoors the whole weekend, which was spent in stag hunting, grouse shooting, fly fishing on the banks of the River Findhorn and watching the Highland Games. He drank good Scotch whisky, smoked the finest cigars and enjoyed robust dinner conversation. He felt thoroughly at home.

Each morning he awoke to the haunting sound of a piper signalling the start of the day's Games. Maurice was fascinated by traditional highland sports such as caber tossing and stone putting. In the evening, his dancing skills were challenged by the complicated routines of the reels. He even ate haggis. He felt invigorated and forged friendships which renewed his personal and political confidence.

Word spread that the affable, debonair Lord Fermoy was proving himself a worthy house guest. It became a prerequisite of a good party to have the enigmatic Irish American under one's roof. After Scotland, when he was deemed 'the most handsome bachelor in Europe' by journalists, Maurice immediately became a much sought-after dinner guest, and most weekends he received an invitation to leave London for the country.

He soon began dressing for the part and instructed his Bond Street tailor to send over samples of shooting suits and heavy woollen plus-fours with tweed jackets the colour of the landscape. He preferred a flat cap to a trilby, feeling it made him look more of a country gentleman. He wanted to blend in, and chose a conservative, worsted green suit along with a new dinner suit and packed them ready for his favourite rural destination – Norfolk.

He found great enjoyment motoring eighty miles north of London to the east coast with its narrow roads and spacious landscape. It was much closer than Scotland, and he liked the stark beauty. Through the Fens and on to Hunstanton, he breathed the musky sea air and glimpsed the King's summer residence at Sandringham, hidden behind forbidding iron gates. Now that would be the place for one hell of a house party, he thought.

He drove onwards to the white sands at Holkham, stopping to watch the lapping water and the sea birds soaring over the dunes. Passing by Holkham Hall and envious of its outlook, he walked through the shaded sweetness of the pinewoods across the saltflats towards the stillness of the sands.

On a Sunday afternoon, late in summer, amid the sea lavender and the larks, he realized he had no interest in returning to the city the next day. As the tide poured in, he knew that this was where he belonged.

He wasted no time in choosing the tree-lined market town of Spilsby, close to the birthplace of Alfred, Lord Tennyson. The historic town was near to Bolingbroke Castle, home of Henry IV, and appealed to Maurice because of its quintessential Englishness. After much searching, Maurice took a lease on Hagnaby Priory, a Tudor Gothic country house.

He wrote to Edith:

Your long letter has at last reached me. Your Christmas cable never arrived. I wrote you a letter too, but I never got an answer. So you see I have had bad luck. I am very well. I am looking forward to the time when I shall see you again. You will see I have gone into politics. It is very interesting work and great experience. Here is a picture of my house, which is most comfortable and has a nice garden with it. I think you shall like it. Edith I still have to find a wife. Somehow I never seem to get one. I have been near it several times. With love, yours ever.

As Edith read his letter, the baby kicked sharply under her ribs. She looked at the picture of the Priory within its walled garden and imagined them sitting together drinking tea in the peace and tranquillity of this English country garden.

It was so different from her own home, where she felt bleak since a pan caught fire and caused substantial damage. She sighed at her daydream and picked up a newspaper account she had found. A smiling Maurice was pictured at a recent society party, surrounded by scantily dressed dancers. She could hardly bear to read it again.

It said that a wealthy princess called Vlora was doggedly pursuing Maurice. This woman, born plain Irish-American Peggy Kelly, was already twice married to millionaires, then divorced and widowed. Her third marriage, to the future King of Albania, was now disintegrating and it meant only one thing – she was hunting for a future husband, and now she had Maurice in her sights.

Edith read one sentence over and over, 'Maurice reached Paris still uncaught, gazed into the blue eyes of Princess Vlora, and in their depths saw the spirit that was Peggy Kelly's.'

It was impossible not to feel jealous. There was the chance that a twice divorced gold-digger might become Lady Fermoy. Princess Vlora had the right connections and more than enough money. Edith wanted to scream at the hypocrisy. Here she was, on the point of giving birth, maybe to his child, while Maurice was thousands of miles away flirting with an array of beauties. She was expected to say nothing. As Edith gazed at his picture, she felt Maurice was taunting her.

Yet she could not stop herself adoring him. The thought that he could be with other women made her angry and want to weep. Most of all, it made her wish never to be hurt again.

The child kicked once more and she rubbed her belly, protective of the baby growing inside. She needed to know who this new life belonged to. It would not be long now. She would find out – as soon as she laid eyes on the child.

She looked around at the darkened walls and the half-repaired staircase, and to where the fire had almost destroyed part of the roof. She told Maurice how brave the boys were and how courageously Henry had acted in the face of such danger. How her husband was promising to have everything back to normal soon. Deciding this was the moment to reveal the secret she had kept from Maurice these past months, she added, 'We must be ready for when the baby comes.'

TEN

'I Love England'

After the pace of London, Maurice relished his new country life. The rambling Priory was perfectly set within beautiful grounds, amid open fields and fresh country air. He was so taken with the place that he immediately tried to buy it, thinking he could settle here for good. He'd sit in his study and from the window watch the nightingales and rabbits playing beneath the crooked magnolia tree. And when he needed solitude, he would walk to the small private chapel in the back garden to pray, or spend time in quiet contemplation.

He had left the critics behind and here found space to breathe. Rising early was still a habit he could not break, but Maurice enjoyed the clear dawn light. Each morning, while the grass was still dewy, he went into the garden where there was a small hand pump connected to the underground water system. The plumbing was so primitive that Maurice had to grab the handle and yank it back and forth for five minutes to fill up the house tank. He found it a useful way to start the day before the rigours of his working life closed in, and wondered how many hands before him had done the same.

Maurice hoped to stand as a Member of Parliament for Horncastle, a local farming town. But within this closed community working farmers and country folk were suspicious of outsiders. They were not likely to take kindly to a lord trying to further his political career, seemingly at their expense. His title and his lack of experience were both stumbling blocks to winning votes. But Maurice believed he stood a chance if he could talk knowledgeably on agricultural and country issues, so he immersed himself in finding out about their way of life.

As a younger man in America, he had looked after his grandfather's herd of cattle, gleaning a basic knowledge of dairy and arable farming. He put this to good use in Horncastle by offering his services as a labourer to a local farmer to learn the more practical side of agriculture and getting hands-on experience.

Although the campaigning hours were long, he did his best to meet as many constituents as he could. His informal style and willingness to get his hands dirty raised eyebrows among those politicians who urged him to follow a more conventional electoral trail. But Maurice realized there was a dignity in knowing these people. Straight-talking people needed straightforward answers.

At his selection meeting, he fiddled nervously with his cufflinks and went over the important points of his speech in his mind. It was crucial to make an immediate impact with the public and the committee. There would be no second chance.

The hall was packed, with standing room only at the back for the last-minute stragglers. Word had quickly spread about this maverick lord who wanted to become their MP.

Maurice peered from behind the curtain and, seeing the

rowdy audience, thought he might be sick. Placing his pen in his inside pocket, he wiped his hands on his jacket sleeves and tried hard to calm himself. This was the biggest crowd he had ever addressed, and his mind went blank. There was no time to recover, however, as the chairman's voice rang out, 'Please give a warm welcome to Lord Fermoy.'

Walking on stage, Maurice was greeted by a series of shuffles and coughs whilst the audience studied this elegant new man, who looked to be without a care in the world. Yet his legs were numb and the sea of anonymous faces terrified him.

Steadying himself with his hands either side of the podium, Maurice began falteringly, almost apologetic, running through a résumé of his time at Harvard and election as a trustee for the university. He noticed a woman yawning. One man shook his head with bored inevitability. All his high hopes were rapidly fading.

Maurice shifted uneasily from one leg to another and changed the subject. He hoped from his own work experience to find common ground with the farm hands and spoke about his army career and the fight for freedom. But he sensed he was losing them. Then he switched to his time on the railroad. 'I was working for a wage like all of you,' he said.

A gruff voice from the audience shouted, 'You're a lord. What do you know about us?'

Another joined in, using a fake American accent, 'Hey Yankee boy! Tell us something new!'

Maurice froze. Every pair of eyes fixed on him, awaiting a reply.

He lay down his notes and seemed to blanch.

'Come on, Yank, do you even know where you are?'

Maurice bowed his head, willing the jeering to stop. But the noise only got louder as the ringleaders stamped their feet and slow hand clapped. Maurice could take no more and replaced his speech deep inside his pocket and turned away from the podium.

But he did not leave, walking instead down the stage steps into the heart of the audience.

'You know Americans have the greatest respect for this country,' he shouted above the din. 'Because of what you all represent.'

The commotion started to settle, and Maurice lifted his arms to quell the remaining rowdy listeners. 'Americans think of themselves as a kind of eldest son who broke away to run their own show. Everyone needs independence and to be listened to. I understand the need for pride.'

The labourers in the crowd, used to being at the constant beck and call of their bosses, fell silent.

'It is true, I was raised in America, and I make no apologies because I am proud of my heritage. But let me also tell you that my father was Irish and I was born in London. So I am a bit of a mongrel.'

The quietening in the room encouraged him to carry on.

'And in that respect I'm little different to an American Jersey cow . . .'

Maurice held his breath and waited. There was a small rumble of laughter.

'Because there's hardly one of the beasts that doesn't boast an ancestry in Great Britain. This *great* country.'

A single pair of hands clapped and he relaxed a little.

'In many ways I am fortunate and I am blessed. But I know something of hardship. There were no luxuries in my trench in France.

'And my grandfather left home at the age of ten, working in a post room as a young boy under hard men who thought nothing of giving him a beating. Even though he would come back exhausted, he still made time to study because he believed he could better himself. And yes, he made a lot of money, but he always lived by the same principles – a decent wage for an honest day's work, enough food on the table to feed his family and money in the bank for when times get tough.'

He paused as a bead of sweat trickled down the side of his cheek.

'I still live by those principles. Just like you.'

Out of the corner of his eye he spotted an old man with a stick hunched over in his seat. Maurice walked over to him and placed his hand on the man's shoulder.

'Those who are lucky should live useful lives,' he began, 'and strive to help others. And I want you to know that is why I am here. And that is what I intend to do.'

A single hand clap started in the centre of the crowd and then slowly rippled through the audience until Maurice was facing a wave of sound. Gamely, he cast his eye along the rows and tried to address each individual personally.

'Thank you, but I have done nothing,' he said, waiting until silence came. Then pointing his finger towards the sky he added, 'Yet!'

'Now, any questions?' he asked, moving back on to the stage feeling more comfortable.

He left that night with part of his dream fulfilled. He had the full backing of the committee, having been unanimously endorsed as the Conservative candidate for Horncastle, and gained the respect of those he hoped to represent. He was on his way.

As far as Maurice was concerned, Prime Minister Stanley Baldwin could not call an election soon enough. He was ready to knock on every farmer's and labourer's door to get his message across. He hoped his empathy and positive outlook would make up for his lack of experience. At last he was doing something he loved and something that mattered. Politics was proving to be a powerful drug, and one he felt unable to leave alone.

Samuel Pattison, the resident MP for Horncastle, caught wind of his opponent's surge in popularity and knew that his own position would be under threat unless he fought back quick and hard. He launched a personal attack on Maurice, saying he epitomized everything the Labour Party reviled. Lord Fermoy was wealthy, titled and had barely stepped foot inside England. How could he understand the needs of Lincolnshire farming folk? Striking at Maurice's Achilles' heel, Pattison promised that his party would heavily tax those with personal fortunes over £5,000. It put Maurice's vast wealth centre stage of the debate and at a time of increasing hardship was an attempt to discredit him as a 'toff' protected by his personal fortune.

Whatever he did, Maurice could not deny his background, it was a sticking point he could do nothing about. Maurice may have been on a crusade to become a Member of Parliament, but he was not yet home and dry.

Edith lay on the bed feeding her new daughter when Frau Hund knocked gently on the door.

'You don't have to do that,' said Edith, as her mother placed a tray with freshly made oatmeal pancakes and a glass of milk on the table.

'I know I don't,' she replied. 'But you are my baby too,

remember.' Watching her granddaughter, Frau Hund smiled contentedly and said, 'That one came out hungry.'

Edith raised her eyes heavenward in agreement and she took the newspaper from under her mother's arm.

'Thank you,' said Edith.

'It's important to keep your mind active,' replied her mother.

Edith opened the paper and out fell a letter concealed between the folds. Frau Hund bent down and gave the baby a kiss before quietly leaving the room. Edith shouted after her, 'Thank you Mama,' and holding the loudly suckling infant, struggled to open the envelope. Tearing along the fold with her little finger, she pulled out a black and white photograph together with a handwritten note and read:

Edith,

I was very glad to get your letter today and to have a photo of the baby who looks too beautiful for anything. I was very sorry to hear of the fire and all that happened this past summer. How fortunate the fire didn't do greater harm. The election took place the other day, I failed to get in. I had a hard fight against a man many years older who had done this for ten years. I made an excellent showing – he got 10,797 and I got 9,158. So you can see it was pretty close. I gained no end of experience and hope to do better another time. It is a great experience and I'll never forget it. I am glad that you are so happy and your life is so full. At present there doesn't seem the slightest chance of finding a wife. I often wished you lived on this side of the ocean. Bless you with love.

She cuddled her daughter closer and wished he could see her downy jet black hair, tiny bear cub ears and chocolate brown eyes. Sitting up, Edith stroked the baby's forehead with her finger and said softly 'How could they do that to him, my little lamb?' The baby cooed.

Hearing heavy footsteps on the stairs she stuffed the letter beneath the sheets. Henry came in beaming, but his expression momentarily froze when he saw Edith with her back towards him. 'I'm not sure you should be out of bed.'

'I'm bored,' said Edith quickly, laying the child in her crib. 'I'll go mad if I stay in this room a day longer.'

He took hold of his wife's wrist and checked her pulse. 'It's a little faint.'

Edith snatched her arm away as the baby started to cry. Henry tutted and in his best bedside manner said calmly, 'You must promise not to lift anything, then I might allow you downstairs.'

He gathered the sleepy infant on to his right shoulder and began patting her back. 'This is what she likes,' he said. 'Do it like this after each feed.'

Edith watched blankly and thought better of saying anything. She walked over to the wardrobe and chose a loose-fitting dress. Carefully she said, 'We must think of a name. I can't call her Lambie for ever.'

He stopped patting the baby. 'I want to call her Edith.'

She waited a moment before turning round. 'Really?'

Henry nodded. 'How could anything be more perfect than you?'

The rigours and disappointment of the election campaign behind him, Maurice went to relax in the glorious Swiss resort of St Moritz, where the silent snow falls and icy roads reminded him of New York.

The fresh mountain air and exercise always made him fall asleep the moment his head touched the luxurious pillows. He would wake refreshed and pick up his hickory skis that still smelt of pine tar and candle wax after his over-zealous polishing. Arriving at the slopes before anyone else, he liked to be first to slalom through the virgin snow past the fir trees as he concentrated on keeping his skis parallel over the white alabaster landscape. Only the aches in his limbs prevented Maurice from staying out until nightfall and he had promised himself to keep something in reserve for the final night's skating competition. As a former ice skating champion, it was the one event he really looked forward to, and although he would never admit it, he loved to show off.

Nightly parties were held at the grandiose Palace Hotel. The restaurant was subtly lit with delicate coloured lamps to create the impression of a flower grove. Maurice chatted happily with the guests as they were led one at a time to the hotel's precarious balcony and lowered to the terrace by a dangerous-looking gondola.

There he met Lady Diana Duff Cooper, the only original survivor from the Great War's 'corrupt coterie' of influential and intellectual aristocrats. She was beautiful and flamboyant, and rumours of her illegitimacy only added to the intrigue already surrounding her.

She stood beside her adoring husband, Alfred, whose connections were equally impeccable. A close ally of Winston Churchill and Herbert Asquith, he was being tipped for a heady ministerial career. Diana air kissed Maurice enthusiastically and Alfred shook his hand firmly.

Maurice thought they were a golden couple and envied their closeness. They sparkled in each other's company but were just as forceful apart. Although Alfred was five years his junior, he seemed to have made a success of his life, while Maurice, approaching middle age, was nowhere near to finding a wife. The men had quickly become firm friends and in a quiet moment, rather out of character, Maurice confided in Alfred about his long search for happiness.

'I don't seem to find the right person. I'm rather old-fashioned, I'm afraid, and don't like modern girls. I wish I could say that I was engaged to be married – but there seems little hope!'

Alfred reassured him that there really was someone out there for everyone. 'Maurice, you worry too much. The ladies love you. You will find your Diana, I know it.'

Maurice wondered how everyone could be so assured about his future, when he was filled with constant doubt.

He awoke for the first time in the early hours of the morning. Perhaps it was too much wine or not enough dancing, but feeling restless and unable to settle, Maurice lay beneath the heavy covers, thoughts buzzing around his head.

Here in Switzerland he was surrounded by attractive, available ladies yet still struggling to find love. Each time he embarked on a potential liaison he felt something was missing and soon lost interest. He wanted someone he could talk to, a woman to laugh with, a friend who understood him. A woman he could love as much as Edith. Many times he wondered if perhaps he did not have the heart for marriage and would remain a bachelor for ever. But he did not have the luxury of choice. Now that he had a title, he had to produce an heir. A single life was impossible when he had duty to fulfil.

In trying to establish his career, he had suppressed the romantic side of his nature. In spite of his outward affability, Maurice had been keeping his distance from people.

It was easy to hide behind wealth and charm, but he had been subtly avoiding talking about himself by expressing great interest in other people's lives. This only made him all the more attractive and ladies never stopped falling in love with him. But his real love affair was with England, as he tried to explain to Edith,

> Yes, I live surrounded by beautiful trees and garden. I believe this county is even more beautiful than people say. It is like a huge garden – no eyesores – inhabited by civilized people and all are excellent masters of the English language and their voices. It sounds as if you are happily married and settled for the rest of your days. Just think we first met ten years ago. How time flies! I don't care if I never return. Yesterday on my way back here there were so many American tourists and they were so noisy and had such dreadful voices that I was ashamed of them. There is nothing more pleasant than the perfect English voice. They don't jar. You haven't sent me the snapshot I have asked – please do.
>
> I love being here as a free person – nobody is prevented from drinking mildly when they wish to. America is the laughing stock of the world with her bootlegging crime. I lived the best years of my life there and saw America at its best. Much love.

At the end of the summer he was invited to a dance in Grosvenor Square, where he met the acerbic and witty Nancy Mitford. They Charlestoned to the Clifford Essex band and Maurice was immediately bewitched. Her constant teasing, which sometimes verged on cruelty, appealed to his sense of the ridiculous.

151

As the oldest of six daughters of the second Baron and Lady Redesdale, she had no care for the conventions and crassness of the upper classes. Nancy had an unconventional childhood at Asthall Manor, on the family estate in Oxfordshire. She was never allowed to go to school and was taught by a series of governesses.

Maurice was fascinated by Nancy's grandfather, Thomas Gibson Bowles, a former MP for the Norfolk port of King's Lynn. He questioned Nancy about this part of the world as he was being lured to the area by the Conservative Party grandees. His performance during the Horncastle by-election had so impressed officials that they believed he would be a huge asset in Parliament and had been working hard to allocate him the safe seat of King's Lynn.

The timing could not have been better. The election of 1923 had produced a hung parliament and another election was not far off. Maurice intended to be well prepared for the campaign and it did no harm to cultivate his friendship with the Mitfords, even if it meant putting up with the relentless teasing about his American ancestry, which was a particular affectation of Nancy's.

He told Edith, 'I don't know when I will get back to the States. I love England and the work here. I am standing for Parliament again. It is hard work and I am out each night addressing audiences and making myself generally useful.'

He gave up the lease on Hagnaby Priory and moved to Heacham village in Norfolk, famous for its association with Pocahontas, the young American Indian princess who married a Heacham landowner and tobacco planter named John Rolfe. One of Maurice's first duties was to unveil a statue of the princess at the local church. Heacham was within a mile of shingle and sand beaches, where he could breathe in the pungent smell of cockles, clams and winkles in the heavy sea mist. He took a large house appropriately called the Shooting Lodge, liking the name and considering it a good omen. Driving through the village with people waving him past, he felt every inch the English gentleman, even stopping along the way for tea and scones.

His arrival in Heacham coincided with a national crisis particularly felt by the Norfolk community. There was a slump in corn prices with farm hands' wages slashed to a meagre twenty-five shillings for a backbreaking fifty-hour week. These people were in dire straits, and Maurice was desperate to help. All thought of travelling back to America faded as his political vocation took on greater urgency. At last he could prove his worth. And his cause was helped considerably when a few days before voting started in the 1924 general election, an extraordinary scare campaign hit the headlines. A newspaper published inflammatory extracts from a letter purporting to be from Soviet chairman Grigory Zinoviev, aligning the Labour Party with Communism.

Support for Labour plummeted, and the Conservatives won a landslide victory with 161 extra seats in Parliament. Maurice romped home at the polls as the proud new MP for King's Lynn. The Zinoviev Letter later proved to be a fake, but it was too late for the Labour Party: the damage had been done and the Conservatives, including Maurice, were riding the crest of a wave.

Writing from his new office in the House of Commons, Maurice told Edith:

It was very thoughtful of you to send me the flowers from California. It was nice of you to say

153

that you were glad I was an MP. It is certainly a very great honour and I fully realize my great responsibility and I am also doing the best to act to the best of my ability. I'm still continuing with my charity work, it's the only thing I enjoy doing, making others happy.

My plans for the summer are uncertain. I had hoped to return to America, but being a Member of Parliament one has to be near at hand. Everyone comes to me about every kind of thing and I ought not to be far away for long. To go to USA takes a long time – if I could only fly over.

Edith, although deeply disappointed, made herself feel better by teasing him about his appearance in photographs she had seen in the papers. But he did not take kindly to her comments and tetchily replied, 'I don't think that I have changed much and I know that I am not any heavier! It must have been a poor photo.' His sensitivity amused Edith and she laughed at his fragile ego. He may have found his true passion but he was still gullible.

The following summer an early morning rumbling startled Henry awake, followed by the persistent ringing of the telephone. It was Edith calling from a house in Santa Barbara.

'I'm so frightened,' she said.

He could hardly hear her on the crackling line. 'Is it a quake?' he asked, fearing the answer.

'A bad one.'

A series of shakes had kept the people of Santa Barbara up all night. They had fled in blind panic into the streets waiting to see if the bellicose thunder coming from deep under the ground would rupture the surface. Everyone asked the same thing – was this another big one?

'Is it safe there?' she shouted.

'Yes. We must be on the edge. Is Lambie all right?'

'Okay . . . just crying.'

Henry breathed a little easier. 'And the boys?'

'They're looking after her.'

'I'll be there as soon as I can. Stay calm,' he yelled. 'And try not to worry.'

He heard a stifled sob as the line went dead.

Waiting for the aftershocks were the worst time. Henry had seen more injuries caused by panic than by actual earthquakes. He lost count of the times he had fixed broken limbs and stitched gashes after people crashed into one another at the threat of another rumble.

Throwing on his trousers and flicking his braces over his shoulders, Henry grabbed for his shoes and ran out to the car. For several minutes he tried to hand crank the engine of his Chevrolet into life. His wrist ached and his thumb was sore. Whenever he was in a hurry the car seemed happy to take its time to fire up, coughing and spluttering like an old man waking.

'Damn thing,' he muttered under his breath. 'Not today.'

Henry was so relieved when the car sprang into life, he let out a small whoop. He drove quickly, pushing the gas pedal flat to the floor, urging the Chevy to go faster. How he wished he had bought the new Ford last summer, but with a young child there had been other priorities. He chastised himself for such false economy.

In Oakland and San Jose dust had turned the air fetid. The oppressive heat had made it impossible to sleep and for once Henry was grateful. It meant Edith and the children were awake and had their wits about them when the quake hit, rather than being crushed in their beds as the walls crumbled.

They were staying near the sea front where buildings were collapsing and crude oil had pushed its way through the sand, turning the beach black. It looked like a war zone. The Sheffield Dam had burst open, sending a wall of water hurtling towards the ocean.

Edith sat trembling, wishing she had followed her instincts instead of Henry's advice. He had encouraged her to get away for a few days, saying a change of environment would do her and the children the world of good. He had bought the tickets and hid them in the sugar jar, waiting patiently for her to find them. She had smiled sweetly and thanked him. But when she boarded the train, Edith had wanted to turn around and go home. He told her she was having an anxiety attack and had given her a paper bag to breathe into.

Now she was squashed beneath the stairs clutching on to her three children and praying it was not the final moment, for there was too much left undone. She still had the boys and her little girl to raise, her life to lead and so many words unsaid. In the dark, with fearful noise all around, she shut her eyes and muttered repeatedly under her breath, 'Keep us safe, Papa, please, please keep us safe.' Edith pleaded to survive. Life was too short and too precious to end like this. And she had a promise to keep to Maurice.

The contrast in their existence struck her hard. He was a wealthy lord taking his place in Parliament, while she was struggling to bring up three children. Neither could have predicted their lives since they met on the train. But they were still in love, despite everything. They had come this far, and Edith knew that whatever happened in the future, she could not give him up.

Edith emerged from the trauma of the earthquake before Henry arrived, already convinced of one thing – that she and Maurice must see and hold each other again. She had been close enough to death to know she did not want a life littered with regrets. She didn't know how or where, but she wrote to say, 'I need to see you again. I will come to you. Whatever it takes, I want us to be together.'

Maurice's letter from the House of Commons was scribbled hastily at his desk between policy meetings. 'I had read of the damage at Santa Barbara, I didn't know that you had been there. What an escape you did have! It was awfully nice of you to say you thought of me during your most anxious period. I have never been in an earthquake. It must be very frightening.'

Her experience scared Maurice into realizing how precious Edith was to him. The thought of her being taken away focused his mind on what was important.

As Maurice hunched studiously over his desk in the House of Commons, his brother Frank stood impatiently by the window, keen to go out on the town. Fifteen minutes later, Maurice stood up, placed his pen back in the drawer and waved for his brother to come along.

'You are quite ridiculous, Maurice. Is this madness of yours still carrying on? There is no point and you know it.'

Maurice shrugged. 'You don't understand.'

'I understand you will be in trouble if this ever gets out.'

'Look, I know I can't allow her to come to England. It's too risky.'

'Good, I'm glad you've seen sense,' said Frank, holding a glass of port to the light.

Maurice screwed up the note and pulled a folded letter from his pocket. 'This is the one I'm going to send,' he said. He handed Frank the thin paper. 'Go on read it.'

'I hope it ends, "I will never forget you . . ."' scolded Frank.

'I wrote it yesterday,' said Maurice.

Frank read: 'I expect to be in America in August. I could meet you in Chicago. If you could come there let me know. I am going on Saturday to Paris. I wish you were going to be there. Take good care of yourself, write soon. Much love.'

Frank downed the port in one large gulp. 'She is married, Maurice. She will never be yours.'

Maurice didn't flinch.

ELEVEN

'I Need To See You'

The bitter cold snow flurries had come early. It was not yet winter, but the roads around St James's in London were already hidden beneath a blanket of shocking white. As the people bowed their heads, there was the monotonous drip-drip of snow falling from brimmed hats. For over two hours the temperature had been falling steadily, and the streets of Pall Mall were slippery underfoot, iced hard by crowds straining to pay their last respects to Queen Alexandra.

Her body had lain in state at Westminster Abbey and in a show of respect, 50,000 people filed past. The great Queen had died at Sandringham struck down by a heart attack at the age of sixty-two. She had done her duty, giving birth to six children, and still managed to outlive her husband, King Edward VII, by fifteen years.

Queen Alexandra grew up in relatively modest circumstances in Copenhagen, Denmark, which gave her an ordinariness which her subjects grew to respect. They saw her as one of them. She was only thirteen and the Prince of Wales sixteen when negotiations began to ensure that the young couple could marry. Five years later Alexandra, hailed as the sea king's daughter, had blossomed into a real beauty and was escorted back to Britain aboard the royal yacht.

Although it caused outrage, her husband's affair with the actress Lillie Langtry did much to raise the public's consciousness of Alexandra's predicament. And she coped with dignified stoicism, until her subjects felt great pity for her. Always more intuitive then intellectual, her eyes betrayed her true feelings and she went through life happily ignoring protocol. Her partial deafness never prevented her being an involved and loving mother who insisted on raising her children herself, rather than leaving the task to nannies.

After a private service at the Chapel Royal, the horse-drawn gun carriage with her body was led from St James's Palace through Marlborough Gates, past a brigade of guards wearing snow-whitened bearskins. The top of her coffin was covered in family flowers arranged in regal splendour. The King, in field marshal attire, and the Prince of Wales, in his regimental Welsh Guards uniform, walked silently behind the carriage, heads bowed, in flawless unison.

Maurice was waiting inside Westminster Abbey with dignitaries and representatives from the royal houses of Europe, including the kings of Denmark, Belgium and Norway.

The Duke of York stared into the distance. The loss of his grandmother had hit him hard. She always indulged him and he, with great fondness, gave her a special place in his heart. His grandmother could always be relied on for affection, in contrast to his own parents, King George V and Queen Mary, who were extremely authoritarian and played little part in raising their children.

Maurice felt huge sympathy for his new friend, whose suffering was all too apparent. The two men had become confidants since Maurice moved into Heacham, ten minutes' drive from the royal estate at Sandringham. As the local MP, Maurice got invited to royal house parties and he and the Duke found they had much in common. They shared a love of tennis with Bertie being the first member of the Royal Family to play at Wimbledon. Although naturally left-handed, he had been forced to use his right hand for everything throughout his younger years, but on court reverted to his favoured hand with winning results. Maurice played regularly for the House of Commons team and as his friendship with the Duke grew, they proved to be lethal doubles partners.

They discovered a camaraderie in their highly competitive natures, regularly challenging each other to a round of golf on the wide open courses near Sandringham. Bertie, playing off a handicap of ten, could trounce Maurice, who found that royalty inhibited his natural swing.

Bertie had a fiery temper when things weren't going his way, but he was really a gentle man, inhibited by a severe stutter. Always seeking the approval of his father, he once wrote to him almost apologetically after winning a tennis tournament, 'I did not lose my head at the critical moment, which was lucky.'

In Maurice he found a confidant and a calming influence, which allowed the two men to express the more extravagant side of their natures. They would jump into fast cars and speed through Bertie's Norfolk estate, or grab twelve-bore shot guns and fly off hunting. Trying to be like two ordinary, if wealthy men in their prime. 'I got 571 pheasants the other day – six guns,' Maurice boasted to Edith.

The Duke and Maurice were bonded by a deep sense of purpose balanced by a flippant humour. Their common touch, ingrained consideration for others and loyalty gave them an unshakeable rapport. Now during this period of national and personal mourning, Maurice wanted to help him in any way he could.

Queen Alexandra's death added to the already depressed mood in the country. Things were not going well for Great Britain as discontent spread through a workforce fed up with exploitative wage cuts and long hours. And the government was struggling with the growing levels of poverty.

Outside Maurice's constituency surgery in King's Lynn, long queues of desperate, angry men and women demanded to know what he was going to do to help them. Children came dressed in rags and shoeless, mothers pointing to open, infected sores on their feet. Fathers begged butchers for pigs' intestines still stinking of manure and undigested swill, to feed their families. Seeing such dreadful poverty and hopelessness on a daily basis, Maurice began to question whether he was up to the job.

As the bitterly cold winter rolled on, coal supplies began to dwindle and many families started burning furniture to keep warm. Mine owners took the unprecedented step of insisting that workers take a 25 per cent wage cut to fund the shortages. If miners rejected these new terms, the owners threatened to lock all the men out of the pits, leaving them with no work or wages to feed their already starving families.

The conflict escalated when newspaper workers refused to print a story denouncing the pit workers as unpatriotic, and the Trades Union Congress called three million members out on strike in support. The effect on the country was catastrophic, with daily living grinding to a halt. White-collar workers had to leave their normal jobs to keep essential services running; lawyers and accountants were expected to drive trains and buses to maintain food deliveries and public transport.

All Maurice could do to alleviate people's suffering was to offer a kindly word and a promise that things would get better. In a House of Commons debate, he spoke angrily at how badly his constituents were suffering in the conditions.

A resident of King's Lynn recently offered to make a free gift to the unemployed of all the available firewood lying in his orchard, provided the men themselves came to fetch it. But the men were forbidden by the manager of the Employment Exchange to accept this offer, despite the promise that the necessary horses and carts were to be lent free of charge. What are the reasons for this?

I am going tomorrow into districts where smallholders have had to stand by and see over 1,400 tons of plums and apples hanging on the trees and rotting. If we are to save the fruit growing industry in which we are told there are 40,000 people in the area, we must do something at once. I can see no harm in the restriction of imports. I spent thirty years in a protected country, in the United States, where they have a licence.

I think I am right in saying that in no civilized country today is the outlook of agriculture poorer. That is due entirely to the high cost of production and the slump in prices. There is no question that it is the biggest industry we have. There is no question we must take care of those men who have taken land since the war and are trying to make it a paying matter.

Everybody knows the depression which exists . . . and all who have read in this morning's *Daily Mail* a letter written by a lady living in my division will bear out the fact that the area around King's Lynn is experiencing the worst period it has had for many years.

When the strike eventually broke and the miners drifted back to work, Maurice was greatly relieved. He wrote to Edith,

England has just concluded a very disastrous year – a seven-month coal stoppage. Thank heavens it is all over – and times look better. It hasn't been an easy thing being an MP. England is having a very grim time of it this winter. I was very interested in all your ideas about running the house, your budget, and what you bought with fifteen dollars.

I've just come in from a game of golf along the ocean front. I won 3 and 1. Do you play golf? I've got to go and see a nice old lady 'laid to rest' this morning – such is my lot – to take part in all these things.

The pressure of the job was intense, and during a parliamentary recess he decided to go to a health spa in France to recuperate. He had been drinking heavily in the evenings and vowed to give up, in an effort to lead a more healthy lifestyle. He told Edith,

Vichy is a great place to reduce. I have lost over ten pounds, one has to go 'on the wagon' and take baths and certain waters. It has done me a world

of good. The cure takes three weeks. I'm going to
Paris to see my mother and brother. My mother
has a very beautiful flat in Paris and she makes me
very comfortable.

I am wondering how you are. Your last letter
wasn't very cheerful, things sounded as though they
weren't going well. Do tell me.

Thinking of Edith unhappy filled him with sorrow. He
hated the idea of her crying, and felt impotent to help.
Since the earthquake, her letters had become more urgent,
'I need to see you,' she wrote. 'When will you next be in
New York? I can arrange to meet you.'

He missed her, and away from his other duties indulged
his melancholy trait. As he unwound in France with little
to distract him, he could think of little else but returning
to America. Scanning through his diary to find a time
when he could leave England without causing too much
disruption, Maurice reasoned that his constituents needed
him to be focused, and seeing Edith would straighten out
his thoughts. For once he decided to be selfish, he had
hesitated too long. If there were any ill consequences, he
would just have to bear them like a man.

On returning to London he booked a cabin aboard a
transatlantic liner to New York during the summer. He
would use the pretext of attending a class reunion at
Harvard.

I am sailing on August 5th for New York. I am
enclosing a snap. You see I haven't changed much –
and I am sure you are the same. Edith I'll do all
I can to see you. Write me a line, 285 Madison
Avenue. Much love.

The moment Edith opened his letter, the sallowness of the past few months faded and her eyes shone with a renewed sparkle. His words meant so much to her. Maurice had listened to her pleas and done what she most wanted. Although separated by an ocean, she could rely on him to make her feel better. Suddenly she did not feel so alone.

For the first time in months, she asked a neighbour to drive her into San Francisco. The brightly coloured stores and bustling streets had for a long time felt mundane and uninviting. But now she longed to see the city again.

'I must buy a new outfit, all my dresses look so shabby,' she said to Henry.

For once he did not mind her spending money, he was just glad she seemed to be getting back to her old self. 'Get your hair done at one of those fancy parlours and buy something special,' he said.

In downtown Magnins Store, she found a calf-length skirt and a matching simple velvet bodice the colour of rich chocolate with a delicate pattern down the front. The tailored cut emphasized her waist and Edith whirled around, admiring herself in the mirror. As she span, she wondered what Maurice would think on seeing her. She felt dizzy and stopped spinning, to look at her own face.

Beneath the familiar features she saw deceit. The expensive price tag felt tainted, because she knew Henry wanted her to have it. She saw a woman prepared to take from all those around her, to destroy everything she had built. A betrayer planning a secret meeting with her lover. She tore at the fastenings on the clothes, frantic to get out of them, as if they were burning her flesh. In her underclothes, she stepped closer to the mirror, pinching and pulling the skin around her cheeks as hard as she could, until her face was red and marked with punishment.

Over the next few days, Edith struggled to justify her dark secret. At the back of her cupboard, encased in delicate tissue paper and still in its original box, lay the suit she had bought. It repelled her to think of it, to contemplate the reason behind wanting it so badly.

'So what did you buy?' Henry asked.

'Nothing much,' she replied.

'That's a pity. A wasted trip then,' he said.

'You could say that,' said Edith, just wanting him to go away.

He looked around at the uncleared pots and the pile of laundry.

'Perhaps you could sort out the house now that Lambie doesn't need so much care. It is bad for the soul to live in chaos.'

Edith looked at him, and the old feelings came back. Her head was numb. All she could do was agree, too afraid to say what was in her heart. She would never leave Henry. He had always been a good man who cared and loved her in his own way. She never wanted to hurt him, but could not stop herself from pushing him away. A wasteland lay between them which neither could bridge. Henry would never understand the need in her, and the more she pursued it, the more afraid she was that he would uncover the truth. It made her hate herself and Henry. But most of all, it made Edith feel caged.

Each night was the same. They sat in silence until twilight, when Henry would cross the room, touch Edith lightly on the shoulder and say, 'Goodnight, my dear.' She listened as he climbed the staircase, pausing deliberately on the same step to place his newspaper more securely underneath his arm. He was now sixty-five years old, while Edith had yet to celebrate her thirty-fifth birthday. When

Henry had left the room she wanted to scream after him, but she did not have the words. She would sit alone downstairs, craving her imaginary life with Maurice.

The following week, rocking in her father's chair, she came to a realization. She knew that to continue loving Maurice and keep Henry happy, she had to be brave and bold. Take the risk and live with it. However selfish and stupid and open to condemnation, Edith had to become a woman of deceit.

Amid the lies and the loneliness, here was the truth. It was a matter of survival.

In early September, gloved porters guided Lambie and her mother through the private underground pathway from Grand Central Station to the lobby of New York's Roosevelt Hotel. It felt very big. It was hardly the place for a boisterous little girl, and Lambie wanted to get out of her fussy party dress.

They had spent a long time getting ready, cleaning and washing, braiding and brushing hair and chattering about the exciting adventure they were having. Mommy's friend was coming to see them, and she had to behave like a good girl.

A big, black man in a porter's uniform came over and played hide and seek in the smooth ocean of marble. He hid behind a column and then waved his hand. Lambie giggled each time he disappeared and then came back and pulled a funny face. Her Mommy was checking her hair in the shiny brass stair rail, brushing it down with her fingers. She pinched her waxen cheeks and they were going red.

'Are you thirsty?' asked the porter.

Lambie nodded and he reached for a paper cup, passing

her a drink from the water fountain. It spilt on the floor. Her Mommy was very quiet and didn't tell her off. She didn't even seem to be breathing as she held on to the rail. Mommy was standing on her tiptoes and staring towards the entrance. Then her face lit up like a thousand stars and a man was running towards her with a huge bunch of lilies in his hands.

'Hello,' he said breathlessly, kissing her Mommy on both cheeks. 'We must never stop meeting like this!'

Her Mommy examined his left hand, checking his fingers.

'I'm so glad,' she said. 'You've become quite a pillar of English society since we last met.'

He shook his head and said shyly, 'Hardly.'

'You even sound British! I bet you call the sidewalk a pavement nowadays.'

'But I still take an elevator,' he said taking her hand in his. 'Some things never change.'

Lambie skipped in step with the porter's stride as he accompanied her back to her mother.

'Thank you for watching her,' said Edith taking a dime from her purse.

The man with the flowers looked down at Lambie and smiled. Her Mommy knelt down and whispered in her ear, 'Say hello to Lord Fermoy.'

Lambie stepped forward and, holding out her hand, did as she was told.

Her Mommy looked sad as Lord Fermoy crouched down and shook her tiny outstretched fingertips. 'Good day, Princess. What a pretty dress you're wearing.'

Lambie giggled and moved a step closer.

He looked up at Edith, who gently nodded.

'I bet you're clever too, just like your Mommy.'

169

Lambie nodded vigorously and said, 'But I don't like spinach.'

He whispered, 'Neither do I, but that will be our secret.'

Lord Fermoy stood up and whispered something in her Mommy's ear.

'Yes, that's right,' she said softly, her eyes flicking back down to Lambie.

As they left the lobby Lambie pulled on her Mommy's skirt and asked, 'What did he say?'

'I'll tell you another time,' she replied. 'We're going out now.'

Just fifteen minutes' drive away, the Big Top sat like an airship on the horizon. Lambie was told that it was full of fierce animals and clowns who kept falling over. She held her Mommy's hand tightly, while Lord Fermoy queued for tickets.

'We're on the front row,' he told Lambie. 'You'll almost be able to touch the tigers!'

She sat between Lord Fermoy and her Mommy, and when the lights went down, the ringmaster cracked his whip. Everyone jumped and Lord Fermoy gathered her up on to his knee and she felt safe.

'Don't worry, they can't get you,' he said, when the lions appeared.

Her Daddy had said there were special doctors for animals, and she thought maybe Lord Fermoy could be one of those. When the clowns came into the ring he laughed so much his chest moved up and down.

They had candyfloss afterwards and Lambie got some stuck to her dress. Her Mommy didn't seem to notice and laughed a lot whenever she looked at Lord Fermoy's face.

Then Lord Fermoy treated Lambie to an ice cream which was so cold her lips went numb, and she had to press the silver spoon hard against her tongue to feel anything at all. He asked, 'How old are you, Lambie?' and 'When is your birthday?' and 'Do you like California?' She didn't know what California was, so she pushed the empty spoon back into her mouth and pretended she couldn't talk because her mouth was full.

'I live in England,' he said.

'Do you live in a castle?' she asked.

'No,' he smiled.

'Not quite,' said Mommy, and then they just looked at each for a long time.

Later in their room, after Lord Fermoy had left, her Mommy said, 'A special lady is going to look after you tonight.'

'Why?' Lambie asked, stroking her Mommy's brown skirt.

'Because I have to go out with some people and you will be bored.'

'I won't,' said Lambie sleepily.

'You will, darling. Now be a good girl and Mommy will be back before you know it.'

As they strolled down Madison Avenue towards Broadway, Maurice's hand slipped through the loop of Edith's arm. They fell into step and an easy silence followed. Maurice pulled her closer to him. Edith looked up at his contented face, a little rounder than the last time they met but still as kind and lively. She wanted to sing out loud.

'You've come home,' she said, caressing his fingers. 'I can't believe you're really here.'

'I'm not,' he joked. 'I'm Frank Roche.'

She slapped him on the arm. 'Don't do that!' she laughed.

Maurice stopped walking and turned to face her. 'How I miss this life with you.'

'Then stay?' she asked, afraid even to blink.

He looked skywards. 'I'm afraid it is not possible.'

'Love is very simple,' said Edith, curling his hair around her fingers. 'Very simple indeed.'

Maurice kissed the tip of her nose. 'When I left New York, it was to do what is right. Sometimes I haven't always managed that, but it has made me who I am. I want to be a useful man who changes people's lives.'

'You changed mine,' smiled Edith. 'And being with you makes me want you all the more.'

'But life is not always about getting what we want,' said Maurice, 'even though I would love nothing better than to stay.'

'Then do,' insisted Edith. 'You say you want to – why not?'

Maurice looked Edith in the eyes, searching for the right words. He held her hands and leaned back a little. 'This is the hardest part, for both of us.'

'Do you have to tell me now? I don't want anything to spoil today.'

He kissed her hands. 'But I'm the only one who can.' Very gently and without inflection he said, 'One day I will marry. I have to. I need a son and heir. And for that I must be with someone else.'

Edith said, 'I expect nothing.'

'You continue to amaze me,' he said, in awe of her resilience. 'You know what we have is strong. This is a love few people find. These are the lilac days.'

'I know what we do is wrong, Maurice, but when I'm with you I really don't care.'

He kissed her again and brushed his lips across her face.

'Now, you must teach me to dance the Lindy Hop, so I can tell everyone in England I learned it from my very special American lady. How lucky I am to have you.'

Back home in Marin County, Edith found the unease within the house almost unbearable. Jack suddenly announced he was going to military camp where Maurice had done his initial war training. The news stirred poignant memories and Edith ticked off the days to his leaving with silent dread.

Edith saw her tall, handsome son climb nonchalantly into the car and wave goodbye for the short journey to the train station. Jack looked every inch a man, but to Edith he was still her first-born child. They had learned much together and now she was watching him go with a beaming smile and not a care in the world. She watched the car get smaller, disappearing to a dot in the distance, and felt as if her heart would break.

'He will be fine,' said Henry. 'The military's an honourable profession for a young man, and a good choice given the state the country's in.'

'He's only a boy,' she said. 'He doesn't know what he's doing.'

'Edith, you would be well advised to stop trying to control everything and everyone,' he said.

She shut up, worn down by the constant bickering between them. As the days passed Edith had no desire to leave the house, and her coffee sat cold as she lounged in her night clothes way beyond midday. A newspaper lay open on the floor. Edith knew what it said almost word for word. It linked Maurice to a woman called Mary Carter. She buried her face in a cushion, fed up with being strong. She had read Maurice was 'engaged to be married', yet it was not long since they had walked together towards the theatres of Broadway. She knew one day this would happen, but it seemed so soon.

Her mother came in and hesitantly asked, 'Henry wants to know what's wrong, Liebling.' She patted her daughter's hand. 'Why not get dressed and come down so I can fix you some lemon tea?'

Edith shook her head. 'Tell him I have a sick headache. Please.'

Frau Hund saw her daughter's swollen eyes. She lowered her voice. 'Is it your Englishman again?' she asked tenderly.

Edith broke down.

'Shh, shh,' said Frau Hund. 'I will not judge you, Liebling.' She cuddled her daughter. 'I just want you to be happy. You are smart, you will work it out.'

Lambie stood in the doorway and ignored Frau Hund's attempts to usher her away, running in and pulling on Edith's night-gown.

'Why are you crying, Mommy?' she asked.

Edith shook her head.

Lambie clambered up on to the bed and put her arms around Edith's neck, hugging her tightly.

'When will you tell me what that man who gave me the teddy bear said?'

Edith squeezed her daughter and whispered, 'he said he loved you and . . . he said, "To think she could be mine."'

'What does that mean?' said Lambie.

'It means you're very special and you shouldn't ask any more questions.'

TWELVE

'Life isn't Easy'

The Shooting Lodge
Heacham,
Norfolk.

My dear Edith

I have just received two letters from you. How
little changed you were and I loved your dear
daughter – you ought to be very happy. I can't tell
you how pleased I was to see you again and how
I wished you could have arrived a week sooner –
that would have made it perfect – however I'll be
over again – certainly next summer, if I get in at
the election. I was very sad to have you write that
you are unhappy. What is the cause? Money? Is
married life going unwell? Do write and tell me the
cause. Life isn't easy for any of us. I have many
depressing times here with my work and there are
many other worries too. I have so many begging
letters and cases of distress. I know we are going to
meet, even if we are sixty. Here is a snapshot taken

at the bowling green – anyway it is something to send you – the church in the background is 13th century. Hope everything is better for you when you get this. Love and kisses, Maurice.

Since returning to France, Fannie was on a mission to find Maurice a wife. Having failed to get him and Frank married off before they reached middle age, she applied herself with greater urgency. She became a self-appointed matchmaker. Most would consider it a humiliating task, but not Fannie. For her there was sport in the challenge. Playing mind games relieved the boredom of having little to do, and it amused her.

By the late 1920s, Fannie was making the most of her inheritance, which was generous enough to allow her to spend months abroad. She had become a *grande dame* of European society, establishing a flamboyant lifestyle in Paris, socializing with the rich, the famous and, sometimes, the infamous.

Frank lived nearby and became her escort. The pair would enjoy dances and dinners, and sometimes they would travel south for a spell at the spa in Vichy, where the bubbling spring water was reputed to have incredible rejuvenating properties. Losing weight became less of a chore in such lavish surroundings, and was an excellent diversion from the rich fare of fine French restaurants.

However, the fashionable allure of Europe was not always enough to keep her away from New York. There she could mischievously indulge her predilection for supplying the gossip columns with tittle-tattle. Having excellent connections, and to keep things interesting, she tipped off the newspapers whenever she sensed that one of her sons had a new love interest.

Maurice and Frank were reluctant to confront the old lady, especially since she was well past her seventieth year and still retained a zest for life which they both rather admired. They knew that beneath her showmanship she had their best interests at heart. Fannie just wanted to live long enough to see her twins settled and to know they were looked after. They usually treated such newspaper reports with the contempt they deserved, and hoped to clear up the mess later.

When the furore over Miss Mary Ridgley Carter hit the headlines, however, Maurice felt things had gone too far. For days, reports claimed that he and this preacher's daughter from Philadelphia were on the point of exchanging vows. But Maurice hardly knew the poor girl, whom he had only met casually, and steadfastly ignored the statements, adding fuel to the rumours that he had taken advantage of Miss Carter's virtue and then humiliatingly spurned her. To protect her daughter's honour, the young girl's mother, Mrs George Calvert Carter had publicly expressed her dismay, confirming Mary was willing to move to England, even though the climate and people were much colder than she was used to.

Things were now dangerously out of hand, and Maurice contacted Frank on vacation in Rhode Island, to demand that the record be set straight. The following day, a statement appeared in the *New York Times* denying that Maurice had any intention of marrying Mary Carter and reiterating that he had no idea where the rumour came from.

'What would mother do without us to keep her so stealthily employed?' said Frank.

'But I tire of being at her beck and call,' moaned Maurice.

'She won't give in until you walk up the aisle,' said Frank.

'What about you?'

'Maurice, it is never going to be me. It's all on your shoulders, I'm afraid.'

By the end of 1928, Maurice was preparing for another election but he was finding the pressure of work and his mother's meddling a difficult combination. Writing to Edith from his study in the Shooting Lodge, he spoke of his worries:

> I have been laid up with an awful carbuncle on my back. However, it is healing now. It has been very painful. It is the first time I have ever suffered from such a thing. I will send you a photo of my garden when I have one taken. It is a dear little place.
>
> I am very busy now because the General Election takes place around May. I do hope I will keep my seat – and I think I will. I have worked very hard for five years here. You must remember the world is a very ungrateful place and they do forget. At any rate I have done my best. I am looking forward to the time we shall meet, much love Maurice.

The annual Armistice Sunday services helped Maurice to put his own problems into perspective. He wrote, 'I've been to three different services today: 11 a.m., 3 p.m., and 6.30 p.m., all very impressive. Edith, it is estimated that if the graves of the British were laid side by side three feet apart they would extend 568 miles in length. So you can see what took place in those war years, even if things don't seem to look very bright. I hope your next letter is more cheerful.'

But news was slow to improve, however. The economy continued to reel and unemployment to grow as the 1920s neared their end. It was a dire time for Britain, and tackling poverty was at the forefront of Maurice's electioneering. Edith's money worries prompted him to consider his own position and he confessed that life as a bachelor gave him a freedom most never enjoyed.

I have been very fortunate in finding out early in life the value of money well spent. How easy it is to waste money on useless things. I agree with you about being in debt. I dislike it myself. I make promises, like to pay the King's Lynn hospital a thousand pounds. It is a promise I made to their building fund, new extension work.

What a wonderful thing – the wireless! I'm now listening to a beautiful concert in Queen's Hall, London – it sounds so perfect – it might be a few miles away and it's really 123 miles. I've just had my dinner. I've got used to eating alone. England is just lovely now – today was real warm – with perfect sunshine – tomorrow I am shooting partridges, which is great sport – this snapshot shows you how I dress. The days are drawing in, one realizes that the long winter is coming. Much love.

Hunting had become Maurice's favourite pastime, and many weekdays were spent in the company of Bertie, the Duke of York. The two would prowl the grounds of Sandringham and bag hundreds of pheasants, as they discussed the local gossip as well as the crisis in the country.

Constitutional uncertainties drew Maurice even closer to the crown when Bertie confided to him that his father's health was failing. King George V had been taken seriously ill with pneumonia and was hovering close to death. In desperation, surgeons removed sections of the King's ribs to aid his breathing, but he was so weak that his health went into further decline.

Bertie had been called upon to form a council of state with his elder brother David and the Prime Minister to take over the King's royal duties. Until the King fully recovered, Bertie was expected to continue handling his father's affairs.

As he lay ill in bed, the King reviewed not only his own mortality, but also the character of his successor. Even at death's door, George V felt a duty to stabilize his family's future. He possessed a dour style which had brought royalty back into favour through its earnestness, and he feared that the more flamboyant character of his eldest son, David, might well damage the integrity of the monarchy.

The relationship between the King and his first-born had always been precarious, and privately George V considered David too frivolous and flippant for a man with his destiny. David, good-looking and charismatic, enjoyed the good life. He struggled to show much respect for his royal duties and loathed the monotony of state business. As the world's most eligible bachelor, he preferred parties and the company of beautiful women – and more often than not married women, such as Mrs Freda Dudley Ward and Lady Thelma Furness.

George V had more in common with his second son, Bertie. Both men were serious and respectful, but also took time to relax by hunting and shooting. However, the relationship had flash-points, as George V was an irascible man and his quick temper conflicted with Bertie's sensitive nature. As a young boy, Bertie had often fled in tears from his father's bad moods which aggravated the young prince's severe stammer. The King's pedantry was notorious among staff, who were ordered to set all the clocks in Sandringham half an hour fast so he could get up early and benefit from extra shooting time.

Bertie was never expected to do more than live in the shadow of the heir to the throne and, despite their differences, he could forgive David most things in view of the expectation and responsibility heaped upon his brother. Bertie enjoyed a freedom, denied to his brother, which allowed him to be at ease with friends like Maurice. He didn't have the burden of looking over his shoulder to see who was watching with disapproval and waiting to trip him up.

Bertie was further protected from the strains of duty by his marriage to Elizabeth Bowes Lyon, who finally agreed to his proposal at the third time of asking. Theirs was a strong marriage, and her open manner and quick mind gave Bertie stability, sympathy and a perspective he could trust. The Duchess of York, along with their bright-faced young daughter Elizabeth, were popular figures and charmed the cantankerous King, further helping Bertie establish a good relationship with his father as he got older. Her influence had gained Bertie considerable benefits, and he was happy to see the Duchess and Maurice becoming great friends.

Bertie reciprocated Maurice's concerns by advising him to find a wife and start a family. He referred Maurice to the matchmaking capabilities of his wife. The more they socialized, the more Maurice appreciated the difference a good marriage could make. He stopped looking for reasons not to marry and began to think about the benefits of a lifelong union. Sharing his days with another could be about compromise and companionship, much more than love.

During Christmas 1928, the King looked unlikely to see out the year and crowds kept a vigil outside Buckingham Palace, awaiting the latest bulletin on his precarious state of health. In a desperate attempt to keep him alive, he was taken by ambulance to the seaside resort of Bognor to see if that would help his recuperation. It turned out to be the right decision, because slowly but surely, and to everyone's surprise, he recovered.

Maurice rejoiced at the good news, knowing it would take the pressure off Bertie. He wrote to Edith:

We are all delighted over the King's recovery –
nobody ever thought he ever would. He had double
pneumonia. I thank you for your picture, which is
extremely pretty. I was very glad to hear what you
were doing and all about your children, you ought
to be very proud. Take good care of yourself my
best love.

Each time she received a letter from Maurice, Edith's mood would lift for a few days, but Marin County had none of the excitement of kings and queens, palaces and shooting parties. How could she compete? Instead she just had the daily grind of hard work to protect her from too much day-dreaming.

She felt it was inappropriate to show her true feelings to Maurice when he had so bravely revealed his own dilemma. And what would it bring her? She was married, he was a lord living in England. There was no future together as a couple and her insecurities could only jeopardize what they already had. It made finding the truth all the more difficult.

'Look, now he's getting married to a minister's daughter!' she muttered to herself. 'And even if he's not, I know he wants to.'

Henry walked into the kitchen for supper carrying a pale blue envelope addressed to Edith.

'I found this,' he said.

Edith felt the blood rush to her face. 'What does it say?' she asked.

'I don't know,' he replied, 'It's addressed to you.'

He handed her the envelope and stood watching as she slipped it into her pocket.

'Aren't you going to read it?' he asked.

'Later,' she replied. 'It's a letter from a old friend in England. Someone I've known for years.'

Henry hovered, as if he had something to say. 'Maybe we can take a trip sometime.'

'It's a long way,' she said, pouring him some tea.

Perhaps he was just being provocative. How he could contemplate spending money, she did not know, as things were very bad in California. Since October, the Wall Street stock market had been in free fall, causing the worst economic crash in American history. There was widespread unemployment, the beginnings of shanty towns and soup kitchens, with many people wandering around homeless and starving. There was no government support, so doctors' bills were way down the priority list. But people still got sick and Henry would continue to treat them, whether they were rich or poor. Edith had regularly found piles of his unpaid bills stuffed into the waste bin and she was already working longer hours at the surgery as they had laid off most of the staff to cut costs.

'Henry,' she had said, 'why are you throwing patients' bills away?'

He did not look up from his plate. 'Because there is no point in pursuing the poor for what they do not have.'

'But how do we pay our bills if you turn the surgery into a charity?'

He did not answer.

'Henry, be realistic.'

'I am a doctor. I took an oath to treat everyone. That is an end of it.'

It was going to be a hard road ahead, with fuel and food very expensive. The car was old and Lambie was growing fast. Frau Hund had promised to help out where she could, but Edith was noticing the signs of ageing. Now her mother hobbled to the store and it was only a matter of time before she became housebound. But Henry would listen to none of Edith's economies, content to bury his head in the sand.

'What about introducing a regular payment scheme to cover some of the cost?' she suggested.

'Sometimes, Edith, I do not know what it is that you want from me,' he said, walking from the room.

They never spoke of it again.

Trapped by indecision and the constant scrimping and scraping, she was relieved when several hundred acres of land were sold to the military for the development of a new air force base at Marin Meadows. Thousands of servicemen and their families would move into the area, boosting the local economy and bringing new blood to the County. It certainly breathed life into the vicinity but there was a price to pay. Thousands of extra vehicles clogged up the routes in and around San Francisco, making every journey slow and laborious.

On a boiling hot Labour Day, after a trip to Yosemite National Park, Edith was stuck in the worst traffic jam in the County's history. She could not go forward and there was no going back. She just had to sit it out to the sound of blaring horns and bad-tempered motorists. Ned was playing cards with Lambie in the back, who refused to look at her hand and cried, furious with the heat.

One motorist stopped his vehicle in the middle of the road and swore. 'If this is progress, then God help us all!'

Inside that cramped, confined space she gazed at the snake of cars stretching into the distance and grew frustrated with the lack of control over her life. As the hours wore on and they edged back home, she chastised herself for never having left America, or seen Europe. Henry's suggestion played on her mind. She dreamt about visiting a place like England, somewhere she had only read about in books and magazines. It was the country Maurice had made home, and he spoke about it with such affection, that she promised herself that one day she would make the trip. She wanted to master part of her destiny as Maurice had done. He had the wisdom and knowledge of a worldly man.

For the rest of the tedious journey, she composed her next letter.

The world seems a crazy place when you have barely a few cents to rub together. I am trying hard to budget and provide the children with all they need. But then does it really matter? I feel like I am on a merry-go-round, searching for something

I will never find, instead each time I return to where I started. But one day I will come to England, to see your world. Good luck with your election, I know you will do well, your integrity will not go unrewarded.

Maurice was not to be disappointed at the polls. He had proved to be a worthy Member of Parliament, and his constituents trusted his track record and showed their continued support at the ballot box. He was returned as an MP, but the Conservative Party were not so lucky, and failed to get back into power. Promising to sort out rising unemployment, the Labour Party came to power in 1929 with Ramsay MacDonald as Prime Minister but with no overall majority in the House of Commons.

Immediately after the votes were counted, Maurice wrote to Edith and announced:

By now you have heard the good news that I have been returned as Member of Parliament. I fully deserve it. I am so busy now – I got sixty-five telegrams. I was extremely glad to hear that my victory was a great one because I increased my majority from 2,526 to 3,695 – everyone was very pleased indeed. It was a very strenuous election. Edith it is very nice of you to say you have every confidence in me.

I worked very very hard and I had two outsiders here to try and beat me. I do hope you will come to England next year, but don't bring the car because of the duty and bother, besides I have an excellent one with a good chauffeur.

I am planning to go to the Riviera next month,

where I shall see the sun again. Here in England that is never possible. As you know my brother is working in a bank there and my mother also contemplates living in Paris in the future. Things are upset here by the coming into power of the Labour Government – they will try and reform all the nice old English customs I am afraid and crush the rich with taxation. Edith I do like to hear from you. Take care of yourself, with much love and affection, Maurice.

The next twelve months were busy. He had moved all his furniture out of the Shooting Lodge and headed a few miles down the road to Sedgeford Hall. Over 150 villagers marked their appreciation for all he had done by clubbing together to present him with a silver salver representing the freedom of Heacham Village.

He then left for Vichy, knowing he must lose a few extra pounds and regain some fitness. He had neglected himself physically in pursuit of his career and was now topping the scales at over fifteen stone. Having concentrated on his parliamentary work and very little else, he had an expanding waistline and hated it. To play tennis at his best he must get rid of the rim of flesh that appeared over his trouser waistband and made his jacket buttons rebelliously pop open.

Frank remained irritatingly lithe and trim, and when faced with this slimmer version of himself, Maurice felt envious. He had tried to diet before leaving the country, but his hectic schedule, late-night voting and his love of candied fruit meant he had not lost a single pound. He was due to play against Lord Kinnaird in the forthcoming tennis tournament and he intended to put on a decent performance. It was exactly the motivation he needed. Looking in the mirror, he turned to view his profile from both sides. There was no denying that his rounded face was starting to show signs of age, and on holding a hand mirror to the back of his head, Maurice saw that his hair was thinning and the grey flecks had become rather too abundant.

Determined to get back in shape, when he stopped in Paris *en route* to Vichy he played tennis against his brother. After two arduous sets he abandoned the match, citing pain from blisters. Frank rarely beat his brother and knew that his success had nothing to do with chafed skin.

'You've let yourself go,' he teased.

'Never!' replied Maurice.

'Let this be a warning to you and your wretched blisters, mother has seats at a concert tonight. With the usual French gastronomy après.'

'If I must,' said Maurice.

'Come, you are in Paris!' said Frank. 'Enjoy the freedom. And the cuisine.'

Maurice grimaced.

'At least with a box, if you don't like it you can fall asleep and no one will know a thing,' said Frank.

Their mother was waiting in the foyer with a cigarette held precariously on the end of a long holder, ready for Maurice to light. A swirling line of smoke drifted upwards as she waved the twins towards their seats.

Maurice settled back in their plush box and read the programme, straining in the dim light to see which musician was next. It was a young Scottish prodigy, Miss Ruth Gill, who was to play a piano concerto.

When a musician walked on to the stage, Maurice usually liked to close his eyes to concentrate on the sound

188

of the performance, but not this time. As Miss Gill struck the first notes, the melody drifted away and he found himself captivated by the pianist's fingers and how they moved dextrously over the keys. Her entire body was like a medium for the music. He could not take his eyes off her, the striking profile of her face and the richness of her hair. He blinked in the darkness and pushed his opera glasses firmly against his eyes. He was transfixed.

A month after Paris, Maurice, somewhat trimmer, was invited to another concert at the Royal Albert Hall, in London with King George V, who had now recovered well enough to socialize. The soloists included Ruth Gill, whose lifelong ambition was to play for royalty. And she was mesmerizing, giving one of the finest performances of her career.

Maurice knew he had to meet this woman. He combed his hair and eagerly awaited the post-concert soirée. Keen to impress, he sipped champagne to steady his nerves, pulled in his stomach and watched from a distance.

'Who is that man over there who keeps staring at me?' asked Ruth.

'That, my dear, is the highly eligible Lord Fermoy, MP for King's Lynn. And he appears to be most enchanted.'

Petite Ruth Sylvia Gill, just twenty-two, was the daughter of a Scottish colonel from the small village of Dalhebity in Aberdeenshire. Ruth had an austere upbringing governed by the strict morals of the Scottish church. Emotion was viewed as an unnecessarily indulgence, and from a very early age she channelled her innermost feelings into music.

Her father, William Gill, was a career soldier who had worked hard for his respectable middle-class position. He drilled into Ruth a profound sense of service and steely ambition. Meanwhile her mother, Ruth Littlejohn, a doctor's daughter, instilled in her the importance of community spirit, insisting that they spend many long hours visiting the sick and poor.

As a small girl, Ruth practised every day, perfecting her scales and learning intricate tunes. She had a rare natural gift for the piano and took easily to its complexities. Where other pianists were plagued by stage fright, Ruth rarely suffered from nerves. She seemed to be born with an unshakeable confidence.

Young men, drawn to her beauty and slender frame, found her unstinting self-belief somewhat daunting. They did not know how to handle this combination of Scottish primness and fierce social enterprise. It soon became clear there was no hope of courting the aspiring Ruth Gill unless they could further her tenacious ambition. She had a plan in her head and was saving herself for someone of high status.

When she gained a place at the prestigious Paris Conservatoire under the personal tutelage of the virtuoso pianist Alfred Cortot, it was no great surprise. Past alumni included the composers Georges Bizet and Claude Debussy, and yet Ruth took the accolade in her stride. She could not wait to get to Paris and begin working alongside the world's top musical talents. It was where she felt she belonged.

She dedicated herself to being the best, and in order to be note perfect, she would play the piano until her fingers ached and her shoulders were sore. She existed for music. And to better herself. Her immaculate dress and manners only added to her sense of perfection. Nothing was wasted – neither time nor opportunity.

Her ambition to become a concert pianist was one she would fulfil. Everyone expected great things from her, and privately she knew she could do it.

It was to be a brief romance. For Maurice there was no reason to delay his proposal. He had at last found a woman who was pretty, pure and young enough to give him the heir he needed. He did not want anything to go wrong, nor any interference with his young fiancée's mind. Above all, he did not want anyone else snapping her up.

Ruth was under no illusions. This was not a love match. But it did not matter who was deceiving whom, as they were both getting what they wanted. For Ruth, the relationship provided a sensational rise to the upper echelons of polite society. Maurice was a lord, popular with the royal family and had close friends in the Cabinet. He was a man who exuded power and influence. And he had set his mind on her – a middle-class girl with no past from Aberdeen.

Maurice proposed in June and promised to marry her before the end of the summer. He was forty-six years old and waiting would only reduce his chances of seeing any children grow up. He also recognized that a beautiful young Lady Fermoy would be a major asset on the political circuit.

There was to be one trade-off. She must renounce her musical ambition. If she was to marry Maurice, all those years of preparation and dedication had to be put to one side. She must be a full-time wife, mother and social companion. Ruth had to decide between her career and her desire for social status. It was no contest. Despite having spent her entire life striving to be a concert pianist, she chose Lord Fermoy. With Maurice she would enter the church a commoner and leave as Lady Fermoy – titled, rich and with homes on both sides of the Atlantic.

To confirm their forthcoming union, a formal announcement was placed in *The Times*. 'Lord Fermoy and Miss R.S. Gill. The engagement is announced between Lord Fermoy, M.P., Sedgeford Hall, King's Lynn, and Ruth Sylvia, youngest daughter of Colonel W.S. Gill, C.B., and Mrs Gill, Dalhebity, Bieldside, Aberdeenshire.'

With Maurice's connections, the wedding could have been held in almost any church, but in keeping with tradition, Ruth insisted they return to her home town in Scotland. It was not often that a lord graced the small town of Bieldside and the simple episcopalian church of St Devenick's.

The austere beauty of the church's white plaster walls and oak panelling so enchanted Maurice when he first saw it that he later made the 900-mile round trip from King's Lynn to hear the banns read and to meet the officiator, the Bishop of Aberdeen, Canon Forster.

Maurice impressed Ruth's reserved parents not only with his title, but his knowledge. He and her father, now a local landowner and farmer, had a good deal in common. Maurice was interested in William's career as a soldier, and they found common ground discussing the Great War. Mr and Mrs Gill looked forward to their future son-in-law's visits and soon forgot about the age difference.

For all his joy, Maurice still dreaded breaking the news of his marriage to Edith. He knew he must tell her, but every time he settled at his desk, his mind went blank. He thought of telephoning so he might inform her gently, but each time he lifted the receiver he was overcome with cowardice. He reasoned that Henry might answer and would wonder who was calling. It would be dangerous to create a fuss. Ruth knew nothing about Edith and he was determined to keep it that way.

Late one night, annoyed with himself for having waited so long, he finally put pen to paper and wrote a short note, succinct and without frills. Before he had time to change his mind he sealed the envelope and took it to the post box. There was no sense of relief and he did not want to think about the effect his letter would have upon her. 'I have a real piece of news for you,' he wrote. 'I am getting married in August. I am sure you are pleased to have me happy. When I have a snapshot I will send it.'

The wedding was a plain affair, with Ruth's father insisting on paying his share of the costs. They invited relatives and a few close friends. There were to be no bridesmaids and only simple flowers.

Fannie, as ever, wanted to be part of the action. She had waited so long to see one of her sons married that she was not going to let this momentous occasion pass unmarked. She arrived with a large suitcase of clothes and produced a beautiful antique lace shawl, which she insisted Ruth wear as a veil, for something old and something borrowed.

Ruth accepted her offer and wore it with a gown made from ivory satin and a head-dress that completely covered her hair, highlighting her fine cheekbones and youthful features. She carried a sheaf of pure white lilies, inter-twined with wild Scottish ferns and a lucky sprig of heather.

The couple emerged from church arm in arm, Ruth with a beaming smile and Maurice looking reserved. During the photographs, she kept touching the string of pearls she had received from him as a wedding gift.

The couple left for a short honeymoon at the golfing

resort of Gleneagles before Maurice returned promptly to their home at Sedgeford Hall in Norfolk, mindful of the need to get back on the campaign trail. The Conservative Party was determined to form a national government in 1931 and take charge of the economy. Over the next few gruelling days, he worked his way through seventy campaign meetings. After seven years in the job his popularity was at an all-time high, and he hoped to guarantee several thousand personal votes on the strength of his record.

Getting out among the people was nothing new for Maurice, but it did surprise Ruth. He would regularly stroll down King's Lynn's High Street with his shopping basket on his arm, never too grand to do his own chores. Also, determined to maintain his fitness, he would jump on his bicycle to cycle from Sedgeford into town.

'It is all right if I leave my jigger here?' he asked the fishmonger one day, pointing at his bike.

'Fine by me,' said the shopkeeper.

'How much is your salmon?' Maurice enquired.

'Ten bob a pound.'

'That's ridiculous,' exclaimed Maurice, genuinely shocked. 'How can people afford that?'

As he was about to leave, an elderly lady came in for fish scraps for her cat. But when she was told the price, he watched her dejectedly counting her change and realizing she could not afford them.

'Why don't you allow me to split the cost with you?' Maurice suggested.

'Thank you, but I couldn't possibly,' she said. 'I don't rely on charity.' As he went to open the door she added, 'And what would Lady Fermoy say if she found out you were offering to pay for another lady's shopping?'

Maurice was duly returned to Parliament at the 1931 General Election with over 13,000 votes, the largest majority for decades. As he waved and thanked his supporters, he stopped for a moment as he realized that marriage had given him an extra dimension. In the few short weeks since the wedding, Maurice and Ruth had become the golden couple, inundated with offers and invitations and given the pick of banquets and engagements.

Among them was a very special invitation. A request to dine at Sandringham as personal guests of the King and Queen. Ruth smirked when she saw the royal insignia and made absolutely sure it was one invitation she answered herself.

THIRTEEN

'A Dreadful Woman'

The phone was ringing incessantly in Sedgeford Hall, but no one knew where her ladyship was. Ruth Fermoy, wandering the grounds of her new home, refused to be hurried. She loved the privacy of the property enveloped by high walls and surrounded by acres of open fields. Each time she drove up the sweeping driveway past the large, wrought-iron gates, she felt very pleased with herself.

Her arrival had added spice to gossip, as locals had assumed that Lord Fermoy would always remain a bachelor. But Ruth was immediately in demand, proving herself to be far more than just an ornament at her husband's political meetings.

Ruth had an amusing turn of phrase and an ability to charm, especially men. When the newly-weds had returned to Norfolk they had been clapped and cheered into King's Lynn, and charities clamoured for her patronage. She agreed to become the president of Sedgeford's Nursing Association. It was the very best of beginnings.

However, today she was irritated that her morning

constitutional was being interrupted. She walked quickly past the ancient cedar tree and into the house, snatching at the telephone receiver. It was Maurice, sounding perturbed.

'You have to come to the Guildhall now!' he said. 'And put on your best dress.'

'What on earth for?' she asked.

'I'm being inaugurated as the Mayor of King's Lynn and you are supposed to be here. Get ready, the driver is on his way.'

As he was the first man in Britain to hold a peerage and the posts of Mayor and MP simultaneously, it was not surprising that this had slipped his mind. However, Maurice's schedule had been so demanding in the weeks after their marriage that he'd forgotten to inform his wife that she would be required at the banquet.

Ruth arrived to rousing applause, with not a hair out of place and no trace of a last-minute dash. Taking her place beside Maurice, her face was one of pure triumph as she listened to his acceptance speech.

This is a great honour,' he began, to a deafening round of cheers. 'During my year of office let us hope better times fall and Lady Fermoy and I will do all we can.' Encouraging everyone to do likewise he raised his glass, 'The royal family!' He then nonchalantly offered to pay for a new fire engine that was desperately needed by the King's Lynn fire station. The crowd cheered and chanted 'Matrimony, MP and Mayoralty'. Maurice was more than ever the local hero.

Ruth, keen to make her presence felt, paid homage to his charitable nature in her first public speech, 'It is a great pleasure to find that the man I have chosen is so keenly loved. I feel I have many friends here.' She was learning fast. Clinging to the coat-tails of Maurice's popularity was going to be easier than she imagined.

Edith was finding it hard to accept that Maurice had taken a wife in just a few short months. The speed with which it all happened gave her little time to adjust. There was no drawn-out courtship or prevarication. Maurice did not even ask if this was the right thing to do. From the moment he laid eyes on Ruth, his mind was made up.

After all this time, Edith felt she deserved more, an attempt at explanation or at least some acknowledgement. Shocked and numbed by the curtness of his marriage note, Edith wondered how he had the audacity to go on writing idle chat, as if nothing had changed. Torn between wanting to know about his life with Ruth and wishing to know none of it, Edith was miserable. One thing was patently clear: she could not compete with a woman half her age, particularly one so beautiful and fresh.

Edith no longer concealed her anger from Henry. Although he had grown accustomed to her lack of sleep and temper flares, he did not like the constant wrath aimed in his direction. Henry indelicately suggested it was due to her age.

'You are going through the change of life, my dear,' he said.

Edith threw his book across the room and yelled, 'What do you know?'

Henry quietly picked the book off the floor and laid it back on the table, brushing down the cover with the side of his hand. 'More than you think,' he said.

A newspaper containing Maurice and Ruth's wedding picture lay untouched on her desk. She could not throw it out, but could not look at it either.

She was not strong enough to see the man she loved with his arms around another woman. It was a cruel irony that, as her own looks were fading, Maurice had chosen someone so young.

The paper sat on her desk unread and untouched for almost two weeks, until her mother, fed up with seeing an old edition collecting dust, picked it up.

'Do not touch that!' snapped Edith.

'Why ever not?'

'I like it where it is,' she answered.

Frau Hund bristled at being spoken to in such a manner and stubbornly flicked through the newspaper, pausing at the centre spread.

'What have we here?' she said. 'It's your Maurice Roche.'

'Please, Mama, don't,' pleaded Edith.

'And who is this woman?'

Edith bit her lip until she felt blood mingling in her mouth.

Her mother looked at the photograph, then back at Edith. Back and forth, as if something was not quite right. Then she said slowly, 'But, my child, she looks just like you . . . this woman could *be* you.'

Edith tore the paper from her mother's hand and stared at the page. Maurice stood awkwardly, half smiling, on the steps of a church, but his eyes showed a man lost in thought. It might have been a picture of a father with his daughter, so marked was the age difference. This was not the face of a man who had found his soul-mate and wanted no other. This was the benevolent look of a man who had acted wisely but without emotion. He had asked Edith to be happy for him, and now she understood why he needed her blessing.

Edith held her mother's hand and began to think more clearly. She realized that Maurice was not leaving her. He still sent letters, as he had always done, and his words, written in secret, took on new meaning.

Frau Hund folded the newspaper in half. 'It's hard to see what looks you straight in the face,' she said.

Edith broke into a weak smile. 'It's the pain of knowing it can never be.'

'Then hold on to what you have,' said Frau Hund.

Edith washed her face, 'I'll never stop loving him, no matter what.'

Ruth was soon mixing in the highest company. She betrayed no nerves accompanying Maurice to the grandest of occasions. If she ever felt daunted, she did not reveal it, least of all to her husband.

Maurice wrote to Edith:

We had the honour of dining with the King and Queen the other night. They were easy to talk to and very charming indeed. I sat next to the Queen and Ruth the King. On the previous day I had shot with the King – we killed 535 pheasants. Edith my garden is beautiful at the moment, the daffodils are hiding but there will be much coming.

Maurice's political career was doing well and he was promoted to parliamentary secretary to the Minister for Transport. He took a lease on 48 Upper Grosvenor Street in London. Here he could deal with the demands of the ministry and parliamentary business, including the late-night sittings. His city residence allowed him to put down roots in the capital.

This London home has proved a great pleasure.
I have lived ten years in a hotel and it is a treat to
have the peace and quiet of a London home – to
say nothing of the carpet. Today Ruth and I are
motoring to the river. It isn't a very promising day
but the country will be pretty. Everyone here is
interested in the great Irish sweep – we have four
tickets. It is so nice of you to remember my
birthday. I can hardly believe that in three years'
time I will be fifty years old.

For the first time in his life, Maurice was struggling
with money. Paying for two homes and a young fashionable wife cut deep into his pocket. He told Edith:

We got into debt with our London home; although
it was well worth it, we still have a lot of small
bills to pay off. We had an Italian cook who was
very expensive in his ways. Also, Edith, we fed
twelve servants in the staff dining-room. When we
leave here, we go back to Norfolk to The Mill
House, Dersingham, King's Lynn. Make a note of
this address so that you can send future letters
there. It is a charming house, furnished, with a
really charming garden. We are on the King's
estate, so that will make it nice. We are still
enjoying the shooting. I am looking forward to
some this week. Last Saturday I have never seen
the moor look more beautiful. I am glad to see that
things are looking up on Wall Street. The
depression can't go on for ever. With love and
kisses, Maurice.

This new move brought Maurice to a brick-built former mill house set high above Dersingham village. It had views of the sea on one side and gently rolling hills of arable farming on the other. It was a perfect setting for what the couple believed would be a family life. Ruth was young and healthy and looking forward to the day she would be mother to a brood of children.

As the months wore on, however, Ruth failed to conceive. At first Maurice assumed it was the upheaval of the wedding and the move; then the busy calendar of events as Lord and Lady Mayoress. Staying in Westminster and travelling around the country put a strain on the couple and made it hard to find time to be together. After a year passed, Maurice feared it might be his age.

'What an irony, having waited this long for a family, and yet time is the very thing against me,' he confided to Frank.

'There's plenty of life left in you, Maurice.'

'I hope so. I'm not sure what will happen if we don't have children.'

Ruth started to fret, knowing only too well that her role was to provide an heir. She dare not speak of her fears to anyone and the couple found it awkward explaining away the lack of children to inquisitive parents and eager constituents.

After two years of trying, Ruth finally became pregnant. Yet rather than remain in Norfolk, she got her way after she asked to spend her confinement at her parents' home in Bieldside. She wanted to go home to her mother's steadying hand, believing that would help her overcome the fear of birth.

Maurice was so relieved at his wife's news that he agreed to her request and, taking a break from his parliamentary duties, accompanied her to Scotland.

When Ruth went into labour, Maurice raced to catch the first available train. At the hospital he waited around, away from the delivery room, pacing, worried about what was happening as Ruth struggled to bring their child into the world. She was very young to be going through such pain, and he wished he could be by her side. As the doctor came to tell him it was over, he lit an enormous cigar and grinned. Amid the jubilation, it almost didn't matter that the baby was a girl, and he wrote to Edith:

I want to tell you the good news. My wife had a daughter yesterday, weighing nine pounds. We were delighted as you might expect. We had been married two years and were rather worried until this child appeared. I have always loved children and this will be a great interest in my life.

Giving Ruth all the time she needed to recover, Maurice remained in Bieldside despite pressing engagements in London. Within a few days he was writing to Edith from his in-laws' home with news that had thrilled his wife.

It was very sweet of you to write me that last letter. Since writing Queen Mary has asked to be the child's godmother, what an honour to our Mary Cynthia Burke Roche! She will have to live up to it! For the moment her eyes are blue. She is supposed to look like me. We are having her christened in the crypt of the House of Commons on the 5th of October. The crypt dates back to 1275 and only Members of Parliament can have their children baptized there. She is over ten pounds now. As you say health is everything, and

I can still play a good game of tennis and beat men of my own age!

Jack slumped back into the house, looking weary but happy. He had returned from military training with a new maturity. But his old routine made him restless and he appeared bored with Marin County. He admitted to wanting to meet up with his real father, Forrest Travis, who was now living in England. He and Ned had not seen the old scoundrel since they were small, but while training to be a soldier, Jack yearned to discover what sort of a man his father was. Forrest's absence had initially made him feel sad, then angry. But as he grew older, he wanted to speak his mind.

Edith stayed quiet, hoping the idea was as fanciful as her former husband. But when Jack mentioned that he had been writing to Forrest, she knew she could no longer ignore her son.

'Jack needs to travel,' she told Henry.

Henry looked up from his book. 'Young men like to find themselves, that is natural enough.'

Edith muttered. 'He says he's going to England. He wants to see Forrest.'

Henry placed his book on his chest and shook his head in disbelief. 'I presume you persuaded him otherwise.'

'That's not the answer,' she said. 'Jack's smart, it won't take him long to figure Forrest out.'

Henry's mouth pinched up at the edges. 'It will end in no good. And who will pay for this trip? You know how I feel about Forrest.'

'If his mind is set, we could help,' she ventured.

'No,' said Henry sternly. 'I will not waste hard-earned money on that man.'

'It's not for Forrest, it's for Jack.'

'Why won't Forrest pay?'

'There's some problem with money right now.'

'Always is. Jack should get this nonsense out of his mind.'

'It's important to him.'

'Well, I am not putting my hand in my pocket for Forrest Travis.'

'Perhaps I'll get work at the air base then,' she said defiantly.

'Edith, I know you think England is the Promised Land, but you've hardly been concentrating at the surgery. I don't think taking on another job is a solution.'

She felt her spine stiffen. 'If Jack wants to go, I would like to help him. I owe him that.'

Henry saw her bristle but continued all the same, 'Then he must start standing on his own two feet, or he'll end up just like his father.'

Edith angrily took him at his word, and after six months of scrimping and saving, mother and son had got together the $350 fare. She wrote to Maurice of her son's impending visit and hoped he would be prepared to spare Jack a little time while he was over. Perhaps show him the sights of London?

Maurice was delighted to help out. 'Do tell him to look me up. I'll have him here for a weekend. I think Henry should have helped in one way or another but he *didn't*. I'm so glad you feel the way you do about England. It is a joy to live here, thank God.'

Nervously, Jack waited at the quayside to board the boat bound for Southampton.

'You're on your way,' Edith said, looking up at her tall son.

'It feels different now,' Jack said.

'You'll be fine,' she assured him, pushing a flop of hair out of his eyes. 'Forrest will be at the other end to meet you.' She kissed him. 'Send me a postcard from London.'

'I won't forget this, Mom,' he said, waving.

'Check you've got the gentleman's number I gave you in case there's a problem?' she shouted up to him as he waved from the deck. But he was too busy jumping up and down to hear her.

After five days at sea, Jack sailed into England. His stomach churned even more than when he first walked into military camp as he searched along the quayside for his father. But Forrest was nowhere to be seen. Jack slumped on to a chair in a cafe near the docks, wondering what could have happened. Night fell and he tried to sleep in the passenger lounge, not knowing where to go or what to do.

'Where are you headed to, son?' asked a policeman. 'I've seen you hanging around for a while.'

'I'm looking for my dad,' he replied.

'You've been waiting a very long time,' said the officer suspiciously. 'Perhaps you should call him?'

'I've lost his number,' he said. 'He promised me he'd be here.'

'Is there anyone else who can help you?' he said, checking Jack's passport and tickets.

'No, sir,' Jack said.

'Then I'm afraid you'll have to move along, son. You can't stay here all night.'

After a sleepless night on a cold park bench, Jack was wet, hungry and angry. He boarded the next available boat home, not seeing why he should wait any longer. He was on his way back to the States having barely laid a foot on England's shores. It was an experience no one would forget. Forrest had broken his promise.

Edith was horrified and demanded that Forrest reimburse the fare and apologize to Jack. The humiliation and disappointment of when they were married flooded back, and this time she had failed to protect her son. Forrest declined to either help financially or give reasons. It turned out to be a hard lesson for Jack to learn.

Although he had never met Forrest, Maurice wondered how a man could behave with such callousness towards his own flesh and blood. He had little respect for men who did not keep their word. Trying to console Edith, he wrote:

> Perhaps his father tried to get rid of him. What an expensive trip! I'm sorry for you. Perhaps he looked like a charge to the slate, as he didn't have a job. English people are very fair and Jack might not have satisfied them with his answers. This must go and I'm waiting to hear from you. Much love.

The birth of a baby daughter had led Maurice to re-assess his own responsibilities as a father. Having almost completed a third term as an MP, he decided 1935 would be the year to pass on the mantle to a younger man. Ruth was pregnant again and they had hopes again of a son and heir. He therefore decided not to stand for re-election as an MP. He wrote to Edith of his plans for semi-retirement:

> I have plenty to do, Chairman of the local Conservative Party, President of the British Legion, looking after the chickens . . .
> I've had a rather sad day attending a funeral. It

was the first time that I've been to a cremation and
I was much impressed when I saw the brass door
open and carry my friend to that roaring furnace!
    Here is a snap of me taken last month, just
older. That's natural!

With the King's deteriorating health causing great
concern, Bertie needed someone with a wise head on his
shoulders. And Maurice was that man. He could always
be trusted to give an honest opinion, unlike sycophantic
royal advisers. Bertie therefore endorsed Maurice's decision to take life easier and get away from his frantic round
of public engagements. It was not all selfless, Bertie needed
someone reliable to talk to now that his own brother the
Prince of Wales was embarrassingly entwined with an
American divorcee, Wallis Simpson. The affair was causing
terrible rows within the royal family, and Bertie and the
Duchess were appalled by their immoral behaviour. They
made no secret of their views over frequent dinners with
Ruth and Maurice, who shared their consternation. It
helped the royal couple enormously to have such allies so
close.
    Despite his ill health the King maintained his grip on
leadership. In twenty-five eventful years on the throne he
had reigned through a world war and the depression, with
people out of work and desperate. In a show of sensitivity,
the King paid £50,000 back into the public purse from the
civil list, insisting that other members of his family follow
suit. Maurice thought it was a fine example to set in uncertain times. He wrote, 'I heard the King speak at the Jubilee
service at St Paul's. The pageant was wonderful. You never
saw London so gay – the weather was perfect, the decorations and crowds were wonderful to see.'

Maurice had good reason to be grateful for the King's generous nature. Park House, used to house guests staying at Sandringham, had become vacant. It was now rarely used and Bertie asked his father if he would pass the lease over to Maurice, as his friend had mentioned he needed a larger home for his growing family. The King thought it a positive arrangement, believing that his shooting partner would be an excellent choice of tenant and a fine influence on his son. Maurice notified Edith of his new address, adding, 'We love our new house and it is much less expensive to run.'

This was Ruth's third home in four years, but it proved a tremendous move for her. Its close proximity to the royal family, just outside the walls of their country residence, was yet another affirmation of her own importance. She was thrilled and considered Park House one of the finest addresses in the country. However, their first Christmas was overshadowed by His Majesty's continued illness, which took the sparkle out of a usually lively royal family gathering, to which the Fermoys were invited. Maurice told Edith, 'We are all very worried about the King. His life is hanging in the balance – I think he will pull through.'

But it was not to be. There were to be no more reprieves. He had only a few weeks to live.

The King died on 20 January 1936, on the very night when Maurice was preoccupied with Ruth, who had gone into labour. As news of the King's death echoed around the world, Maurice felt split between the sadness of his Majesty's death and elation at the birth of a new life. Frances Ruth Burke Roche was born in her parents' bedroom during the early hours. She was a blonde, long-limbed, blue-eyed baby girl.

Ruth was disappointed that they still did not have the

boy heir they needed and resentful that she would have to go through it all again. Her body had been pushed to its limits over the past few years, and she did not relish the prospect of a third long labour. Looking down at the sweet child in her arms, she could not help wishing Frances had been a boy.

After dawn broke, a note was delivered by hand to Park House, congratulating Maurice and Ruth on their recent addition and wishing the little girl a happy life. It was signed by the Queen, who, even in her darkest hour, wanted her close friends and neighbours to know she was thinking of them.

Maurice wrote to Edith with the news:

> My wife produced a second daughter the other day. We had hoped for a son! All England is mourning the late King. We saw him every day. His heart was just tired and gave out. I'm going to the funeral at Windsor on Tuesday. It will be a magnificent sight.

The new King was David, to be known as Edward VIII. The playboy prince with all his foibles and unconventional love life was finally to be monarch. But there was a blot on the royal landscape.

Throughout 1935, American newspapers had been writing about the future English King's unusual companion, whom he was openly escorting around the French Riviera. Although no such reports appeared in British newspapers, it seemed just a matter of time before the scandal emerged about Edward's choice of woman. Surely he had more pressing things on his mind as he took over the helm of monarchy?

Maurice was disturbed by the new King's attitude but

knew it was not his place to question royalty's motives. Edward VIII's appeal lay in his easy charm and boyish attitudes, and the people warmed to him. However, Maurice wished the King would act with more discretion over his tangled love life. He knew only too well that nothing must be taken for granted when you have a secret to keep.

Although most people spurned and rejected Wallis Simpson, claiming she was scheming and manipulative, Edith liked her haughty manner and the way she kicked against convention. Not a natural beauty, Wallis seemed to have no problem attracting men. She had first married a naval pilot, Earl Winfield Spencer, when she was only twenty, but his violence and excessive drinking had quickly put paid to their early happiness. She later married Ernest Simpson and settled in London, playing the role of hostess, before meeting the heir to the throne at a house party in Leicestershire. Edith liked, rather romantically, to draw parallels between the King and Mrs Simpson and Maurice and herself.

'Who could blame her for divorcing an alcoholic husband?' she said to Frau Hund. 'What is she supposed to do – put up with him, so no one gets offended?'

'Well she did marry him, no one forced her,' said her mother.

'He would have been different when they first met. Men always are,' she replied.

Frau Hund sighed, 'The unattainable is always more attractive. The new King has a very nice face. A bit like a film star.'

Edith had learned the hard way that love and duty are strange bedfellows. She had always felt isolated by her own experience until she heard the difficulties facing the

King. On 11 December 1936 she listened on the radio as Edward VIII abdicated from his most privileged position. It brought back painful memories of the problems she had faced with Maurice. The King revealed to the world, 'I have found it impossible to carry the heavy burden of responsibility and to discharge my duties as King as I would wish to do without the help and support of the woman I love.'

She thought Mrs Simpson was a very lucky woman to have found a man who would give up everything for love.

The abdication stunned Maurice and created several dilemmas. His best friend, Bertie was now to be King, with responsibilities he had never dreamed of, and the future of the royal family on his shoulders. Bertie had no desire to be monarch and was physically and mentally ill-prepared for the task, but he had to bring stability to the crown and the country to prevent a greater crisis across the Empire.

Maurice was worried about the extra pressure on Bertie, who had been unwell after a difficult operation for a duodenal ulcer and whose general health was poor. However, Bertie was determined to rise to the challenge and practised hard with his speech coach to alleviate his stammer. He knew that every word would be broadcast around the world on the day of the Coronation. He relied now more than ever on his close circle of friends.

Maurice wrote to Edith:

> We dined the other night with the new King and
> Queen. Something must be very wrong with
> Edward – they will never return to England, I feel
> sure. The whole country is against them. What a
> dreadful woman Mrs Simpson must be to wreck a

king's life like that. She certainly will pay dearly for
it. We move to London on Monday for four
months. It will be a most interesting season because
of the Coronation. We shall be in Westminster
Abbey all dressed up.

On Coronation day, sitting in the splendour of
Westminster Abbey dressed in heavy ermine robes,
Maurice and Ruth were surrounded by some of the most
powerful and wealthy people in the world. Maurice had
wished his friend well and promised to catch his eye during
the ceremony. They were about to see their best friends
and dearest neighbours crowned King and Queen. The
course of history had been changed by one man's love for
a woman. Maurice and Ruth now had the ear not only
of the King, but also of his Queen.

What a twist of fate this was. Maurice and Ruth Fermoy
had become intimate with the most influential family in
the world, closer than anyone to the royal couple. The
American who had been taunted fourteen years ago with
having just arrived off the boat was today a confidant of
the King of England. As he took his place in one of the
best seats in Westminster Abbey to watch a ceremony that
had remained the same for almost a millennium, Maurice
could not help but smile.

Sadly the glorious occasion was only window dressing
and the world was soon plunged again in turmoil. Bertie's
steadying hand could do nothing to stem the rising tension
in Europe. Adolf Hitler was gaining terrifying powers in
Germany, and the fragile stability of the central powers
was under threat. For men like Maurice, who had served
and knew the real horror of conflict, another war was an
appalling prospect.

Not that he was one to stand idly by. If hostilities started he would once again be ready. But on the eve of Hitler's invasion threats, Ruth announced she was pregnant again. Maurice prayed that this time she would produce a boy child. 'Here is another Christmas tide,' he wrote to Edith. 'How quickly they turn. I wonder how you have been? We had a very anxious time, but thanks to Chamberlain it was all settled for the present. We are expecting our third baby in March. I am hoping for a son and heir.'

In March 1939, Maurice was delighted to be cradling his newly born son, Edmund James Burke in his arms. He had what he had hoped for; his family line was secure. He immediately told Edith, 'This is to give you the good news that Ruth presented me with a son and heir. We are overjoyed with having him. It has been the one bright spot in all the latest anxiety, which has been pretty bad here. I don't think there will be a war – but it will be a close thing!'

Within six months all thoughts of joy were forgotten. Maurice's heart turned cold as the Prime Minister, Neville Chamberlain, announced that Britain was at war with Germany. The world was in chaos and England at grave risk of Nazi invasion.

They had all badly misjudged the situation. As Maurice wrote pleadingly to Edith, 'I would very much like to see you.' He knew in his heart that it was an empty hope, but one he desperately needed at this dark hour.

FOURTEEN

'Utter Barbarity'

Park House
Sandringham
June 6th, 1940

Dear Edith,

Your letter has come as the one bright spot at
this dreadful hour in our lives. Can you imagine
the mental anguish we are going through? Can you
imagine too what might be in store for us. Poor
England. Does she deserve this after a thousand
years of peace-loving peoples? She has established
huge peaceful continents all over the world, where
there is no persecution, where there is freedom of
all kind. Well here we are, waiting for our fate.
What is it to be? God only knows.

It was all too familiar for Maurice. Food was so scarce
that it had to be rationed; the look of fear had returned
to people's eyes; and then the bombs came and lit up the
skies with explosions that pounded the cities. It was over

twenty years since he had been in the trenches, but when the air raid siren sounded, he remembered it as if it were yesterday.

Within three months of his soul-searching letter, London had become a primary target for German aircraft on a mission to fulfil Hitler's dream of crushing the British people. Night after night the Luftwaffe descended, indiscriminately raining down death and destruction in an evil attempt to shatter morale and overpower all resistance.

Hundreds were killed and thousands injured and made homeless during raids on London's East End and the Docks. Each night, huge swathes of frightened people flocked to the London Underground and its network of tunnels to escape the relentless onslaught.

Buckingham Palace was hit while the King and Queen were in residence. If the monarch could not be protected, Maurice realized, no one was safe. Park House was stripped of many non-essential items, with iron railings and other metal objects sent off to munitions factories.

Everyone had to play their part. Maurice's young daughters didn't need telling that life was different now, and after several staff left to enlist they had to get their own hands grimy. Mary and Frances spent their days trawling through the grounds of Park House checking on the animals. The small girls managed to hitch up a pony and trap and used it to trot around gathering chestnuts, which they then cleaned for making into toothpaste.

Ruth stayed at home and took on domestic chores that had once been left to maids and housekeepers. She changed beds, made breakfast and cooked for the first time in her married life.

As the war progressed, Maurice considered evacuating the children to Scotland until the immediate danger was past, but the thought of being away from his family was very hard to accept. Writing to Edith, he confided his fears,

> You can imagine our anxiety over here – over a million men separated from their families and children. This madman Hitler must be got rid of somehow or another. I envy you living on the peaceful shores of California. We do very little at present – never go out at night.
> Thank heavens my children are well. I hope and pray 1941 will see an end to this hateful war. The bombing is something terrific.
> You remember as well as I do what we are going through, anxiety, blackouts. We are determined to see this through. Real winter conditions prevail, skating and the roads in Scotland closed.
> I've phoned my medical friend and expect to be called up in a month. Wish you were here, much love and kiss

Maurice wanted to get back into the armed services, but his age was against him. Now considered an old man at fifty-five, he was not eligible for combat. But Maurice was having none of it and after contacting an old military friend, obtained a posting to France to supply troops with food and ammunition. It was dangerous and sometimes involved working behind enemy lines but his ability to speak fluent French made him invaluable.

Wanting to motivate the young troops, many of who were away from home for the first time, he volunteered to work occasional shifts in the canteen. Without grumbling he poured tea, handed out cigarettes and bootlaces, and then dished up food while waiting at table. The soldiers took to his approachable manner and fell for his natural charm. Maurice had only one aim – to help wherever possible. He would never be the kind of officer who was too proud to wash dirty dishes or sweep the floor.

Aware that troop morale was vital to the success of the war effort, Maurice organized a surprise visit from the 'forces' sweetheart', Gracie Fields. Under cover of darkness he hid her inside a tea wagon and drove to a secret location near enemy lines. Here they tracked down an attachment of British officers and men who had been holed up for several weeks and were in desperate need of a boost.

The troops were grateful, thinking that Maurice was risking life and limb to hand them out a fresh cuppa. But their relief turned to sheer delight when out stepped Gracie Fields dressed in brown skirt and a tight-fitting sweater with a headscarf encasing her blonde hair. The entertainer theatrically handed out biscuits, cake and chocolate and served tea from a five-gallon urn.

'There's no sugar rations here, lads!' she yelled, placing extra lumps in their mugs.

Within seconds, over three hundred men had stormed the van, slapping Maurice on the back for having arranged such a coup. Gracie then jumped up on the back of the army truck and launched into a cheeky rendition of 'The Biggest Aspidistra in the World,' with the men cheering and hollering for more.

How could she refuse? Blowing kisses and waving theatrically, she encouraged the men to join in as she sang 'Wish Me Luck As You Wave Me Good-bye'.

Maurice was a hero. His hard work and willingness did not go unnoticed and he was awarded a commission in the Auxiliary Military Pioneer Corps. Maurice was

At the outbreak of the Second World War, despite the anguish of having to leave his beloved daughters Mary and Frances and his son Edmund *(top right)*, Maurice *(top left)* was determined to join up.

In California, Edith's concerns about Maurice's safety deepened when her eldest son Jack *(bottom left)* enlisted. With the imminent arrival of her and Henry's new grandchild *(right and bottom right)*, she prayed all her loved ones would survive.

Christmas Day [1918]

Dear Edith,

I am thinking of you today. You are at the other end of the world. But I pray that you and the boys are having a happy Xmas together. It has been a nice day here and we have had a good lunch and spent the day sitting around. I hope this finds you well and also the boys.

I received your Xmas card, thank you for your kindness in remembering me.

Much love, Maurice.

Lord Fermoy and his wife Ruth
became firm friends with royalty
and, dressed in their finery,
attended many illustrious social
occasions, including Queen
Elizabeth's Coronation (*top left*)
on 2 June 1953. He remained ever
the gentleman when helping Queen
Mary (*top right*) from the steps
of a church.

He appeared to be in good
health, even playing the odd game
of tennis in his sixties (*middle*).

Just a few months later, Edith
(*bottom right*) was captured
shopping in San Francisco,
unaware that Maurice had died.

Holiday Greeting

WESTERN UNION
· TELEGRAM ·

RECEIVERS NO.	TIME FILED	CHECK

DAY MESSAGE	DAY LETTER	NIGHT MESSAGE	NIGHT LETTER

123 CLIFTON AVE., LAKEWOOD, N. J.

SEND the following telegram, subject to the term
on back hereof, which are hereby agreed to   191

871 NY A 13   COPY

To

AZ NEWYORK NY 105 PM JAN 1 18

MRS EDITH TRAVIS

LAKEWOOD POSTOFFICE LAKEWOOD NJ

MANY THANKS FOR YOUR TELEGRAM CAN YOU MEET ME COMEDY

WRITE CAMP DIX LOVE

MAURICE

143PM

Spurred on by the coldness of the way that she had learned about Maurice's death, Edith refused to wait any longer and obtained a passport *(above)* to sail for England. Never having stepped outside the USA, at the age of sixty-eight she set off to say farewell.

At the steps of Sandringham churchyard she wrote the details of her pilgrimage on the back of a taxi firm's business card *(below)*, so that nothing was forgotten.

WALS TAXIS

(Late Ever-Ready)

★ WEDDINGS A SPECIALITY

7 SADDLEBOW ROAD, KING'S LYNN

(Mr. W. F. Wilmerson)

Telephone : 3 2 6 1

Mrs Howitt,

Box 112,

San Rafael,

California,

U.S.A.

PARK HOUSE,
SANDRINGHAM.

SEPTEMBER 28TH.

Dearest Edith

    Curiously enough I was about
to write and tell one of my daughters is
engaged. It sounds grand, but she will be
The Countess of Spencer. He is very nice
and first goes to Australia with the Queen
They will be married in July next year.
He will come into huge estates after his
father's death.

    Well, I suppose you are doing the
right thing. You must know plenty of peo-
in San Rafael. Death makes a big hole in
one's life.

    The summer is gone. I went to
my in-laws in Scotland. It is dull there,
but we have to give our staff a holiday.
The children went to Ireland and enjoyed
it, sailing etc.

    I'M thinking of returning to U.S.A.
next June for my 45th. at Harvard. We must
meet somehow.

    All well here.

    Have no other news. Much love & kisses.

    your old friend,

Maurice

IN
LOVING MEMORY OF
EDMUND MAURICE
ROCHE
FOURTH BARON FERMOY
MAY 15th 1885
JULY 8th 1955
AND HIS WIFE
RUTH
OCTOBER 2nd 1908

As Edith entered her twilight years (*top right*), she was surrounded by memories of her true love. She contacted several of Maurice's relatives, and met them to talk of her and Maurice's friendship over the years. Maurice's son, Edmund (*bottom*) came to her rest home, and they struck up a friendship that lasted until her death.

A selection of the letters Maurice wrote to Edith during their forty-year love affair.

ordered to return immediately to England, and as he was making his way back to London via the French port of Calais, he twice came under attack from an aerial bombardment. He took cover and was lucky to escape with his life, but found afterwards that many of his comrades had been killed. So as not to worry Edith, he tried to made light of the incident, but even as he wrote his mood darkened.

I've only just returned from France, where I had an exciting escape. The night after I left my billet, it was bombed, twenty people killed. I was bombed too in Calais, several people there were also killed.

You have always been a good friend, one of the truest. How wonderful all those past days look in contrast to this hideous nightmare – and there seems to be no escape. Will we all be bombed and killed?

England is up against it, fighting this huge Nazi machine single-handed. We take all help possible. I'm working for the British War Relief fitting out broken planes. I too have always loved truth. I live for the day when this hateful war ends. How any civilized country can put up with such a policy is beyond me. England will never forgive the Germans for this for years. The utter barbarity of bombing the civilians. Ruthless warfare. I too send a kiss, I long to see you again.

Edith had forlornly hoped that Maurice would stay out of the war, but knew in her heart that it was impossible for a man like him to sit and do nothing. It was not in his nature to turn his back on his country or its people.

Tensions heightened across the globe and Edith's sons were also preparing to do their duty. Yet when Franklin D. Roosevelt won an unprecedented third term in the White House, he declared, 'I have said this before and I shall say it again and again and again. Your boys are not going to be sent into any foreign wars.' But his words rang hollow with Edith. She had heard it all before during the First World War.

'Prepare yourself, darling, it's only a matter of time,' Henry said.

She tried to live for the moment, yet noted that ominously an ever growing number of defence contracts were being handed out, with factories working flat out to meet the orders. In Marin County, 15,000 workers arrived at the new shipyard at Richardson's Bay, which began building tankers at a rate of one every month. The newly opened Golden Gate Bridge helped industry and the shipyard was a focus for employment. When the actor Bing Crosby swooped in to cheer the boys on, Edith realized just how important it was to the government. A postal stamp was issued showing the Statue of Liberty holding her famous torch emblazoned with the words 'For Defence'. Although no one would say as much, war was good for business and unemployment fell for the first time in years.

'It is ironic that death is the answer to the depression,' she whispered to her mother.

'Shh, don't speak so,' said Frau Hund, not wanting to hear.

'Papa would say the same,' Edith said.

'My only comfort is he didn't see another bloody war.'

Edith wrote incessantly to Maurice and sent small treats for his children that he could no longer buy. He replied:

Your welcome box of candied fruit has arrived to give us much pleasure. You don't know how pleasant it is to get this gift! The food situation is very monotonous – especially in sweets. The children will get one each after luncheon and I wish you could see their faces. A thousand thanks. I've been looking around for Christmas presents lately, they are hard to find. However, I've been lucky to find a second-hand watch and other toys.

Hitler wanted to overwhelm Moscow and Leningrad, and both cities were under siege. Meanwhile the Japanese cabinet had been taken over by military leaders who made a pact with Germany and Italy to become part of the Axis powers. They planned to re-divide the world, giving Germany and Italy dominance in Europe, and Japan the rich resources in China and Southeast Asia.

History was repeating itself, and just as they did twenty-five years before, the Americans steadfastly refused to commit to conflict. Across the water, the new British Prime Minister, Winston Churchill, sent out a defiant message, to the British people pledging he had 'nothing to offer but blood, sweat, toil and tears'. There was clear transatlantic discord. Until the day of 7 December 1941 dawned.

At eight o'clock in the morning, the Japanese Imperial Navy launched 360 aircraft to make a surprise attack on one hundred United States Navy ships berthed at Pearl Harbor on the Hawaiian island of O'ahu. There had been no formal declaration of war and no warning. But within two hours, over two thousand people lost their lives in this unprecedented bombing raid on the American base.

Edith shuddered as she heard twelve bombers thunder through the skies from Marin Meadows that morning.

They were destined for Pearl Harbor and got caught up in the slaughter. Within days, Japanese submarines were attacking merchant ships off the Californian coast and shelling oil refineries. The response was swift; beaches along the coast were covered in barbed wire to protect from invasion, and cities were blacked out in readiness for further attacks.

In Marin County, seventy-five deputies were sworn in and ordered to guard the waterfront. And as rumours spread of Japanese atrocities, people clamoured for reprisals. All those of Japanese origin were to be expelled from California. Just as the Hunds had been persecuted in the First World War, so now were the local Japanese community.

At last America was at war, and Maurice wrote to Edith:

I've often thought of you since those miserable Japs attacked America. I'm surprised they didn't lynch them in California for the Pearl Harbour attack. We all admire America – their splendid defence of the Philippines and their gifts to us. This will be a very anxious year for us all. Who would have thought this would have ever occurred? Am glad your children are doing something to help out. We are all busy doing everything possible. When I have a photo I shall send one to you. Much love. Bless you.

Edith could not bear to think how she would survive another war, this time watching her sons leave home, not knowing whether she would see them again. But they were among the first to volunteer and soon on active duty. Under such stress she found her faith once more, and returned to church, praying so hard and long that her knees ached from asking God to keep her boys safe.

'Please don't take them away from me,' she prayed out loud. 'They are both good, innocent boys.'

With her sons gone, Edith's priority changed. Lambie was about to leave home and was keen to find her own way. Henry, meanwhile, after a life devoted to others, was starting to slow down. He had pioneered the building of a new hospital for the town, and Edith watched proudly during the dedication service as he waved at her in thanks for all her support. It was a moment she would never forget and one that made her realize, despite their differences, how much he loved her.

Seeing his life's work embodied in such a way helped Henry to relax, and he entered retirement with a calmer spirit. A similar change had happened with her mother, Frau Hund. Both now in their late seventies, they could be found each night staring up at the clear skies and watching the stars. They would jokingly compete to be the first to spot a constellation.

'There's the Big Dipper,' he would say, pointing up towards the darkened sky.

'Like a fairground kipper,' Frau Hund would reply and laugh.

Edith tutted at their silly rhymes but kept a watchful eye on them. It was like having two playful elderly parents to look after.

The restrained voices of her mother and husband made Edith yearn for the freshness of youth. She missed the sound of youngsters in the house and the gay shrill of sibling shouts. She decided to hold a tea party every Thursday for the neighbourhood children. With many fathers and brothers away at war, and mothers struggling to cope with work and home, there were plenty of takers for her offer.

Frau Hund helped with her special brand of home cooking, and the mothers would bring their rations to bake a World Cake, made with only a dried egg and so little sugar that it drew complaints for tasting too much of flour. But it didn't stop the children asking for second helpings.

Edith became an expert at scraping the thinnest smear of butter and jam over the piles of sandwiches. She used the family's much coveted cigarette coupons to obtain extra food and became friendly with local farmers, who would happily trade a small basket of fruit and vegetables in exchange for a smoke.

Henry was glad to help with the younger children and, after preparing the gramophone player and his records, would arrange the furniture for a game of musical chairs. He laid out his old collection of rocks and coins, which he marked with titbits of information about their age and origin, hoping some of the children would join him in a discussion about geology and history.

Edith had retrieved several of her precious books from the library, and as a grand finale, she gathered the children around in a circle for a story. Watching their expectant, smiling faces as they listened wide-eyed to the adventures of Robinson Crusoe was indeed sustenance for the soul. For a while they forgot about the war and became lost in a world of make-believe.

'Thank you, Mrs Howitt,' they would shyly drawl, unprompted by their mothers, as they trooped out one after another at the end of the afternoon.

'Come again next week!' she would gasp, shaking each small hand.

Then the rest of the evening was their own to sit pleas-
antly exhausted, talking over their own childhoods and
what the boys and Lambie got up to at similar ages. They
went to bed content. Maybe it was a small and rather
unlikely contribution to the war effort, but it felt good to
have the house filled with laughing, excitable children once
more.

Maurice grew more frustrated as he tried to balance his
time as a father with the requirements of his work for the
Royal Air Force. He could only get home once a month
and had too much time on his own to dwell on the many
dangers. Fearing that the Germans would switch their
bombing campaign to the flat, farming lands of coastal
Norfolk, he at last relented and told Ruth to take the children away. He wrote to Edith:

> I bought a sweet dachshund for the kids the other
> day and they love her. The one bright spot in my
> dejected life is my children. They don't know what
> is going on and are in Scotland with their grand-
> mother, with every good care and perfect safety. It
> has been very interesting with the soldiers,
> wonderful brave fellows, what they have had to go
> through in the Belgium Corps, I'm just heartbroken.

With the children away and Maurice focused on his
military activity, he received a most unexpected call. Since
Maurice's retirement, Lieutenant-Colonel Somerset
Maxwell had been the Conservative MP for King's Lynn.
Early in 1943, however, he was killed in action in the
Middle East, and the National Government wanted a
respectable and worthy candidate to replace him.

Although Maurice had never expressed any desire to return to politics, the party knew he was far and away the best man for the job. Maurice could not refuse. Prime Minister Winston Churchill was grateful for his dedication and sent a cable thanking him for his service:

As a local resident you are familiar with the special problems of a county of farmers who have rendered essential service to the national cause in war. Agriculture will have a more than ever important part to play in the national economy when peace comes and needs men like you in shaping the nation's long-term policy.

Maurice was confident he could see off the Independent Socialist member who was standing against him. He told Edith. 'Our Member of Parliament died of wounds and they persuaded me to stand again. We are now in the midst of the election. My opponent is a complete stranger and doesn't live here. I think I ought to win – but there are no motor cars so the vote will be very low.'

Independent candidates had enjoyed a run of successes at by-elections during the previous year, and Maurice's victory was by no means guaranteed. And when only half the electors turned up to vote, Downing Street waited nervously for the result.

They needn't have worried. Maurice's huge personal support again won through and although his former majority was slashed to a paltry 1,679, nothing could hide his delight as he headed down to Westminster yet again.

Edith was aware that the British government wanted to avoid sensitive material working its way into enemy hands, but she was surprised when Maurice's letters from the House of Commons started to arrive sliced open and scrutinized by an inspector. Then a large sticker was used to reseal the envelope, the seal bearing bold, black lettering with the words 'Opened by Examiner' and then a number. This one was 5989.

She wondered what Examiner 5989 looked like: was it a man or a woman? Did they gasp when they saw the contents and who the letter was from? And who it was going to? Or were Edith and Maurice of no interest, just mere titillation for some agent looking for information much more sinister than a transatlantic love affair between a lord and a woman from Marin County?

Such a policy made Maurice laugh. Could an MP manage to get a letter through unopened, he wondered? So he took the liberty of typing his own name and address on the front of the envelope. But it made no difference – the censor still had his way. Edith had to smile when she read his next letter:

This is my election address. I hope the censor
won't take it out. Hitler will gain nothing from it
as it announces that the policy is to win the war –
it will be no news to him! I know you are all as
busy in America as we are here. We only have a
staff of two when we used to have eight! The
children are now able to dress and take care of
themselves. The boy will be four next month. He
wears a kilt and is very sweet. Mary will be nine in
August. Frances is just six. I think I told you they
kept chickens and their vegetable garden.

By February 1944, Maurice was back in the limelight,

calling attention in the Commons to the dropping value of war pensions. After his experience in the RAF he knew what these men had been through and campaigned hard to increase the amounts they were allowed. Within weeks of his return to Westminster, Maurice received a telegram from his brother in New York. Fannie, now eighty-four years old, had suffered a life-threatening stroke. He wrote to Edith with the bad news,

I am anxious right now because my mother has had a stroke, and although cables state she is out of danger, she can't speak. These clots are I believe absorbed in time – but there is always the very great danger of a second attack. I am expecting another cable from my brother, perhaps today.

My life has changed a great deal. I am again in the House of Commons and a great many new faces have turned up. Eight MPs have lost their lives in this ghastly war. Such are the conditions we are living in just now.

Life goes on, sadness on all sides. News of deaths – missing. Never did we imagine that Europe could destroy itself. If there is a God we must be rewarded soon. How can German people stand such tyranny? Why don't they revolt? Keep writing. Much love.

Maurice was distraught, knowing he had to find a way back to America to see his mother. If she died before he held her one last time, he would never forgive himself. He took the opportunity to suggest another meeting with Edith.

He wrote, 'You'll be delighted to hear I am hoping to

visit America this summer. I hope we can meet. We must arrange it, my best love, Maurice.'

Edith smiled on her way to the store and queued for her weekly ration without complaint. She went home and made supper, refusing the help of Frau Hund, encouraging her instead to have a cocktail with Henry. As she absent-mindedly peeled the potatoes and examined the fat on the tiny piece of meat to find the lean parts, Edith dreamed of what it was going to be like to see Maurice again. He was risking the trip, at last.

Looking into his face, hearing his voice, feeling the touch of his hand on hers made her skin tingle. How could a woman in her mid-fifties feel seventeen again? But she did. She would make a dress, try and get hold of some new nylons. Should she dye her hair or leave it grey? They had so much to catch up on, so much to talk about. Her mind raced with questions. She sent him pictures of the children – the boys in uniform and Lambie at graduation – but none of herself. She did not want to pre-empt their meeting, and hoped he would be as pleased with her as before.

Then, just weeks before Maurice was intending to sail to America, General Eisenhower announced the invasion of Europe had begun. It was the largest land, sea and air operation ever known, involving Allied troops from many different nations. Almost every available British craft was commandeered and ordered to set sail for France on the night of 6 June 1944.

Leaving ports after midnight and fighting against heavy winds, the huge convoy arrived before dusk at strategic points along the French and Belgium coast. This was to be the big push to liberate Europe – and a battle they could not afford to lose.

Despite casualties running into the thousands, Winston

Churchill appeared upbeat and told Maurice that the operation was going well. 'Many dangers and difficulties which appeared extremely formidable are now behind us.'

Maurice was torn between concern for his mother and the nation's fight for survival. With all the ships in action and the highly charged political climate making travel treacherous, there was now no possibility of his returning to America. He trusted Edith would understand and promised he would try again.

His letter, delayed by the fighting, arrived almost two months after she last wrote to him. Terrified that Maurice had been badly injured during the conflict, when she saw his familiar handwriting she breathed a huge sigh of relief, and hurriedly opened the envelope, hoping to discover his arrival date. Quickly scanning the letter she could find no such news. It read,

> Thanks for the photos. I wish you had sent one of yourself. I was interested in all you said. I never got to America as D-Day made it impossible to get away. Let us meet after the war, either here or in New York. You have no idea of all the mental worry we have all had with the flying bombs. I've gone grey but still keep myself fit and well. The news is good, what a relief when it is all over. Bless you and love.

She was saddened and disappointed. Her anxiety about his safety was swept aside by crushing disappointment and frustration. She lived for him, and had waited so long to hear from him in the hope of seeing him again. How she longed to tell him of her love and fears, and to feel his love in return.

Who knew when the war would end? In the beginning no one expected it to last beyond a few months, yet years had already passed and there seemed to be no end in sight. She hardly dared to hope any more and began to doubt whether she would ever see Maurice again. It had been difficult enough with an ocean between them; now they were driven apart by this madness. They had survived one world war, she hoped they could another.

FIFTEEN

'What a World'

There was an expectant but reverent hush across the floor of the House. Maurice had arrived early at the House of Commons to be sure of a good seat. He now sat five rows behind the Prime Minister, staring at the broad back of the wartime leader, who was shuffling his papers in readiness. Maurice could feel a chill of excitement surging through his chest. 'God, let it be good news.'

Seventy-year-old Winston Spencer Churchill rose solemnly to his feet and stepped over the red line to the dispatch box. He pulled his glasses towards the end of his nose and peered intently over the top. His small eyes then fixed on his notes and Churchill's tidal wave of a voice delivered the news everyone needed to hear. 'German armed forces surrendered unconditionally on May the 7th. Hostilities will end officially at one minute after midnight tonight, but in the interests of saving lives the "cease fire" began yesterday to be sounded all along the front.'

The war in Europe was over. Hitler had been defeated. Five years of desolation, death and hardship were ended in that moment. 'Advance Britannia! Long live the cause of freedom! God save the King.' The House erupted with cheers of joy.

Churchill left the House of Commons and walked purposefully to the Ministry of Health in Whitehall, where a large crowd had gathered.

Stepping on to the balcony he shouted, 'This is your victory!' The people roared back, 'No. It's yours!' Churchill waved and yelled, 'God bless you all. In all our long history we have never seen a greater day than this.'

Maurice remained sitting quietly in the Chamber, absorbing the news. Before leaving, the Prime Minister had thanked MPs for their honourable conduct during the war years and the resolve they had shown in pulling together. Maurice felt the tension slip from his shoulders. He could at last leave political life with a clear conscience, his duty done. The war had drained him. Whatever else he was going to do now, it would not involve the pressure of office.

Maurice walked slowly through the House of Commons; it was not a day to rush. He wanted to savour the peace after the endless days and nights of calamity. MPs were laughing and patting each other on the back. He made a cup of tea in his office and sat down at his desk, arms behind his head. His children would at last be safe. A glorious prospect. They could be a family again.

Sitting there alone, he thought of Edith. The nature of their love meant that much was suppressed, but for a few seconds, with the country revelling in freedom, he could think about her. He imagined her laughing and dancing, and heard her gentle teasing whenever he got above himself. It was almost too much. He had prayed for the end of the war many times. What he might do, how he

233

would feel. But he never thought it would bring him to these tears.

Thinking of times to come, he started a letter to Edith, but was disturbed by a fellow MP urging him to join colleagues for a celebratory drink.

'At this time of day?' quizzed Maurice.

'Licensing laws have been suspended for the day, old chap. Didn't you know – the war is over!'

Maurice carefully folded his unfinished note and placed it inside his coat pocket. He would make time for that later, but now was the moment to be among the people. Walking into the late afternoon sunshine, he was faced with glorious pandemonium on the streets of Westminster. At first, Maurice thought the gentle touches on his head must be a spring shower, until he looked skywards and found that his face was being sprinkled with fluttering confetti. Here was liberty! Flags as far as he could see, draped around people's necks, hanging from the buildings, wrapped around street lamps. An old man came up to him and shook his hand. A young girl swinging half-way up a lamp-post reached out and kissed him on the cheek. Small children perched high on their parent's shoulders looked happily bewildered. Exuberant singing and the clattering of dustbin lids filled the air.

Many people hopped on to bicycles and cycled furiously down the Mall. Maurice watched from a distance, then moved forward slowly to join the growing crowd as it wound towards Buckingham Palace. The golden statue of Queen Victoria was already decorated with people gripping on and chanting, 'We want the King!'

Maurice raised his hands aloft and cheered as King George VI and Queen Elizabeth appeared on the balcony,

time and again, along with the Princesses. In the fading
light the crowd went wild, waving, clapping and
screaming, 'God save the King!' Nothing else mattered.
Victory was theirs.

Returning at midnight to his club, Brook's in St James's
Street, he dismissed all thoughts of sleep, still absorbed
by the excitement and noise from the surrounding streets.
Feeling in his pocket, he took out the letter to Edith and
continued to write of the day's momentous events.

You can't imagine our joy at the end of the war
with Germany. I was in the House of Commons
when the Prime Minister made the announcement,
which was received with great enthusiasm. London
and the country gave rejoicing. The floodlighting
came on and thousands went to Buckingham Palace
to see the King and Queen appear on the balcony.

Maurice felt jubilant, but his thoughts soon turned to
those still embroiled in conflict. There might be peace with
Germany, but the fighting continued in the Far East.
Reports of dreadful atrocities there sent shivers down his
spine. Maurice could not celebrate further until the war
had ended on every front, and all the boys were back
home with their families.

The experience of war had left people hungry for
change, and Labour's promise to nationalize industry,
transport and even the Bank of England struck a nerve
with workers who had long felt they deserved better. The
Labour Party also had one huge trump card – their plans
to introduce a National Health Service with free medical
care 'from the cradle to the grave'. After the physical and
emotional scars of conflict, they promised to end the

tragedy of watching loved ones die because they could not afford a doctor.

> Now we are preparing for a General Election – the
> result of the Labour Party refusing the Prime
> Minister's appeal to remain in the coalition until
> the defeat of Japan. It will be a bitter election with
> all sorts of distortion and blame. I am not standing
> again for many reasons. Taxation is terrific and I
> just can't afford it and I want a little peace of mind
> now that I am sixty. There are so many problems
> ahead to settle the world peace. Much love.

Within two months of peace being declared, the political landscape in Britain had been dramatically transformed. Churchill was unceremoniously ousted, the British people rejecting their wartime leader's warnings about the evils of socialism.

Working-class men had served alongside officers and seen comrades give their lives. Now they wanted recognition for the role they had played in Britain's triumph. By the end of the war, no one under the age of thirty had ever voted in an election, and they were no longer willing to doff their caps to aged politicians. A younger generation wanted a part in the running of their country; they saw themselves as the future of politics. It was the Labour Party which promised to respond to their demands and were swept to power under Prime Minister Clement Attlee with a majority of 146 seats.

Maurice had chosen the right moment to go. Having left at the top, he could enjoy life and still mix in the headiest set. He proudly announced to Edith:

Ruth and I have dined with the King and Queen twice and on Sunday they are coming for a cocktail. We are expecting the American Ambassador to spend the weekend. He was at school with me and went to Princeton.

I am going to Paris this week with some Members of Parliament. It will be very interesting to see things and how the French are looking since their liberation. I had to have a new passport and here is what I look like at sixty. My mother looks as though she won't last much longer. Much love, bless you.

Frank had just sent an emergency cable to Maurice saying their mother had collapsed and was gravely ill at the family home in Newport. He wanted his brother's approval to seek specialist care at a medical centre, because it was increasingly difficult to care for Fannie at home.

Maurice agreed, knowing that at his age he was lucky to have had his mother this long. She had always been there for him, her indomitable spirit and unique sense of humour as infuriating as it was engaging. Now he could not imagine life without her. Preparing himself for what he might find in America, Maurice booked a passage on the first available boat out of Southampton. There was very little time to do anything other than pack a few belongings, kiss Ruth, hug the children and go to Fannie's side. He felt acutely vulnerable as his car swung out of Park House for the start of a very long trip.

He arrived in America to depressing news. Fannie was near death having suffered a devastating stroke. She looked terribly emaciated and her throat was dangerously swollen, making breathing and feeding difficult. And despite round-the-clock care, she was not responding to treatment. Frank had already organized three nurses to work in shifts to tend to her every need. The house had the air of a gloomy hospital rather than a home. Every day was hard as their mother grew weaker, and it was impossible to find ways to help.

'We must be prepared for the worst,' said Maurice.

'I think this is the time to get her to hospital,' said Frank.

'Maybe,' replied Maurice, 'but this is her home and the place she loves best.'

They looked at each other, quietly weighing up the options. Both were aware of how things had changed, and that the time had now come for them to protect and parent her.

'Then that is what we will do,' said Frank sadly. 'She always ran the show – why change now?'

Maurice winked to acknowledge his brother's brave words and they walked, heads held high, back into their mother's room.

Shortly afterwards he wrote to Edith with the news she had passed away, 'My mother died aged ninety. It was all for the best. The sad thing is she couldn't speak.'

On 6 August 1945 American Pilot Colonel Paul W. Tibbets sat at the controls of his B49 Superfortress bomber going over pre-flight checks. He'd painted his mother's name, Enola Gay, on the nose of the plane and watched as the front bay was loaded. He was all set to take off carrying the most destructive bomb the world had ever seen.

The twelve-foot long explosive, nicknamed 'Little Boy' after President Roosevelt, was armed and ready. The flight was uneventful, until Tibbets reached the Japanese city of Hiroshima. When the plane was directly overhead, he released the load and nose-dived to the right. Forty-three seconds later, the atomic bomb exploded, erasing five square miles of the city in a cataclysmic fireball, burning as bright as the sun and sending a mushroom cloud miles high into the sky.

Three days later, another nuclear bomb was dropped on Nagasaki and Emperor Hirohito surrendered. Japan had been defeated in the most ignominious of ways.

Edith read the headlines, relieved that her boys would now come home safely. The years had taken their toll: her face was more lined, and her body weary. But the news of Jack's imminent marriage thrilled her. The young couple promised Edith that she would soon become a grandmother. The excitement of holding a baby in her arms would roll away the years and make her feel young. It had been a very long time since there had been a newborn child in the house, and she sanded and painted the boys' old wooden crib in readiness. She wanted her life to be filled with hope once again.

Every Sunday she would walk to church and quietly light a candle. It was Edith's way of trying to cleanse the world of hate. She wanted her grandchild born into a better world, without the madness that surrounded them. She wondered whether that would be possible.

And, with his mother dying, Maurice wrote a letter, which started, 'I hate to confess it, but I was in America for August, but I just couldn't manage to get out to see you.'

She read the lines over and over in disbelief. She thought of all the trivial tasks she must have been doing when he was here. She would have been making the beds, buying gas, sleeping. She really thought that she loved this man so much that she would sense when he came home. Yet there had been no shiver down her spine, no hunch or special feeling. No inkling of his presence. He had been closer than ever, there was only the width of the country between them. She could have caught a train, hopped on a plane – driven, for God's sake – to be with him. She would have done anything to see him again.

Edith's thoughts were interrupted by shouts from upstairs.

'The pain is back,' Frau Hund moaned.

'I'll get your tablets.' She went to her mother. 'I could get the bed moved downstairs if you like,' said Edith, stroking her mother's forehead. 'You would be more comfortable there.'

Frau Hund shook her head. 'When my time comes I will die in my bed, not where people eat their food.'

She had been deteriorating for several months, and walking was nearly impossible, yet she stubbornly refused to accept more help. Henry came and did what he could to make Frau Hund more comfortable, but she was slipping slowly away. Day by day her voice grew smaller and she had lost interest in talking. Edith tried sitting quietly, reading aloud from the newspaper, consulting her mother on the more difficult crossword clues. But Frau Hund would only stare out of the window, watching the clouds drift through the ever changing sky, becoming part of the rhythm of the wind and patter of the rain.

When Edith looked at her mother, she realized that even if Maurice was in New York, it would have been impossible to get away. She had been fooling herself. Henry could never look after Frau Hund alone.

In her heart, she knew she must remain in Marin County until the end of her mother's and her husband's days. Having come this far she wasn't going to let them down. She returned to Maurice's letter and read the rest.

'It was wonderful to be there for VJ day. I spent most of my time at Newport. The Americans couldn't have been nicer. I saw a great deal of the Duke and Duchess of Windsor. And my brother also arranged many parties.'

She was puzzled. He had always boasted that the King and Queen were among his best friends. Yet in America he was openly dining out with the exiled former King, whose illicit love affair almost brought down the monarchy. What was Maurice up to?

As a man who thrived on variety when he came to America, Maurice would happily embrace invitations to dinners and parties. It may have been a life he had left behind, but it was one he had never forgotten. Doing as he wished reminded him of his single days as plain carefree Mr Roche, and he was flattered to be invited on his own by such esteemed friends.

She doubted he had gone home and told Ruth the company he was keeping. How could he? His wife was such a staunch ally of the Queen, and the two women had only feelings of bitterness towards the former Mrs Simpson, and a strong sense of betrayal.

Edith hunted in her drawer for Maurice's older letters. She had a suspicion that he and Ruth were not getting on quite as well as he indicated. The war had meant long separations, and many couples were finding it hard to pick up the pieces of their former lives. Why should Maurice and Ruth be any different? After all, Ruth was a young woman in her thirties while Maurice was an old man. Of course there would be problems. As Edith knew only too well. She posted Maurice a box of Robert Burns cigars and then spread his letters over her desk. Looking over the many pages, she knew there was still much left unsaid.

* * *

With all her children at boarding school, Ruth had absolutely no intention of sitting around twiddling her thumbs. She threw herself wholeheartedly into a new career as a Justice of the Peace, hearing cases at the local magistrates' court. It gave her a separate interest and an identity independent of Maurice, and she liked the intellectual challenge. Ironically, Maurice's retirement coincided with one of the busiest periods of his wife's life. He was proud of her achievements, but the two of them were very different.

Now that the children were gone, Maurice filled his days with domestic chores, doing the shopping, looking after the animals and tending to the vegetable plot. He had time to indulge his love of farming, and he rather quaintly kept a pen and paper at hand in order to make notes and work out which crops had the best yields.

The optimism after the war did not last long and Maurice felt betrayed. He was angry that the country had moved in a direction which undermined his work as an MP. The pound had been devalued by 30 per cent and the country was almost bankrupt following a rash of imports that could not be paid for. The meat allowance was cut to a shilling's worth a week and there was no end in sight to rationing.

The Labour Party was struggling as it dealt with strikes and widespread discontent. Maurice did not take kindly to being told his car could only be used for business and that all foreign holidays were banned. It was not how he had envisaged victory. The thought of Edith basking in glorious Californian sunshine only added to his sense of frustration. He wrote,

The country is paying a good price for turning out Churchill. In London, the men sit in their coats reading the newspapers. Candles on the counters in the shops and no heaters in the hotels. Homes are freezing cold, misery all round. Food very scarce and rationed.

He sat back, trying hard to force the more optimistic side of his nature to win through.

However, it never hurts a nation to go through this. I believe luxury, over-eating is the worst thing for one's character – and just makes one no good! I am glad to write with the news that my children are all well, pink cheeked, healthy. Much love.

Amid the doom and gloom of post-war politics, a royal romance emerged. Princess Elizabeth, eldest daughter of King George VI and Queen Elizabeth, and Lieutenant Philip Mountbatten, a dashing Greek naval officer, had fallen in love. Knowing the young couple well, Maurice was heartened by news of their impending marriage.

I've had a lot of invitations at the Royal House, Sandringham. We dined there one night – twenty-four for dinner. Ruth sat next to Philip and found him charming. I sat next to Queen Elizabeth and Queen Mary on the other side. They are so easy to talk to. I shot there on Thursday. We got 750 pheasants, some high birds. I got a hundred to my own gun.

The children had the Kent and Gloucester children to tea today. The Duchess of Gloucester came with her two boys. Very sensibly brought up, no bad manners, or spoilt. We had favours – lovely chocolate cake. They ran about the house afterwards playing hide and seek.

It seems so funny to be living this life after my long years in New York. I look at your photo. You look very pretty in your grey hair. As you say. What a world.

He wished he could turn around and see Edith standing there, smiling. He missed her, but shook his head at such self-indulgence. I must be getting old, he mused.

On 20 November 1947, Maurice and Ruth were well seated in Westminster Abbey as the royal bride made her dramatic entrance. The twenty-six-year-old groom waited nervously at the head of the aisle.

There had been concern about mounting such a flamboyant royal show when the country was in crisis. But Parliament reasoned that the union would be a cause for celebration, capturing the nation's imagination and instilling a sense of togetherness. Outside on the streets, people crowded in their thousands for the briefest glimpse of the happy couple. And for those who could not make the trip, broadcast cameras had been allowed into the Abbey for the first time. Pictures flashed across the globe showing the nation enjoying this wedding and supporting the Crown.

The cheering crowds led Maurice to reflect on how he would feel when the time came to walk his girls down the aisle. He knew it wouldn't be that long, and hoped he could do his duty as a father.

Princess Elizabeth came through the Abbey dressed in a gown inspired by Botticelli's painting *Primavera*, embroidered with ten thousand seed pearls. As Maurice rose to sing the first hymn, 'Praise my soul, the King of Heaven', he stumbled over the words, a lump in his throat.

Afterwards, along with other special guests, he and Ruth were treated to a grand supper with twelve wedding cakes, one of which towered right above their heads where they sat. That night, while the details and scene were still fresh in his mind, he began his letter to Edith. He knew how much she would expect from him. In spite of the time difference, she had promised to be listening on the radio.

What a wonderful time we are living in. You must have been up at three in the morning to hear the broadcast of the wedding. It was a great moment, we could see it all beautifully. There were twenty-eight foreign crowned heads all dressed in their best.

The reception two nights before the wedding was a fine show. It took place at Buckingham Palace. The King and Queen, Queen Mary spoke to us. The French people of southern France had sent three thousand carnations and these were all placed around the rooms. What a sight. They went to the hospitals afterwards.

I was glad to hear your news. As you say, life is difficult. We have had every kind of restriction since the war. The masses of the people still back this government because they feel the Conservative one will drop wages.

I am no longer in the House of Commons, but manage to be busy, with many irons in the fire. President of the British Legion, King's Lynn Cycling Club, Bee Keepers (I know nothing about bees),

Patron of Bowls Clubs, it helps to pass the time.
I was very shocked by the death of
ex-ambassador Winant. We were at school,
together. I saw him several times during the war.
He could have had a useful old age as some
university head, or lived in some garden spot of
America. I suppose something 'cracked'.
I wish I could send you a Norfolk pheasant.
I shot with the King yesterday and we got 300.

Still puffing on his cigar and a little worse for wear from the day's celebrations, he expressed his thanks at her well chosen gift. He added,

They are really the only things that give me any
pleasure. I smoke one each night sitting round the
fireside. Here we only have Jamaicans, which are
no more than soft coal owing to the dollar
exchange. There is not another thing I would ask for.

Edith's mother died in her sleep, in her bed, just as she had wanted. In the morning Edith found her and stayed holding her hand and stroking her tranquil face until Henry ushered her gently away. When he came downstairs he handed her a lock of silvery grey hair.

'Always keep a part of her,' he said, placing the curl into a plain envelope.

Although Henry was by Edith's side he did not want to talk much about Frau Hund's passing. His working life had been filled with death, and he protected himself by never dwelling on it.

'Move on,' he always said. 'Don't get lost in what you can't change.'

Edith sighed at the differences between them. He found solace in his books and radio, whereas she needed to talk.

For a while, even Maurice's letters could not bring much joy. She sent him a note admonishing him for his description of the royal wedding. She did not need to know about the poor quality of his smelly old cigars! 'Tell me how the bride looked,' she implored, all the while tutting quietly to herself, 'What a typical man.'

When next she received word, there was a large envelope sitting in her mail box. Maurice had gathered together cuttings on the wedding from the entire British press and parcelled them up to try to make amends.

'Well, maybe not that typical,' she thought.

SIXTEEN

'Not a Bad Seat'

Edith and Henry were seated at the restaurant, waiting patiently for Lambie and her new boyfriend to arrive.

'So I guess they're serious,' said Henry, pouring out their water.

He was always nervous meeting his daughter's dates, especially when not on home turf.

'Just remember not to call her Lambie. You know how she gets embarrassed,' said Edith.

Henry adjusted his tie and tapped his foot, flicking absent-mindedly through the menu.

'She's in love,' said Edith. 'Better get used to it, Henry.'

Lambie waved from the doorway and walked over arm in arm with Arty, in his merchant seaman's uniform. 'He's a fine-looking boy,' whispered Edith and smiled at the approaching couple.

Art confidently held out his hand to Henry. 'Pleased to meet you, sir,' he said. 'I've heard plenty about you.'

Merchant seaman Arty Hodgins, a tall man with a steely glare, had been teaching navigation at the Marine Academy when Lambie first laid eyes on him. His dark, curly hair and prodigious self-assurance made him a popular figure with the girls.

'He's just got back from Russia,' Lambie explained to her father, who had heard little of this young sailor.

Henry felt the tight grip of Arty's hand. 'Good to meet you at last, son,' he said. Moving closer, he hid behind the menu and whispered, 'If the truth be told it's good to meet someone who likes the ocean. Let's have a beer and talk about fishing.'

As the evening unfolded, Henry was impressed with the composure shown by Hodgins. And there was no doubting the respect he showed their daughter.

'He makes her laugh,' Henry told Edith in the car on the way home.

'You know he's a war hero?' Edith said.

Henry raised an eyebrow. 'He never said a thing.'

'Far too modest,' said Edith. 'He's got an OBE.'

'A what?' asked Henry.

'It's a medal, Order of the British Empire, awarded for service to King and Country. And he's not even British!' she laughed.

'Must have done something pretty smart to be decorated like that.'

'His boat was torpedoed and sunk by the Germans in the Arctic Circle. The captain was beaten up and taken away, leaving Arty in command of thirteen men on three small rafts. All he had was a loaf of black bread and a week's water ration.'

'Go on,' he urged.

'Even though they were closer to German-occupied Norway, Arty ordered the men to start rowing for Russia. But they started to get weak and when there was no sign of rescue, some of the men refused to go on. Arty knew their only chance of survival was to stick together, so he took out his gun and forced them to keep going.'

'He's a tough customer,' said Henry.

'They went for sixteen days until the men were collapsing with exhaustion. Then, out of the blue, a search plane spotted them. They were taken to Murmansk where they spent the winter in real primitive conditions, but at least they were alive.'

'Maybe I won't take him fishing then,' laughed Henry.

'He's more than capable of coping with our Lambie,' smiled Edith, as Henry reclined in his seat pressing an imaginary brake every time she accelerated.

That night, long after they had gone to bed, a storm cracked overhead, making the house shake, yet Henry slept on, oblivious to the rumbles and flashes. Edith flinched with each flare and crept down the long hallway to make the house secure. The darkness, illuminated by a momentary electrical snap, did nothing to settle her nerves. She had always hated storms for their sense of foreboding.

Outside, the wind was growing stronger and the weather-vane on the rooftop clattered in an angry spin. Edith strode from room to room, hastily tightening all the windows.

In the kitchen, the blinds knocked rhythmically against the glass and she was startled by a dark shadow swaying wildly in front of the window. Edith scolded herself when she saw it was only the bird feeder bobbing back and forth. As she struggled to close the shutters against the beating rain, they slammed with such force, that a photograph on the table fell to the floor.

Edith screamed, then laughed at her silliness, picking up the frame and wiping off the dust with the sleeve of her blouse. It was an old family picture of Edith, Lambie,

Frau Hund and Henry. Three generations of women, arms around each other, and the man of the house standing behind. Her mother and daughter had moved on from Edith's life, and soon it would be Henry's turn. A thunderous boom echoed in the distance.

Edith could sense the sweet smell of her mother's perfume, as if she was standing beside her in the room. She stood perfectly still, breathing deeply, clutching the picture to her breast. As the perfume faded she broke into a quiet sob. But the rain's rhythmic splatter kept on coming and she ran back to bed, her head a jumble of childhood memories.

The following afternoon, the doorbell rang. Edith was checking her bank account and did not take kindly to being interrupted. The ring changed to a tapping, and she remembered that she was expecting a delivery from the food store. The polite knocking became more insistent and her screen door vibrated. She walked briskly down the hall, expecting to see the eager young delivery man.

Peering through the screen, the man on the other side had a strange familiarity and Edith took off her glasses to get a better look. She opened the door slowly and the hinge gave a tired squeak.

'Hello Didi,' he said.

'What the hell are you doing here?' she said, pushing the door wildly as if trying to bat him off the front porch.

Edith looked right and left down the street to see if anyone was watching. 'What do you want, Forrest?' she said, shocked to be looking at her former husband for the first time in years.

'I came to see my girl.'

'She grew up,' she said, annoyed that she felt flattered.

'Let me in, so I can be real sure.'

251

'Henry is here.'

'Is the old Doc still alive? He must be a hundred.'

'I'm amazed you're still going,' said Edith.

'That's a nice greeting, after I've come all the way from Ireland to see you,' he replied. 'Remember how Doc used to take me in his horse and buggy when he did his rounds? I thought he was wonderful, even when his dog bit my ass and he had to cauterize the bite.'

She could not stop herself from smiling at how he had winced for a week whenever he sat down. 'You still owe him five dollars for the pleasure,' she reminded Forrest.

He took a step closer. 'I'll never forget the drive to Saratoga that summer with the wind blowing your hair like catkins and the moon lighting up your face. You sure were a doll.' His hand rubbed the top of her arm as she leaned on the door frame.

'You've got five minutes, Forrest,' she said, pulling him off. She moved back to allow his angular frame to slide past. He made an exaggerated bow and removed his sodden cap to reveal a thick crop of black hair.

'I'll have a coffee since you're offering,' he said.

She laughed at his cheek and made it weak, adding a little honey. The years showed on his weather-beaten face, but his lines were in all the right places. His eyes creased into a friendly fan whenever he smiled, which he still did more than any man she had ever met.

'What made you come?' she asked again.

'I got a postcard from an old friend, a full nine by six inches of the Golden Gate bridge. He invited me over and I couldn't be this close without stopping by.'

He delved into his pocket and handed her a piece of crinkled paper. 'I bought you a gift,' he said, looking decidedly pleased with himself. 'It's a sweepstake ticket. When

you win, book us the best suite on the boat back to Ireland
– the boys can fly first class!'

'You always were a dreamer. I thought you would die
in Ireland with your silly thoughts for company.'

'Ah, my beloved Ireland, where there are too many gales
off the Atlantic and enough rain to make your bones ache.'

She sipped her tea and then said too breezily, 'Have you
heard of a place called Fermoy?'

'It's about an hour from Dublin by train, I think. Why
do you ask?'

'A friend I know used to live there.'

'I see,' he said. That smile again.

He leaned forward and said, 'We were great friends,
Didi, we shared a life.' He was so close she could smell
his whiskied breath.

'You are obviously very well, Forrest,' said Edith.

'Well thank you,' he replied, his grin only disappearing
when she added, 'Very well pickled, that is.'

He looked at her with real intent. 'Dammit, I never was
as good at English as you. We made the boys, didn't we,
we had fun . . .'

'You got drunk. You got us both in debt. Then you
wouldn't come home. That was our life, Forrest.'

He stretched his arms out towards her. 'Things are
different now. Listen, what would it cost me to live in San
Francisco and keep you in scotch and martinis?'

Edith heard the sound of Henry rousing upstairs.

'You have to go,' she said nervously glancing around.

'I always thought he was too much of an antique for
you.'

'Henry is a good man who has raised your sons to be
fine citizens. You owe him everything.'

He hesitated. 'Truth is . . .' he leaned forward and stole

a kiss on her cheek. 'I know in a house this size, you must have a spare room.'

'Go home!' she hissed. 'You don't belong here.'

'I could be the one to get up and make the breakfast – imagine that, Didi – and bring you a tray in bed.'

She leaned forward until she was close enough to see a cluster of unshaven whiskers down the side of his face. 'You're drunk, Forrest. Get out!'

'Ah, back to my beloved Ireland – where there is nothing but lovely green scenery and . . . yer fancy Fermoy man?' He looked at her with a sideways glance. 'Not even a movie house to help forget for a while, no nipping off to better oneself in the land of the blarney – *mais non, ma chérie. Au revoir.*'

She turned and saw Henry standing at the bottom of the stairs.

'What was he doing here?'

'He'd come to annoy me,' Edith shrugged.

During the late 1940s, Britain struggled back on to her feet and the food shortages started to ease. But the hardships had a positive effect on Maurice, who was feeling much fitter. Retirement was suiting him, and he worked to offset the excess weight from the constant round of socializing, which lately had begun to pall. The same small talk and visiting bores sometimes made Maurice feel claustrophobic. He preferred the physical exertion of harvesting crops or running local clubs, which helped to keep his mind active and his spirit grateful. He wrote to Edith about the pleasure he got from the land:

We have had a terrible wet summer and it has given very little outside sport. However, the crops

will be heavy, potatoes, wheat, etc. There is no
doubt there is more of everything in England –
especially vegetables. The strawberry crop has been
excellent, and green things – peas, tomatoes.

I have never felt better, very largely I am almost
a teetotaller – only when there is a free cocktail
party or wedding. I feel so well in the mornings
when I haven't had a go at the whisky!

Ruth and I went to Aberdeen for her father's and
mother's fiftieth wedding anniversary. It was gay,
a big reception, dinner and it was daylight till
11 p.m. We gave a joint family present.

I have been to my boy's school for a parents'
day. He seemed very pleased to have me there.
They had ice cream and strawberries. One hundred
small boys. The rest of my time is spent in helping
round the place, attending to local charities, church
fetes, British Legion.

I miss my children. They are all at boarding
school. Mary wears her mother's clothes. We are
going to her confirmation.

Tomorrow Ruth and I go to London, where we
dine with the Argentine Embassy. These dinners are
large and they have all their food sent straight
from the Argentine, turkeys, chicken, butter, etc.
They have plenty of footmen to serve. The King
and Queen come here for the weekend. He may
come and play a game of tennis with me. I am
always looking forward to the time when we may
meet, the travelling restrictions can't last for ever.

'Well, this must go. I have known you so long.
Much love and kisses.

255

In Sandringham, the royal family's wealth and position shielded them from the daily hardship of post-war Britain, but could not prevent King George VI from suffering chronic health problems. Like his father, he had endured years of illness and one day, while shooting with Maurice, he casually mentioned a pain in his legs.

After much persuasion, Bertie consulted his doctors and was diagnosed with arteriosclerosis, a hardening of the arteries. Despite the agony, he continued with his engagements until the pain became so intense that there was a real fear that he might lose his right leg. Surgeons convinced him they could help by making a four-inch cut to the right side of his back, severing the chain of nerves. This was to prevent the artery from constricting and to increase the blood supply to his leg. The King agreed to have the operation, although it meant the cancellation of a tour to Australia. The surgeons who performed the delicate technique, in the Buhl room on the first floor of Buckingham Palace, stressed how vital his aftercare was. The King was ordered to get plenty of rest and sit for hours in an electrically heated bath.

During his long recovery there was the uplifting news of a baby boy born into the royal family on 14 November 1948. Prince Charles's chubby cheeks and rounded knees reminded them all of Prince Albert, Queen Victoria's consort. Princess Elizabeth and Prince Philip, who had been married just over a year, were thrilled at their instant success in continuing the royal line.

A male heir for the British monarchy was a reason for optimism, but Maurice felt more cautious, understanding the future pressures on the little prince. He had seen how Bertie had suffered from the pressures of the office and knew it was no easy task. He told Edith, 'I've seen Prince

Charles. He is a nice baby. Poor thing – I often wonder what things will be like when he grows up.'

Rejuvenated by his first grandchild, the King refused to let health problems stop him from leading a normal life. Maurice was optimistic that after good medical care, his friend's illness would be behind him.

The King seems to be doing well. How he ever got this trouble I can't see. He has very thin legs.
I have seen them while he was playing tennis with me.

My brother seems to be quite happy in Paris. He spent a month with me in January. Plays golf.
Aimless life.

My sister's son has been here too. I don't understand these modern young men. He upsets my house by remaining in bed till eleven each morning. I was always up and down at eight. He doesn't like girls either. Not like his Uncle Maurice.

Although he had promised himself he would no longer play a part in domestic politics, Maurice had always remained loyal to his old party. It was impossible not to have strong opinions in the present climate. Russia now had an atomic bomb, and scientists in America had developed an H-bomb, potentially a thousand times more powerful than that dropped on Hiroshima and Nagasaki.

As China and Czechoslovakia fell to Communism, people in the West feared that their very way of life was being threatened. Senator Joseph McCarthy was rooting out any 'red' sympathizers and accused high-profile personalities and government officials of conspiring to undermine democracy. Comedian Charlie Chaplin and the playwright Arthur Miller were called to account for themselves by the Un-American Activities Committee. Many Americans believed that Communists were infiltrating their society, and actively encouraged the witch-hunt.

With the onset of a new decade, Britain was hoping for better times. The Welfare State had proved to be a great success, but socialism was struggling and a General Election was looming. Maurice wrote to Edith:

It is going to be a dirty fight. I don't know just what the result will be. This Labour Government has been a great failure, but as followers of Truman, the money is being wasted like water.

This country is up to its neck in debt, spending too much buying votes as Truman does. Australia and New Zealand turned out their Socialist governments, perhaps we may do the same. I am rather disturbed because my brother in America is having a bad time with his nerves. He has nothing to interest his mind. He is at a rest centre right now.

It is a glorious day here, no wind, sunshine. I shall go for a walk with the dog, posting this letter in Sandringham.

We dined a short time ago at the big house. The King's legs seemed very much better. I saw Prince Charles the other day, he is a sweet child, little is he aware of what is in store for him.

I can see you in California bathed in sunshine – Oh how I would like to spend a month there – just lazily doing nothing. Thanks again for all the pleasure you have given me. Much love.

Maurice still mourned the loss of his King's Lynn seat,
which in 1945 the Conservatives had lost for the first time
in many years. He reminisced to Edith.

Well, we did our best but the Labour candidate got
in by only 270 votes – the Liberal lost us the seat.
It's just as well, as the country would have given
Churchill a good ride for his money. They have to
face the Trade Unions for wage increases now too.
No houses for the poor.

This is a very big week with the French
President's visit – dinners at the Mansion House,
Buckingham Palace, etc., the City is decorated for
them – you very likely will see it on the films.

Am going to a concert this evening, after a
political meeting, after-election summing up.
Tomorrow a 'bring and buy' sale for a good cause,
so my old age is occupied.

The other night we dined with the Royal Family.
I sat between Queen Elizabeth and Queen Mary,
not a bad seat. I get on well with them both. After
dinner we saw a poor film.

Another Christmas has come and gone. We have
a nice French girl to be with the children. The
place is full of Xmas presents.

Today we had our first skating. It seemed so
queer to be on the ice again after so many years.
I learned it in America at school where we had one
hundred days of ice each year in New Hampshire.
Those were the happiest days.

There is some excitement here over the
Coronation stone being stolen. It does no good to
anybody taking it. There is no way of selling it –

just stupid. There isn't much more to say. Much love dearest Edith, till we meet.

Edith read his letter while looking over the neat lawn and the once white picket fence. She remembered her parents pottering in the garden, the day Henry first walked her home, the birth of Lambie – all fine memories safely stacked within the walls of this house. After all these good times, however, they were finally leaving the past behind. There was no point in kidding themselves, Edith and Henry were grandparents and what they needed was a smaller, more manageable home.

Edith especially did not want a big house to run any more, with bedrooms gathering dust and chairs nobody sat in. She was tentative about uprooting Henry, but he said, 'As long as you're there, that's all that matters.'

So she picked up some glossy brochures, the sort that claim you can move to paradise, and chose a brand new bungalow. It came with a modern Franklin stove and an 'au naturel' garden with two pine trees and an abundance of red geraniums. Everyone said it would be easier to move with Henry than without him, though she knew they were just being kind – but to whom, she was not sure.

Edith longed to be able to open the front door and take her chair on to the sunlit porch. One large bedroom and an easy-to-clean hardwood floor would do nicely.

'Drop your watch and it's fatal,' Henry tried to joke.

Time passed slowly until moving day, and she was packing Maurice's last letter in a box. She carefully concealed it inside pictures of her parents and the children.

'Can I help you with that?' asked one of the removal man, still chewing on his lunch.

'No, I can manage,' she replied. 'This one stays with me. It's family.'

Maurice had been relieved to see the return of Winston Churchill as Prime Minister. He was seventy-seven, but his wartime experience guaranteed that he would place good Anglo-American relations high on his agenda. Maurice said, 'Well, I hope Churchill will do a good job in America with Truman. He is the only man that can do it for this country. I hope he does.'

But Britain's volatile domestic problems had already been overshadowed by events in Asia. North Korea, aided by Russia, had invaded its southern neighbour in June 1950. American troops, under the command of General Douglas MacArthur, had been flown in to help the beleaguered south. British forces soon entered into the conflict, setting the Communist bloc squarely against the West. Churchill's fighting spirit re-emerged as he declared, 'Once again, America and Britain find themselves associated in a noble cause. When bad men combine, good must associate.'

Maurice was appalled that, less than five years after the end of the Second World War, ordinary men were again being asked to make the ultimate sacrifice.

Well, I don't want to think of what is coming soon, but the news of what the enemy has in line is frightening. Poor American boys being killed like flies. I am glad about Ike. Thought he would never make it with all the mud being thrown. We are pleased over here. Let us hope Churchill's visit to Washington will produce something. We're all so tired of this Russian menace.

I went the other day to see an American

cemetery, near Cambridge. 5,500 gallant Americans lie there. Beautifully kept. They gave everything. A thousand thanks.

I am really very well, though I sleep badly these days, I don't know why.

Maurice was in a line of stop-start traffic, trying to get home before dark. Suddenly the car in front braked hard, forcing Maurice to swerve to the opposite side of the road. An oncoming car had begun to overtake and could not pull over. There was a loud crash as the two cars collided head on.

Badly shaken, Maurice checked himself. Nothing but a couple of small bruises. He looked over and saw the bonnet of the other car badly damaged. The driver was slumped over the wheel. Beside him was a woman, and on the back seat two terrified children sat crying.

Maurice was in shock, unable to believe what had happened. The man was dead. A simple manoeuvre on an ordinary road had left a family fatherless.

He went over the events in his mind to see if there was anything else he might have done. But even the inquest could not fully determine what had taken place.

The coroner concluded there was no question of overt negligence, to Maurice's great relief. He informed Edith of the verdict. 'The man whose car I hit, died of heart failure. Fortunately the police had his record of his heart trouble, so I got a five-pound fine for careless driving.'

Although he rarely spoke of it, the incident lived with him. His letters focused on his children, as if compensating for what the other family had been denied. 'I gave Edmund a set of steel-shafted golf clubs which pleases him. I'm taking them to the circus Saturday afternoon,' he wrote, adding, 'I can't understand men who sit home and drink, there are several like that here and I suppose in America too. What a waste of money and health.'

Maurice further distracted himself with a new pet project. The restoration of the ancient Guildhall of St George in King's Lynn, which had the illustrious claim of being one of the first theatres to stage Shakespeare's orig inal plays.

This was the venue Ruth had chosen for the town's first ever arts festival, which she hoped would give a cultural boost to the area by encouraging artists and musicians. There was to be a series of concerts, and Ruth also planned to play. Maurice pestered his wealthy relatives for dona- tions, to ensure everything would be ready on time. He wrote to Edith:

Well, the house sounds comfortable and modern. It was just like you to remember my sixty-sixth birthday. It all passed off like so many previous ones. I must say I don't feel my age. I'm glad to say I'm not in any way damaged by age. I'm playing tennis this evening, no pains or handicaps of any kind. It is the reward of living a good life.

We are having the most beautiful weather at the moment. Glorious sunshine every day. It makes such a difference to life, the rhododendrons are all out, a very pretty sight from my window.

We have been lent a villa on the Riviera this August and are to motor to the South of France early in August. The bathing is wonderful.

On the 24th July the Queen is re-opening an old Hall in King's Lynn. It has been restored after being empty for years. It dates to 1440. We have been very active in raising funds. My brother is coming over from New York for it. He gave the largest single gift – £2,000, which was very generous of him.

Well, I suppose life goes on just the same for you. Prices are high in America as here. With much love and kisses.

The year's end came round quickly and Maurice joined the royal family for the festive season. Maurice and the King talked and joked in one of the largest Sandringham gatherings since the war. They all relaxed and returned invigorated to their duties in the new year. He wrote to Edith, 'Christmas was as you said, surrounded by my children, well, happy. The royal family make it gay. There were several thousand at the church to see them troop out. Prince Charles walking with his father.'

I shot with the King the other day. I thought he was very well, but he looked tired. He smokes a lot too. I'm surprised the doctors albw that with only one lung. We also dined there. I sat between Queen Mary and Queen Elizabeth. They are beautiful at night with their fine clothes and jewellery.

I took Mary and Ruth to see 'South Pacific' the other night. We did enjoy it a lot. The music is lovely.

On the last day of January 1952, the King waved farewell to his daughter, Princess Elizabeth, as she left London Airport for East Africa, on the first part of a royal tour of Australia. It had been decided that she and Philip would cope well with the state visit, and the King had no qualms, believing their fresh approach would win over the Australian people.

As the plane taxied along the tarmac, the King waited in a biting wind, refusing to wear a hat against the cold. He looked tired, but smiled easily alongside the Queen and Princess Margaret. The future for the royals looked good, and there was great pride in their achievements. The King returned to Sandringham, where Prince Charles and his new baby sister, Princess Anne, were waiting to see their grandparents and aunt.

Five days later, Maurice was tramping the grounds of the royal estate, a gun beneath his arm. The King, who was in fine form and wearing his specially designed heated waistcoat, stood next to him, enjoying the cold, crisp conditions and counting the number of hares they had already shot. Maurice joked that the life of a retired man was very taxing.

Maurice returned cold but satisfied to Park House, feeling encouraged that his friend was in high spirits. Over in Sandringham, Princess Margaret played the piano for her mother and father, and they all gathered around the radio to listen for news of the African leg of Princess Elizabeth's tour. Around eleven o'clock the King, feeling tired, asked for a drink of hot cocoa to be brought to his bedroom. A watchman noticed him latching his bedroom window against the cold night air at midnight.

The King had arranged to go shooting again the next day, and when he failed to ring his bell in the morning, the valet went to investigate. His bedclothes were unruffled, and he appeared to have died peacefully in his sleep. Within moments, Dr Ansell, the King's physician, was speeding from the nearby village of Wolferton, but could do nothing.

Twenty-five-year-old Princess Elizabeth had been resting at the Sagana Lodge in Kenya when she was informed of her father's death by her husband. Arrangements to fly the couple back to London were under way within hours.

The King's body was laid in a coffin felled from Sandringham oak and placed before the altar of nearby St Mary Magdalene Church. Several of the green-coated gamekeepers shared round-the-clock guard duty along with foresters and footmen.

Three days later, the coffin was taken from Wolferton station to Westminster Hall in London, where Maurice arrived, deeply upset, to pay his last respects. George VI lay in state on a catafalque with a crimson velvet robe and the Imperial Crown on the coffin.

Maurice did not write to Edith for many weeks following Bertie's sudden death, his grief too raw.

Withdrawing quietly, he walked the moors where the two of them used to be seen out shooting, but this time without a gun. The skies looked darker without his old companion. And when at last he could bring himself to mention Bertie in a letter to Edith, it was with gracious, but sad reserve.

Two months ago today the King died. He seemed well the day before when I shot with him. I sat next to him at luncheon. He didn't complain of being tired or ill. The funeral was most impressive at Windsor. I have lost a good friend.

The new Queen has made a good impression so far. I feel I know her very well ever since I taught her to skate years ago now. The Coronation will be a big thing. Ruth and I will be in the Abbey. It is a great pageant.

Although grieving, Maurice still had his daughters to deal with. The London Season, in which the pair would be debutantes, was almost upon them, and Ruth had been busy organizing their 'coming out' ball. Although there was a two-year age difference between the girls, and Mary would have liked to be first, Frances insisted she was also ready. The young sisters were beautiful, titled and highly eligible for the right kind of suitors.

They had chosen a very smart venue in Park Lane, where the elite groups of guests assembled in their ball gowns and black ties. While Maurice was dancing with the Queen Mother, a particular admirer took his younger daughter, Frances, to one side.

His name was Johnnie Spencer, and he was a thirty-year-old viscount and heir to the sprawling Althorp estate in Northamptonshire. Johnnie was educated at Eton and had served as an officer in the army, where he was commissioned into the Royal Scots Greys.

'He fought in France in the war,' said Ruth.

'Good to know he did his duty,' said Maurice, not expecting that Johnnie would be interested in Frances after the evening was over.

Ruth watched the couple closely, surprised and thrilled with this prospective match. Johnnie was a very fine catch. The Spencers considered themselves true blue aristocrats and could trace their ancestry back to King Charles II. And although Frances was just half his age, Johnnie was far from deterred. An unsuccessful proposal to Lady Anne, the Earl of Leicester's daughter, still rankled, and he was under pressure to find a wife. Frances enamoured him with her feisty personality and razor wit. She was direct in a way that Johnnie had never encountered and, perhaps most importantly, she also adored children.

Maurice understood only too well that Johnnie, at the age of thirty, would be feeling the march of time and anxious to produce a son and heir. However, Maurice was very keen for his daughter to fall in love with a man of her own choosing.

But he had underestimated Frances's determination. Young and impressionable, she could think of no one else but Johnnie Spencer and, as the romance developed, was adamant that she had discovered the love of her life.

In the midst of such high drama, there was much activity at Sandringham as plans for the Coronation were progressing well. Sales of television sets soared when Elizabeth overruled her advisers and agreed to the live broadcast of the ceremony. With ten weeks to go, it was announced that twenty yards of purple velvet had been woven for the special coronation robe. Maurice wrote, 'We talked about the Coronation. They say 750,000 are to be here – just where they are to stay and see the procession I don't know. It will be a mad house. We shall be in the Abbey, well seated and comfy.'

The morning of 2 June 1953 was wet and cold, but did nothing to deter people lining the streets for hours in the hope of a good view. The congregation of eight thousand seated in Westminster Abbey had no idea of the behind-the-scenes disasters.

The orchestra and choir were so large that they could not all see the Director of Music's baton, and two assistants had to relay his conducting. The choristers, up since 5 a.m. and feeling light-headed, had to pass barley sugar sweets and sandwiches under their cassocks to keep them going through the long day. A new carpet had been laid, but its pile was running in the wrong direction, so it bunched up the Queen's robes. Whenever she tried to walk, the metal edge of her golden cloak caught in the pile and she whispered to the Archbishop of Canterbury, 'Get me started.'

At eleven o'clock there was an irrepressible mood of excitement and hope as St Edward's crown was placed on Elizabeth's head and she was crowned Queen Elizabeth II. The congregation shouted 'God Save The Queen!', and the princes, princesses, peers and peeresses, including Maurice and Ruth, placed their caps and coronets on their heads. Maurice later described the ceremony to Edith as 'too wonderful for words'. A new era had dawned.

SEVENTEEN

'Never Understand'

Park House,
Sandringham.
June 20th, 1953

Before I opened your second letter I knew what
had taken place. Poor Edith. There are some times
when it is hard to know what to say. I know too
what a great loss this has been to you. You must
console yourself that he had a long life and a
happy one. You have my love and sympathy in
these sad hours. God bless you in your hour of
trouble, all my love and kisses.

Maurice struggled for words to comfort her – it was a
sadness that Edith must bear alone. The death of Henry
was no great surprise, for he had lived to a grand age,
but that did not make the suffering any less. Hoping it
might help ease the pain if she had something to look
forward to, he offered to pay Edith's fare so they could
meet when he was next over. Perhaps Chicago? 'I often

look at your photo, where you are entering a doorway with a cafeteria in the background. It is very like you as I remember in the old days. I will never forget meeting you.' He wrote two weeks later to say:

Your last letter took a very short time to cross the continent and Atlantic. I read with interest the clipping about your husband's useful life. You must be very proud. I thought the snap of you and Jack excellent.

You ask about the girls? Frances returns to Paris for the autumn. Mary is looking for a job of sorts, foreign office. It isn't easy for girls like her to get an interesting job as they don't have to earn their living.

I am going to London to see the finals at Wimbledon. Little Mo will win the Ladies', I think. The Men's is open.

My brother has developed rheumatism in his knee and has gone for a cure in France – Vittel, it is well known for that ailment. He hates the cure, baths, waters. I don't blame him. He's too fat too.

Have just read about the death of a Harvard class-mate in an auto accident. I never quite forgave him for being a 'stay at home' in the First World War. He went to Washington in the Red Cross. A man should fight for his country. He was able bodied.

Just off to Lynn to buy household things. You are often in my thoughts. Much love and kisses.

Five months after leaving school, his daughter, Frances was running around the Park House tennis courts with Johnnie Spencer. In the middle of their match, when he

271

was getting well and truly beaten and refusing to play on, Johnnie got down on one knee and asked Frances to marry him. She threw her racket in the air and accepted without a second thought. Johnnie, perfectly mannered and a stickler for tradition, asked if he could change into his suit and tie.

'It won't help you win the second set,' said Frances.

'But it might help convince your father of my intentions,' laughed Johnnie.

Johnnie charmed Maurice and brushed aside any worries about her youth and inexperience. He persuaded Maurice that he loved her for who she was and believed they would make a good match. Maurice happily gave his permission for Johnnie to take his daughter's hand in marriage. He also knew that the union of the Fermoy and Spencer lines would catapult Frances closer to the Crown.

The Queen Mother found Johnnie most affable and told Ruth he was very suitable. They both felt sure that, at the tender age of seventeen, Frances could be moulded to the responsibilities of a viscountess and her impetuosity brought under control. The women predicted a good and lasting partnership.

The engagement provided the perfect opportunity for Ruth to cement her friendship with the Queen Mother. Since Bertie's death, the two women had become great friends and accomplices, and Ruth had been rewarded with an OBE. It was recognition beyond her wildest dreams, and she reciprocated by asking her Majesty to become patron of the King's Lynn Arts Festival. The Queen Mother was more than happy to help and took her role very seriously, driving herself the eight miles from Sandringham to King's Lynn every evening, and sometimes twice a day, during the festival season.

It was going to be a busy summer. Ruth wondered how she would cope with the demands of Frances's betrothal as well as the festival. With members of the royal family participating in both, she could not afford any hitches, especially as the preferred wedding venue required royal dispensation from the Queen.

There had been speculation at one time about Johnnie being a potential suitor for Queen Elizabeth. She had appointed him as one of her trusted equerries, but her marriage to Philip put paid to any amorous ideas he might have had. There were no hard feelings, and the two remained good friends.

The Queen found Frances more complicated and had never really warmed to her enthusiastic and high-spirited nature. Yet she would not stand in their way and gave her blessing.

The wedding was set for a year after the Coronation. Maurice could never have envisaged returning to Westminster Abbey so soon for such an auspicious occasion. He proudly realized that the Fermoys were to become part of the Abbey's history, Frances being only eighteen and the youngest twentieth-century bride to be married there. He told Edith his cheerful news,

> Curiously enough I was about to write and tell you one of my daughters is engaged. It sounds grand, but she will be the Countess of Spencer. He is very nice and first goes to Australia with the Queen. They will be married in July next year. He will come into huge estates after his father's death.

Maurice hoped to return to America to see Edith and his old friends but within days, his plans had changed as the enormity of the wedding's arrangements started to grip. He wrote to Edith:

I don't think I'll be able to make the Harvard reunion now with the wedding. It all costs money. We are busy with our lists of wedding guests. They number hundreds. With the Queen, Philip, the Queen Mother and Princess Margaret the crowds will be huge. My sister, brother, nieces too from the States.

Here is a very poor snap I'm sending to give you some idea of Frances.

I know how hard it must be to make a new life after all those married years. It is very difficult for me to advise you. Too bad you can't join up with some nice woman in sharing an apartment, they are hard to find, I know. Where you could share a car and a flat.

Mary and Edmund leave today for a skiing trip to Austria. It will be a change as there is no snow in England. I shall miss them. The second girl, the one engaged, is remaining here.

Had two days' shooting here with the Duke of Gloucester as host. Sat next to the Queen Mother at luncheon. The Queen's children were in church and behaved very well. Anne wore no hat and was very sweet.

There is very little shooting this year owing to the very bad hatching period. But I have plenty of public work on the side. Today I'm presiding at the opening of a chrysanthemum show and going to a local play.

I would love to see you if you come over.

Before the marriage could take place, Johnnie had to fulfil his duties escorting the Queen on a two-month royal tour of the Commonwealth. Frances was distraught that her new-found love was going to be out of the country. Johnnie was not above the occasional grand gesture and asked Frances if she would mind posing for a painting. What her fiancé had not told her was that he had arranged to have the portrait completed within twenty-four hours, so he could take it with him on the voyage. Ruth chaperoned Frances down to the cabins to say farewell and discovered that the bleary-eyed artist had already been sneaked on board for a theatrical unveiling of the canvas.

It was, however, a clumsy *au revoir* as Johnnie, given the job of recording the ship's departure using the Queen's own cine-camera, kept his eye firmly fixed on Frances. Wearing full dress uniform, he struggled to wave goodbye and record the view as they left port, his regimental sword flapping at his side.

Maurice, only too aware of the effect distance has on a relationship, reassured Frances that time would pass more quickly if she kept busy. With a wedding to plan there would be plenty to occupy her mind. As Maurice mopped up the tears at Park House, he sensed the next few months were going to be tense.

Frances found their time apart very hard and she pined. Maurice agreed with Ruth that the best option would be to send her to finishing school in Florence, where she could also shop for her wedding trousseau. It was an expensive decision for Maurice, as Frances did not stint when she saw the range of *haute couture*, and comforted herself by adding to her already extensive wardrobe.

It was Johnnie who was miserable, so with the majority of the tour complete, the Queen gave him special permission to disembark at Tobruk, in Libya. Then, rather than sail back to England, Johnnie flew home to be with his fiancée. He returned to great celebrations with the Fermoy family.

Somewhat relieved, Maurice wrote to Edith, 'Well, the winter is behind us in England. We have followed the Queen's journey through New Zealand and Australia. It seems to have been a success.'

For three months before the wedding, the tradesmen's entrance to Maurice and Ruth's London residence in Wilton Street, Belgravia turned into a delivery site. There was a constant stream of parcels and messages of good-will. 'We shall be busy right up to the day,' Ruth insisted to Maurice, who by now had grown weary of detailed discussions about table decorations and menus.

The number of wedding guests had swelled to over 1,700, and Maurice was not best pleased. He insisted that Ruth edit the list to a more manageable and affordable number. There followed tense discussions both in and out of Frances's hearing, and eventually a compromise was reached. All 1700 guests would attend the ceremony in the Abbey, but only 900 personal friends would be invited to the reception at nearby St James's Palace.

Maurice was content to oversee the seating plan, attempting to gauge who would get on with who and trying to remember those who must at all costs be kept separated.

He read that his daughter's betrothal had been dubbed 'the wedding of the year' by journalists. It was the talk of society. With just a couple of days to go he wrote to Edith, so absorbed with the task that he repeated the guest list:

My daughter is getting married on Tuesday. We are
having the Queen and Prince Philip, which is a
great honour of course. My brother and sister and
her daughters are here too for the great event.
I will write you all about it. I have no other news.
Bless you and love.

Light drizzle fell on the morning of the wedding, but a
huge crowd congregated, eager to catch a glimpse of the
royal guests in their best wedding finery. Maurice was
amused to learn that a verger was sniffing the air to differ-
entiate between guests and the public, a subtle perfume
apparently suggesting a society guest, while an overpowering aroma gave away the others.

Seated at the very front of the Abbey, Ruth, ever the
perfectionist, wore a turquoise blue taffeta dress with a
feathered hat dyed exactly to match. But there was no
sign of Frances. Although it was fashionable for the bride
to arrive late, the Queen was at fault. Her car had been
snarled up in traffic, further delaying the wedding car. The
only way for Maurice and Frances to avoid the dreadful
faux pas of the bride turning up ahead of the monarch
was to drive even slower.

'Well, at least she can't complain about anyone else
being late!' Maurice quipped. But Frances failed to see the
funny side.

Out of the silence he told her, 'You look beautiful.
Johnnie is a very lucky man.'

Frances reached for her father's hand. She wanted to
kiss his cheek but fretted it might leave a lipstick mark
on his skin and smudge her own make-up. Instead she
blew him a kiss.

When the Queen's car emerged from the traffic jam, the

crowds cheered at the monarch, unaware of the farce that had just taken place. Ten attendants sheltering under cover jumped to attention, removing their shawls and velvet cloaks, ready to take their place during Frances's grand entrance.

An overpowering scent of lilies hit Maurice as they entered the Abbey, and Frances began to tremble. Taking hold of her arm, he steadied his daughter. She looked like a princess in her dress of woven silk, embroidered with crystals, rhinestones and diamond-encrusted flowers. Now he was pleased that no expense had been spared.

Seven bridesmaids, including Frances's sister, Mary, moved forward to follow behind the bride and her father. The skirts of the girls' white spotted muslin dresses fanned out as they shuffled behind the bride, the younger ones fiddling with their long white gloves and blue sashes.

Arm in arm, Maurice and Frances smiled at each other and began the long walk past the Tomb of the Unknown Warrior, where Maurice bowed his head slightly. Adjusting her diamond-tipped tiara, Frances's veil fell softly around her fresh cheeks. When she saw Johnnie, she began to appreciate the significance of what she was about to do, and her wedding bouquet quivered.

The sea of familiar faces – friends, family, workers from the Althorp and Sandringham Estates and especially the Royal Family – made it hard for Frances to contain her emotions. As they neared the candle lit High Altar, Maurice gently released her and gave an encouraging nudge towards Johnnie, passing over his precious Frances for a future with the Spencer family.

The Bishop of Norwich solemnly pronounced, 'You are making an addition to the home life of your country on which, above all others, our national life depends.' There was a hush across the Abbey.

Their vows completed, the couple walked slowly to the side of the Abbey to sign the marriage register and were followed by the Queen,

Prince Philip, the Queen Mother and Princess Margaret, Johnnie's parents, Jack and Cynthia, and Maurice and Ruth. They all inscribed the certificate. It had gone beautifully, and Maurice put his arm tenderly around Ruth's shoulder.

Outside the Abbey, a guard of honour with eight soldiers from Johnnie's former regiment proudly held their swords aloft. The weather had lifted and Johnnie blinked into the sunlight, smiling at his new Viscountess. Walking beneath the arch of glinting steel towards the waiting photographers and cheering crowds, they felt invincible.

The ceremony over, Maurice relaxed and heard a bystander shout, 'You're a lucky man.' Maurice acknowledged him with a wave and went to a group of elderly ladies. One dressed in her Sunday best placed her hand on his lapel and adjusted the carnation in his buttonhole. 'Can't be askew for the Queen, my lord,' she muttered.

The invited guests moved on to St James's Palace for the wedding breakfast and Maurice tapped his breast pocket to reassure himself that his wedding speech was there and not, as he irrationally feared, still on his desk in Belgravia. He rarely enjoyed public speaking, especially in such celebrated company. His maiden address in the House of Commons paled against the anxiety of this special moment.

'Seeing you prepare for a speech is like watching a game of chess,' said Frank. 'First you move your fork slightly to the left, then your knife goes to the right, and the glass . . . well, goodness knows where that will end up!'

Maurice had tried hard over the years to keep still, but

he never lost the urge to fidget. As he rose to speak, he pushed his hands deep inside his pockets to stop them waving about. He did not want to appear overawed today. His daughter had elevated the Fermoy family beyond anything his grandfather could have believed. Surely even he would be proud of Maurice now?

Looking over at Frances, the child who was born as one King died, Maurice knew she had not yet grasped the world she was about to enter. Frances would set off on honeymoon and return to a new home and a new way of life. She would now come to Sandringham only as a visitor. His little girl suddenly looked all grown up. Seeing Frances and Johnnie together, he hoped the love they had found would last a lifetime.

Henry's death gave Edith endless time. Lambie would bring her family round and show off her first-born son Hal, named after her dear father. Edith loved watching the little chap stretch out and kick his legs on the sunny front porch, wearing the little cowboy suit she had made for him.

'A right little Howitt,' she told Lambie.

Edith's move failed to curb her desire for travel and her wanderlust mingled with her new-found independence. She decided she now had time to visit Maurice. Yet whenever she thought of that journey she found herself making excuses, putting obstacles in the way of the trip. Although she yearned to see him, having the freedom to do so was not enough.

She missed her friends. And Henry. Life was so different as a single woman, and silly little things brought the strangeness home. Whenever she shopped, it was now for one. If she walked down the street, she found herself stopping to talk at every corner to avoid the silence of home.

Some women even saw her as a threat to their husbands and never answered her calls. She now locked the door last thing at night when Henry always used to, and turned off the light to lie in the dark alone.

Frances's wedding had put Maurice on the front pages and he was again in the public eye. Edith had no desire to feel hunted; stolen moments needed a strength she could not find. The wedding brought home to her the ordinary events of existence; the birthdays, weddings and deaths that would always be, for them, separate times in separate worlds.

Yet, down the years, Maurice had talked quite openly about his family and the small incidents and adventures that made up his daily life. Edith felt part of the pleasure he had in first seeing Mary, Frances and Edmund. How much it meant to be a father and the people he had met along the way. All this she knew.

Edith did little things to show she cared and to keep Maurice close. She collected a series of articles in American magazines, so he could see how Frances's wedding had been reported there. She laughed when he replied:

I was very glad for the newspaper clippings.
Curiously enough a man I thought was dead wrote
me he had seen it on the television in Buffalo! Also
a friend from Philadelphia. The bride is back from
a lovely trip through Italy and Austria.

I have a piece of news. Mary is now engaged
too. She is to marry Lord Kemsley's son, Hon.
Anthony Berry. A very nice man, 29, Editor of the
Kemsley Press. They will be getting married in
November. Two weddings in one year is quite an
effort for my wife, as you can imagine.

281

As I am typing this I hear that an agreement on a cease-fire has been reached. Let us hope this Potomac Agreement may pave the way to World Peace. Our festival begins on Monday. The Queen Mother received the 'Freedom of Lynn' and unveils a portrait of my wife. We shall have the house full of guests. Well, I haven't anything more to add. Much love and kisses.

Another letter quickly followed with confirmation of his first daughter's marriage.

Mary's wedding is on November 25th. My brother says he is coming over for it. It won't be as 'grand' as Frances's but we shall make it just as nice. Wedding at St Margaret's, Westminster.

Last weekend was particularly nice. I was entertaining an American couple. Like most kind people they bought champagne, cigars. We played bridge after dinner. They were very lucky in being able to hear the Duke of Edinburgh read the lessons in church. They had wonderful sunny weather too.

Things look better for the world. Why we have to fight these days I'll never understand.

Edith loved his optimism, but decided to write and tell Maurice she could not face the long journey across the ocean alone and her trip would have to be delayed. For the moment she felt safer at home. 'After the events of the last few months, I have decided it would be better to postpone my trip until I feel a little stronger. After all, you don't need me crying on your shoulder, as well.'

Maurice realized he had been so preoccupied with his daughters' weddings that he had not understood the depth of Edith's suffering. Her letter shocked him. He hated thinking of her like that. The guilt and unease shook him out of his complacency and he decided enough time had been lost waiting for the right moment. Once his duties as a father were complete, he would go to her. He would sail over to New York.

When she got his note, Edith ran on to the front porch waving the letter in the air, cheering to herself. It was remarkable to think that at sixty-six and seventy years old they were about to meet again. Their love really had survived. Against all the odds.

Maurice was waiting very quietly in the hotel bar. He had been there for over an hour and his third drink had slipped down easily. Probably too easily. He still felt incredibly nervous.

On the wall several large clocks ticked ominously, each marked with a different city and a different time. London – 1 a.m.; Paris – 12 a.m.; New York – 8 p.m. The barman raised his eyebrows and pointed at his empty glass Maurice shook his head and rubbed his hands together.

'No, thanks,' he said, looking at his wristwatch even though he knew the time.

'So where do you hail from, sir?' asked the barman.

'Just up the road,' replied Maurice, not wanting to talk.

'You sound kinda different from the folks we get around here.'

'That's because I've been too long away,' said Maurice.

'Well, here's hoping you have a swell time now you're back.'

'I intend to,' he replied.

Maurice brushed his grey receding hair straight back, wondering if he should have had it cropped by his barber before coming over. He opened his newspaper and spread it out over the counter, tracing an article with his finger as he read the print. It made a change; it had been impossible to get a newspaper for nearly a month with all the strikes at home. What an irony that he'd had to come to New York to find out that MPs had just voted to retain the death penalty.

'So what's happening?' asked the barman. 'Anything new?'

Maurice shook his head and walked towards one of the padded booths at the back of the room. He manoeuvred himself into the seat and sat doing nothing for a while. It had been a long journey over on the boat and, despite the luxury of the cabin, he had not slept well.

His sweating brow was the tell-tale sign. The clocks showed ten past the hour. She was always late. It used to annoy him when he was a young man with all the time in the world. Funny, he thought, that all these years later, with time now running out, he no longer minded.

One thing that never changed was the slow crunching in his stomach at the prospect of seeing her again. He was seventy, but the same excitement he felt on that train a lifetime ago made him queasy.

He heard a voice and knew.

'Are you waiting for someone?' she asked.

'Forty long years,' he said.

Edith was standing by his chair, the light anointing her laughing face. He looked at her, the fur draped around her neck, a stylish black bag swinging in the crook of her arm. And, of course, the pillbox hat. In all the years they had known each other, Edith had never failed to wear a hat when they went out. And today from underneath, silver hair fell around her plump cheeks.

'I'm so glad you came,' she said. 'I can't thank you enough.'

He took her gloved hand in his. 'How I've stayed away I'll never know.'

'You never really left me.'

'Darling Edith,' he whispered, kissing her hand.

'Can I get you guys anything?' said the barman hopefully.

'Can you mix an Old-Fashioned Cocktail?' asked Edith. The barman was silenced.

'Never mind,' said Maurice, leaving a five-dollar bill. 'We have everything we need.'

They could have gone anywhere in New York, but all they wanted was to be together in comfort, to talk and enjoy the precious time they had left.

In the hotel lift, Edith leaned her head on his shoulder and they did not stop smiling all the way up to the fifth floor. Each time the doors opened at another level, they moved apart and stared in different directions. When they reached the penthouse, he wrapped his arm around her and they walked in together.

The fire was lit, fresh flowers were on the table blossoming next to a photograph of Edith.

'You've gone to a lot of trouble,' she said.

'It is my turn to care for you,' he said.

They turned to look at each other in the gilt framed mirror, neither wanting to see the two elderly people staring back, but instead the fresh faces of Maurice and Edith as they were on the train so very long ago.

'How do you do, Mrs Travis?' he said, staring at the reflection.

'And how do you do, Mr Roche?' she replied.

'I'd say just a little older, but otherwise much the same,' said Maurice.

'But are you any wiser?' she asked.

'I hope not,' he said, kissing her forehead.

In the bedroom he beckoned her to lie down beside him. Edith closed her eyes and listened to the hum of traffic and the crackle of the logs on the fire. She was at peace.

'Three days and three nights that changed our lives,' she whispered.

'It might all have been so different,' he said. 'But without you, my life would be unfinished.'

'I could have spent my whole life searching for you,' she said.

'It has always been easy to love you, Edith. That was never the hard part.'

She felt his hand find hers.

They were reunited. Maurice had led a privileged life and been a friend to kings and princes, but as he stroked her hair he realized what he had missed.

'Tell me what you see from your window,' she asked.

'How do you mean?'

'When you sit at your desk and write me, I want to know what you are looking at,' she replied.

He lay silently for a moment, and thought back to his drawing-room at Park House.

'I see the most beautiful fragrant lilac. It blooms all round the garden, this lovely, light purple colour, surrounded by smooth, heart-shaped leaves.' He kissed the end of her nose. 'It's almost perfect,' he said.

Edith looked up at his happy face. Forty years. It had taken them that long. And here they were, lying with their heads on feather pillows, hands gripped tightly. She was looking into the beautiful face of the man she could never have.

'Think of me when you see your lilac, won't you?' she said.

'I always do . . .' he said. He kissed her lightly upon her eyelids. 'I always have.'

EIGHTEEN

'hodie mihi cras tibi'

Maurice went to New York to stay with his brother. He was feeling exhilarated. Seeing Edith had given him a renewed sense of purpose and put him in a buoyant frame of mind. There was a lightness about her that he had never found anywhere in his life. She had promised to meet him again in the autumn, during his next visit to America, and for now he could bask in the contentment of his earlier trip. The fine spring morning and the early sun added to his good spirits.

His brother greeted him with his normal gusto.

'Come, you need a drink,' he said, shaking his hand hard.

'Well, maybe a small one,' said Maurice.

'Something wrong with you?' asked Frank. He was half teasing, but he had noticed that his twin was perspiring heavily.

They sat together making small talk until Maurice said suddenly, 'Remember Edith Travis?'

'How could I forget? If you'd had your way I'd be in the House of Lords and you'd be leading my "aimless life" as you so delicately put it!'

Maurice laughed as he crossed his legs. 'I was young and impetuous,' he said, brushing imaginary specks of dust from his trousers.

'And blinded by love. I really thought you were going to do something stupid.'

'I did. I gave her up.' Maurice sipped his whisky. 'I went to see her, Frank.'

His brother raised an eyebrow and looked over the top of his crystal tumbler, waiting to hear more.

'In New York,' said Maurice.

'Somehow I'm not surprised. What was she like after all these years?'

'Beautiful.'

'Older . . . ?'

'Still beautiful.' Maurice suddenly felt a need to share Edith with his brother. 'We've been writing all this time.'

'But you've never been much of a letter writer.'

'True, but I am in this case.'

'Something tells me she's more than your correspondent, Maurice.'

Maurice paused a little too long. 'And we've been seeing each other over the years, when we could.'

A taut silence stretched between them, Maurice stared into the bottom of his glass.

Frank's face held steady. 'I'm glad for you, Maurice. Honestly. You made some hard choices and you've lived by them. Love takes some finding. I've never managed it, and you discovered a way.'

'There were times when I thought I'd go mad without her, Frank,' Maurice said, struggling to regain his composure. 'I'm going back to see her, but next time for longer.' He fanned his face with a newspaper.

'As long as you're happy,' said Frank. 'But I don't need to tell you that after all this time.' Frank looked long and hard at his brother. 'Are you all right, Maurice?' Seeing his flushed appearance he asked, 'How long is it since you had a check-up? I've got a good doctor friend who'd be happy to see you.'

'Really, I'm fine. Relax, Frank. Look at me, I have never been better.'

The two men shook hands and parted.

Maurice wandered through the streets of King's Lynn with his familiar shopping basket. It was a glorious English June day, sunny and warm. He had left his bicycle at home this morning, deciding to save his legs, and driven the short distance into town.

He was feeling rather tired, which was hardly surprising as he had been so busy of late after the trip to America and the birth of his sweet grandchild, Sarah. He was relieved that, despite his fears, Frances and Johnnie were still regular visitors to Park House and came willingly to show off their first-born.

While in town, Maurice walked into his favoured barber shop, as it had been a while since his last trim and he always preferred to keep his hair neat, a habit from his army days. He also rather needed to sit down for a few minutes and catch his breath. Ruth had been on at him to give up his cigars, but he was having none of that nonsense. At seventy he not only deserved but had earned his pleasures. In fact, he was hoping Edith would send him another box of Robert Burns from America.

He waited, flicking through the newspapers, wondering if he should come back later when the queue was a bit shorter. Then the barber flourished his white towel and indicated Maurice should go to the high-backed red leather chair, the most comfortable seat in the shop.

As the barber tucked the towel into his starched white collar, Maurice suddenly felt claustrophobic. He adjusted his tie, trying to relieve a pain creeping down his side. Removing his handkerchief from his breast pocket, he dabbed the perspiration from his brow.

'Are you all right, Lord Fermoy?' asked the barber. 'You look a bit under the weather.'

'Just a spot of dizziness, that's all,' he said. 'It'll soon pass, must be the heat.'

'I'll get you a glass of water,' said the barber and went into the back of the shop.

Maurice fanned himself with the paper, hating having created such a fuss.

'Thank you,' said Maurice, trying to grip the slippery glass with both hands. He sipped the water, but the cold of the liquid stung his throat.

A crushing pain was squeezing his chest, and his left arm felt as if it had been hit by a huge weight. Each breath in and out was becoming progressively harder. His ears pulsed with the thud thud thud of his own heartbeat. Glass smashed against the hard shiny floor.

The agony from his tightening chest jolted his body. Struggling for air he sucked in hard between gritted teeth.

The barber's head came close, his lips moved again, but Maurice could not discern a word.

Maurice tried to nod, but his heart was racing and he gripped the side of his chest. He struggled to stand up. Maurice was gasping wildly and his eyes stared blankly into the distance. He didn't even have the strength to ask for help, and then his legs gave way.

'Call an ambulance,' yelled the barber, bending down

and scrabbling to undo the top button of Maurice's shirt. 'Quickly!'

And then there was blackness.

After emergency resuscitation he was transferred to the Gaywood Hall Nursing Home in King's Lynn for round-the-clock care. For several days, with all his family sitting at his bedside, Maurice remained stable and to their great relief appeared to be showing signs of improvement. A report was leaked to the press that things looked hopeful.

But it was a false dawn. Maurice never fully recovered consciousness.

Ten days later, on 8 July 1955, he died. He was seventy, and Ruth had been widowed at the age of forty-six. It was now her turn to be consoled by the Queen Mother.

Edmund, Maurice's son and heir, sixteen years old and fatherless, had become the fifth Lord Fermoy. It was a title he would rather not have had in these circumstances.

On Wednesday 13 July, at half past two in the afternoon, the community came together at St Margaret's Church in King's Lynn for Maurice's memorial service. It was the largest gathering in King's Lynn for years, with over a thousand people wanting to pay their respects. What could anyone say of this man loved by so many? How could anyone express what they were feeling? Ordinary people, aristocrats and royalty all mourned his passing.

The vicar tried to sum up their loss.

A gash has been torn in our community. We
honour him as we remember him, the hours spent
in the service of this town, the care bestowed upon
the constituency over many years and the willing

service poured out abundantly to so many of our organizations and societies, the generous help given to so many good causes and to so many in need. If our loss is great, how much greater is that of those he loved so deeply.

Sir Patrick Hannon, a fellow MP, paid his respects.

It would be difficult to recall any member of the House of Commons in my time who brought greater charm and a more warm atmosphere of friendship to the membership of the House than Maurice Roche, whose Irish character and qualities of expansive friendship will long be remembered. Maurice Roche was one of those Anglo-Irish colleagues in our parliamentary life whose memory will be recalled with affection and the sad reflection that it will be difficult to look upon his like again.

For a man who believed that duty was the linchpin of the soul, it was fitting that the congregation stood for the Act of Remembrance and the words Maurice most cherished.

'They shall not grow old as we that are left grow old;
Age shall not weary them, nor the years condemn;
At the going down of the sun and in the morning;
We will remember them.'

He was buried in the small walled graveyard at Sandringham Church, surrounded by princes and workmen. Nothing could have been more appropriate.

Maurice was laid to rest, and each day as the sun rose, his stone would cast a shadow westwards, towards America. To where life had truly begun.

Edith sat by her writing desk, letting her feelings flow. All guilt gone, she penned her languid letters telling Maurice how much he meant to her and the contentment she felt about the honesty they had shared. She allowed the words they had whispered when alone together to spread across the page.

As she wrote, it was as if she had been set free by their last moments. Lying in each other's arms, Maurice had talked of his unhappy times at Park House. He confessed that all the pomp and ceremony gave him little comfort compared to that of true love. That was what he most wanted from life and was now his one regret.

He had admitted that throughout the years, he always wanted her. The aching had never waned. But his life had been destined for duty and honour, and for that he was proud. The sadness came from the false belief that by turning away from love, he had become a better man.

'My children are now all but gone,' he had told her. 'And there is very little left for me.'

Edith had hardly dared ask the question. But as they aged the chances of their seeing each other became slimmer each year. She needed to know while they were together. She was far too old to wait and let things happen. That was for times past.

'And us?' she asked. 'What of us?'

Maurice bit his top lip, as he often did, and lowered his head.

'We have made mistakes, but we're too old to change them now.'

'We could have had so much more,' she said.

'How could we have more than this?' he replied, kissing the top of her head. 'There is no more. We have had it all.'

Yet despite these last precious moments her letters went ignored. Not a word came back. It made no sense. Why would he not reply?

For the truth was, as Edith Howitt kissed another envelope goodbye, she had no idea that Maurice Roche had died.

At first she thought he was busy, so she continued to write her usual chatty notes, telling him anything and everything of her days. The way next door's new rooster crowed so loud she had to put cotton wool in her ears; how she had enrolled at the local college on some European history courses; about the new friends she was making. She filled page after page with her silly news.

As the days turned to weeks she grew more afraid. She was writing almost daily in the hope of a reply. But nothing came. Puzzled, she re-read his last letters to seek a clue. Perhaps a sign that he had intentions of which she was not aware. But there was nothing extraordinary, just the same lovely words.

She delicately lifted a few leaves of the blue writing paper and kissed his signature. He professed his love, ending with 'a good kiss'. What she would do now to feel his lips upon hers.

One of his last notes read, 'Ruth and I went to a wonderful party at the American Embassy on Washington's birthday. The Queen and Prince Philip were there, and all the "tops" including Sir Winston. We stayed till 2.45 a.m. I saw a great many Americans I knew. I saw my daughter this week who is having her baby. All is well so far. Very young to have a baby at nineteen. Dear Frances.'

His daughter seemed but a child herself and Maurice hoped she would cope. How thrilled he had been to know he was about to be a grandfather. Why had he not written with news? He had promised to let her know about the christening.

After staring into the clear dark sky as the moon shone bright one night, she dialled his home telephone number. Her fingers trembled as she waited to hear a ring at the other end of the line, and then the clipped English voice answering, 'Fermoy Residence, how may I help you?' But it never came, because she replaced the receiver, unable to complete the call.

Edith's notes became shorter, but they had a more forceful tone. 'How are you?' she would ask. 'Did you get back to England without a hitch? Please let me know. I am worried about you. All love Edith.'

One by one her letters arrived at Park House. But they were no longer scooped up by a trusted servant and quietly handed to Maurice when no one else was around. Instead, her Californian letters were piled up, unread and untouched, on a table in Maurice's study. Until one day when they could be ignored no longer. Ruth, having recovered from the initial shock of Maurice's death, noted the growing pile of letters from Marin County, California. But she never opened them. One day they were placed in a bag and destroyed. Then she called her secretary and instructed that a note be sent to Edith.

On 7 November the secretary typed a dictated letter. It was posted and forgotten about.

A week later, sitting on her front porch, Edith opened the letter franked 'London SW1'.

I am writing for Lady Fermoy to tell you that Lord

Fermoy died rather suddenly in July. Lady Fermoy
is at present abroad or she would have written to
you herself, and she is sorry that there has been
some delay in answering your letter.

She dropped the letter on the bed. Icy cold, her hands
turned to claws and plucked at the hem of her dress. The
thread came undone and she yanked hard. It still wouldn't
come, so she ripped it.

He was dead.

They had been together, laughing and loving. He had
been warm to her touch. She had kissed him farewell. Felt
his heart, strong against hers.

But he was dead.

Her head was empty, stunned into the silence of the
stars by the power of a single word. Dead. She stood there.
Looking down at the note. Wondering what to do next.
But it didn't really matter any more. Nothing mattered
any more. All those letters, all those months and she had
never known.

Edith had been dismissed and sent away. They had left
her with pen in hand, while they wept and cried and buried
him in the ground. They had that luxury, while she had
nothing except a huge chasm that could never be filled.
And she had no one to tell. No one to mourn with. No
one.

She sat down by her desk and slid open the top drawer
where his pictures, letters and newspaper cuttings lay.
Forty years of love smuggled tight. And who would ever
know? She pushed it shut and forced herself to think.

They might want to sweep her away and put her in her
place. But they didn't know Edith Travis Howitt. She was
worth more than this. Their fancy manners would not

stop her from doing what was right. Hiding behind headed notepaper did not impress her. Four months to post off a letter of explanation was the height of bad manners.

She was free, for the first time in over forty years. There was no one to hold her back and she would not be told what to do.

She would show Maurice how much she loved him and no one could stop her.

Eighteen months later, in April 1957, Edith boarded HMS *Queen Mary* in New York docks. The ship was bound for Southampton. She had never travelled abroad before, and now was sailing half-way around the world. Maurice gave her all the strength she needed.

From the moment she had received notice of his death, she knew she had to come. There was no time to wallow in shame or thought, she had to act. Carefully working out her schedule, Edith instinctively knew when to arrive. Springtime. At sixty-eight years old, she was still being driven by a lifelong passion to be with the man she had loved for so long.

From Southampton she took the train to London and booked in to the Basil Street Hotel, in Knightsbridge. It was good and central and the sights of the city beckoned her outdoors. Parliament, where Maurice had spent much of his working life, and the green parks he loved to stroll through. Settling into her room, Edith ordered a pot of tea and sat on the edge of her bed, hardly able to believe that at last she really was in England.

There was a knock at her door and she opened it to find a bellboy holding out his hand.

'Telegram for you, madam,' he said.

'Thank you, but who could this be from?' said Edith

298

handing the lad a tip. Somewhere in the back of her mind she wanted to believe it might be from Maurice, asking her to meet him. Opening the envelope, she let out a huge laugh. Almost hysterical. The cable read: 'Coming Tuesday, please meet Dublin boat train arriving Euston Station about 12. Please book room – Forrest Travis.'

'He never stops trying, does he, Maurice?' she said, throwing the telegram on to the floor. 'But I am not here for you, Forrest.'

The long straight road into Sandringham crosses land belonging to the monarchy as far as the eye can see. The spring sunlight played off the lush greenness of the trees, casting long shadows across the ground. Fresh grass had just been mowed for the first time that year, leaving the sweet smell of meadow in the air. Birds were nest building, flying busily back and forth to the hedgerows. Edith, overcome by a sense of freedom, watched it all from the window of her taxi as they sped along the lane.

The ancient oaks slipped past as they approached an opening, and the driver from Wals Taxis drew up next to a pathway, leading away into distant hills.

'Down there, love,' he said, nodding towards a war memorial.

'Can you wait?' asked Edith.

'How long are you going to be?' he replied.

'A little while.'

He checked his watch and said, 'Here, take my card and give me a call from the phone box when you're ready. I can be back in fifteen minutes.'

Edith stepped out of the car and felt the crunch of gravel underfoot. It could not be far now. On her left, a high stone wall covered in glistening lichen ran towards open fields. It then lurched left, at a large pair of elaborate wrought-iron gates, marking the entrance to a path which could only lead to the church.

She walked slowly down the path, watching for any sign, something she might recognize. Placing her face close to the small bouquet of daffodils she was carrying, she breathed deeply. They were wrapped in plain paper and tied with ribbon. She felt an overpowering sadness and was glad of the peaceful silence.

Her heart jumped as she spotted a small spire peering through the trees. With Maurice now seemingly within her grasp, Edith felt overwhelmed by the effort of her journey. It seemed as if she had been travelling for ever. She had saved for so long, needing to fulfil this dream but never really believing she would get here.

After all the months of struggle, here she was, and yet she felt so ill-prepared. How easy it had been to make the journey in her head, and how wonderful she had felt each time she imagined it. There had been a safety in sitting on her porch in Marin County. But now all she had was the sky above and the earth beneath. There were no dreams to hold her tight. And she was about to face reality. Her lip quivered. She was not sure she could do this.

'Count, you silly fool,' she told herself. 'Count!'

She took a deep breath and started: 'One . . . two . . . three . . .'

Her footsteps could be heard along the path, and as she stepped up to the lych-gate leading to the church, Edith exhaled loudly and exclaimed, 'One hundred and twenty-two steps!'

Edith's eyes were drawn upward to the markings carved into the wooden lintel. They were in Latin, and Edith puzzled over the unfamiliar words – *hodie mihi cras tibi*. She took out her small address book and scribbled them down. That was for later.

Her body shook as she looked around the tiny churchyard, cradled within a small stone wall, which kept the elements at bay. Maurice was here somewhere, and that helped to calm her. Looking out at the gravestones peppered between the neat, well-kept grass, she muttered. 'Where are you, Maurice?'

She stopped, momentarily wondering if she should read all the inscriptions. But then she saw cascading over the far wall of the churchyard a most perfect-coloured plant. Its delicate hue reminded her of the shimmering light as the sun set across the Rockies. She moved a little closer and knew.

It was lilac.

She had no doubt then where he was. Edith's hand came up to her mouth. 'Oh no!' she said out loud.

His grave was surrounded by lilac, in all its shades and brilliance.

She walked respectfully, placing her daffodils carefully on the top of the wall and, using both hands, twisted three lilac sprigs from an overhanging branch. Then, mixing both wild flowers together, she knelt in front of his stone and placed the simple posy down on the soft ground.

She kissed her fingertip and traced it across the outline of his name hewn into the grey granite. But her eyes were dry. There could be no more tears.

'Together,' she said. 'Nothing can ever separate us again.'

Kneeling, she closed her eyes and waited to hear the sounds Maurice would have known so well from all his years of living here. But nothing came. It was as if in silence they could be together. She had, at last, come to see his England.

She brushed the grass from her knees and walked sombrely back towards the lych-gate. With each step, she remembered the first time she saw into his blue eyes on the train, and when she reached the steps, she thought about what Maurice had said all those years ago on his way to war: 'I will never leave you.'

And he was right.

Glancing around, she saw an estate worker striding down the path carrying his fork.

Edith attracted his gaze and, as if urged by a silent whisper, found herself asking, 'Do you know what the Latin inscription on the gate means?'

Unperturbed by her American accent, the gardener nodded nonchalantly and said, 'Mine today, thine tomorrow.'

As the clock chimed, she said, 'I understand now.'

And when he shall die
Take him and cut him out in little stars
And he will make the face of heaven so fine
That all the world will be in love with night
And pay no worship to the garish sun.

Epilogue. January 2005

Frank George Burke Roche
Frank died on 30 October 1958 in Newport, Rhode Island, aged seventy-four. He never married. He corresponded with Edith after Maurice's death and they shared their grief. He wrote:

> Many thanks for your letter of sympathy in my great loss, which I appreciate. My brother's death was the worst blow that I have ever received, and I am only just now getting over it and enjoying life again. When my brother was in New York in April, I saw by his flushed face that he was suffering from my complaint of high blood pressure, but he refused to see my doctor or take the wonder drug for that ailment. He did not want to know the worst as he was having too good a time. What made it particularly hard for me was that I was taken ill myself in France before Maurice had his stroke and had to come home to be with my doctor, so I never saw him again or attended his funeral.

The last time he wrote it was to say, 'I have just left St Claris hospital after a heart attack and it was the worst ordeal of my life . . . I suppose I was lucky to be alive. But life has lost a lot of its charm, not being able to play tennis again. However there are much worse off than I am. I miss Maurice terrible too. But one has to go on. I hope you are well and happy and God bless you too.'

Cynthia Burke Roche

Maurice's sister married Arthur Scott Burden, who was fatally injured in a polo match in 1920. Two years later, she married Guy Fairfax Cary, a New York lawyer and banker, who died in 1950, aged seventy. Cynthia died at the family home in Elm Court, Newport, Rhode Island on 18 December 1966, aged 82.

The Honourable Frances Ruth Burke Roche

Frances died at her home, 'Callanish', on the Isle of Seil near Oban in Scotland, on 3 June 2004, aged sixty-eight. She is survived by her children, Sarah, Jane and Charles, the ninth Earl Spencer.

Her marriage to Johnnie Spencer produced two other children, baby John, in 1960, who lived for only a few hours, and Diana, in 1961. Diana became Princess of Wales in 1981 after her marriage to Prince Charles. The marriage produced two sons, Prince William and Prince Harry. Charles and Diana divorced in 1996. Diana died on 31 August 1997, aged thirty-six, in a car crash in Paris. Her son William – Maurice's great-grandson – is destined to become King of England.

Frances divorced Johnnie in 1969, and Ruth Fermoy testified against her daughter in the custody case for the children. Frances lost, and then married wealthy wallpaper magnate Peter Shand Kydd. They moved to Scotland but separated in 1990, remaining lifelong friends. She converted to catholicism in 1994. Her relationship with Ruth was always fraught, but Frances adored her father and said of him, 'It did not matter whether you came from a croft, a castle or a caravan, he would always listen. I was much too young to lose him at nineteen.'

The Honourable Mary Cynthia Burke Roche
Maurice's eldest daughter married the Honourable Anthony Berry in 1954. They were divorced in 1966 and he became an MP and was later murdered by the IRA in their bombing of the Grand Hotel, Brighton, in 1984. She married twice more, both times unsuccessfully, and reverted to her maiden name of Roche. She has carried on her mother's work with the King's Lynn Arts Festival.

Edmund James Burke Roche, the fifth Baron Fermoy
Maurice's only son was educated at Eton and Sandhurst and the Royal Agricultural College, Cirencester. He served as an officer in the UK and Germany before leaving the army in 1966 to farm full time. He was a district councillor and Mayor of Hungerford in 1983. A talented pianist, he flew his own helicopter and loved to ski. Edmund was also a successful steeplechase rider and polo player. A troubled soul, he once asked his sister, Frances, why they were so different, 'It's how you come out of the egg,' she replied.

He met Edith Travis Howitt at her retirement home in California and they spent an afternoon talking about his father and looking through her letters and keepsakes. Edmund later sent her this letter.

There could have been no greater and more
delightful surprise than meeting you on the recent
polo trip to Pebble Beach. I was so glad that you
rang up and got in touch and it was a great relief
to be able to find the right way out of Pacific
Grove to come and see you. It was fascinating to
hear you talk of your friendship with my father,
you have no idea how little seems to have been
known in my family about his life in America
before he came over to this country. It was a
complete blank until you started to produce your
wonderful collection of photographs and letters.
I cannot possibly thank you enough for the whole
scrapbook and the interesting newspaper articles.
The one about Frank Work is particularly
interesting. I can understand why my father
must have been especially fond of you. He
was never particularly a great letter writer,
you must have received many of the few he
wrote.

They corresponded and Edmund sent family photographs and cards until Edith's death.

Edmund shot himself on 19 August 1984, aged forty-
five, on his Berkshire estate and is buried next to Maurice
in the Sandringham churchyard. His eldest son, also named
Maurice, inherited the title to become the sixth Baron
Fermoy.

Lady Ruth Fermoy
Widowed at the age of forty-six, Ruth was appointed by
the Queen Mother as an Extra Woman of the Bedchamber,
later promoted to Woman of the Bedchamber in 1960 –

a senior lady-in-waiting role. Ruth was granted the freedom of King's Lynn in 1963 for services to the town. She was appointed an OBE in 1952, CVO in 1966 and DCVO in 1979. Until her death, she remained one of the Queen Mother's closest friends and allies and the two grandmothers were pivotal in the matchmaking of their grandchildren, Prince Charles and Lady Diana Spencer. Ruth died on 6 July 1993, aged eighty-four, a year after the Prince and Princess of Wales separated. She never remarried and is buried with Maurice in Sandringham churchyard.

Edith Travis Howitt

Edith sailed back to America and ended her days happily in a rest home in Washington State, where she was the only resident to have a poster of the Beatles in her bedroom. She died peacefully on 1 March 1976, aged eighty-six. It was her dying wish, expressed to her daughter, that her relationship with Maurice would one day no longer remain a secret.

Edith 'Lambie' Howitt Hodgins

Edith is in her mid-eighties, and her husband Arty is in his nineties. They live happily on America's West Coast, a stone's throw from the ocean. She became a social worker and had three sons with her husband. They have been married over sixty years and love nothing more than getting together with their family and grandchildren. Edith goes to work every day in her own small business and is a very popular and much respected member of her local community.

Jack Travis

Jack, proving that longevity runs in the Howitt family, is still alive and living in Kentucky. He is in his nineties, married and with a daughter.

Ned Travis

Ned completed his musical apprenticeship and joined Louis Armstrong as his drummer. He had a successful career as a jazz musician and married a Communist, but they were childless. He died in his mid-forties.

Forrest Travis

Forrest continued to write to Edith, and they always kept in touch because of their sons. Forrest eventually remarried and lived in Ireland and England. He always had a special place in his heart for the girl he married when she was sweet sixteen. He wrote to Edith for some years after their last meeting.

> I have meant for months to answer your other letter. Do you know after Mom's death you were the only one of the family to write me and I did think it very sweet of you. I find it difficult to answer after all these years.
>
> I have the greatest fondness for you and have always been sorry we did not make a go of it, through no fault of yours. When I think of what an irresponsible idiot I was and what you put up with, it makes me quite ill. Whether you believe it or not, there is no love like one's first love and I quietly treasure it.
>
> I am as ever your devoted old man, Forrest.

Index

with George 181; bitterness
towards Duchess of Windsor 241;
at end of war 234–5; at
Sandringham 243, 259, 264;
reopens King's Lynn Guildhall
263; approves Spencer wedding
272; friendship with Ruth Fermoy
272, 306–7; becomes patron of
King's Lynn Arts Festival 272;
receives 'Freedom of Lynn' 282

Fermoy, Edmund Burke Roche, 1st
Baron 99
Fermoy, Edmund James Burke
Roche, 5th Baron 214, 227, 262,
274, 292, 305–6
Fermoy, Edward Fitz Edmund Burke,
2nd Baron 95, 99, 126
Fermoy, Lady Elizabeth Caroline
(*née* Boothby) 99
Fermoy, James Boothby Burke
Roche, 3rd Baron 16–18, 43–4,
95, 99, 112, 115, 126
Fermoy, (Edmund) Maurice Burke
Roche, 4th Baron 4–6, 16, 43;
meets Edith Travis on train 8–10,
13–15, 18–19, 22–3, 24–6; loses
touch 42; takes job as railway
clerk 43, 44; gives society dinner
in Newport 40; correspondence
with Edith begins 41, 46–7, 49,
50, 51; with her in New York
51–9; sees her at Lakewood 61,
62, 63; enlists 64–6; at Camp
Dix 67–72; brief meeting with
Edith 72–3; serves in France
74–8; postwar emotions 79–81,
89–90, 93; cannot marry Edith
81–2; sends her contract and
money 90–3; writes her letter
after letter 94–5, 100–1; becomes
heir 99, 100; suggests Frank take
his place 101–2; finds Edith is
married 103–8; near-fatal sailing
trip with Frank 110–12; becomes
Lord Fermoy 112–13; and grandfather's will 114–16; meets Edith
again 121–3; sails for England
123–4, 125; in London 125–7;
decides to stand for Parliament
126, 127; postpones ambition

133–5; leases Hagnaby Priory
138, 139, 141, 152; selected for
Horncastle 142–6; fails to be
elected 147; in St Moritz 148–50;
bewitched by Nancy Mitford
151; moves to Heacham 152–3;
becomes MP for King's Lynn
153; at Queen Alexandra's
funeral 160; friendship with
Duke of York 160–2; at Vichy
164–5; with Edith in New York
165, 168–73; and rumours of his
engagement 173–4, 177; and his
mother's attempts to find him a
wife 176–8; electioneering 178–9;
shoots with Duke of York
179–80; advised by him to find a
wife 181–2; is returned to
Parliament (1929) 186; moves to
Sedgeford Hall 187; age takes its
toll 188; marries Ruth Gill
188–9, 191–3, 195; is again
returned to Parliament (1931)
195; becomes Mayor of King's
Lynn 197; dines and hunts with
George V 200; promotion 200;
in debt and moves to
Dersingham 201–2; and birth of
daughter 202–3; plans for semi-
retirement 207; at first cremation
207–8; leases Park House,
Sandringham 209; and birth of
second daughter 209, 210; and
Abdication crisis 210–11,
212–13; at George VI's
Coronation 213; and birth of son
214; and outbreak of war
215–16; serves in France 217–19;
returns to politics 225–6, 227–8;
and the end of the war 232–5;
leaves politics 236–7; and
mother's illness 237–8; sees Duke
and Duchess of Windsor 241;
enjoys farming 242; angry with
postwar Britain 242–3; invited to
Sandringham 243–4; at
Elizabeth's wedding 244, 245;
shoots with George VI 246;
enjoys retirement 254–5; in car
accident 262; with Royal Family
for Christmas (1952) 264; shoots